WOMANLY
DOMINION

More Than a Gentle and Quiet Spirit

MARK CHANSKI

WOMANLY
DOMINION

More Than a Gentle and Quiet Spirit

MARK CHANSKI

Calvary Press Publishing ✲ CalvaryPress.com

Calvary Press Publishing
www.calvarypress.com

ISBN-13: 978-1-879737-60-0
ISBN-10: 1-879737-60-0

1. Christianity—Women's Issues
2. Practical Christianity—Marriage—Motherhood

Printed in the United States of America

10 9 8 7 6 5 4 3 2 1

Again, to my Dianne,
My intelligent, beautiful, and servant-hearted Abigail
who does good to me all the days of her life.

Contents

ACKNOWLEDGEMENTS

The Lord has been so gracious to give me many wise counselors and helpers who have directly assisted me in the writing of this book. I can only mention a few:

Dr. Russell Moore whose encouraging words and helpfulness have been of great benefit; Dr. Joel Beeke whose reading, comments, and recommendations have added gravitas; Dianne Chanski whose mind and example have together provided my most frequently consulted human source; Dorothy Chanski Martin, my Priscilla-like mother, who always had time to talk with her third born; Marcie Filcik whose editorial work and servant's heart have been precious and priceless; Mary Jo Haab whose reviewing, even through a first trimester's queasiness, was very helpful; Randy Stinson whose continued interest was inspiring; Elaine Wallace whose Northern Ireland proofreading added polish; Craig Sietsema and Jon Vannette who encouraged me to write a sequel.

"How did I get into this situation?"

I asked myself as I clung to the tower's exterior, about forty feet above the ground. I really thought I'd have no problem scaling this sixty-foot wall at the Baptist Camp at Clear Lake, Iowa. But the ninety-three degree temperature and the corn-growing humidity were taking their toll on me. Sweat poured down my soaking wet face onto my drenched t-shirt. Slippery moist and burning fingers were crying, "Uncle," as they strove to grip the slick handholds. My heart pounded for relief.

I thought it would be a great father and son adventure. Eleven-year-old Nathan and I would side-by-side accomplish our first wall-climb attempts. While strapping on our rope harnesses, it appeared a bit more formidable than the view from across the lake, but I wasn't worried. I told Nathan, "Remember, no pain, no gain. We can do this!"

But now, twenty minutes into the ascent, I wasn't so sure about my own performance. "Come on, Mark," I thought. "You're a long-distance runner. You lift some weights. You're in good shape. What's the matter? Besides that, look at Elizabeth. She's nearing the top. Are you gonna let her out-climb you?"

Elizabeth is Pastor Mike's wife. She's a petite woman with a very *gentle and quiet spirit*. In appearance, she's the epitome of soft femininity. But with Elizabeth, there's more than meets the eye. Her father was a linebacker for the University of Northern Iowa, and had obviously passed on to his daughter a hefty portion of his drive and tenacity. My nephew had told me that she had been his high school English teacher, and that though she herself looked like a high school freshman, she *subdued and ruled* her classes like a Marine drill sergeant. Nobody dared to mess with Mrs. A.

This makes me think of another *Elizabeth* in American history. Her name was Elizabeth Cummins Jackson, the *great grandmother* of Lieutenant General Thomas J. "Stonewall" Jackson. Stonewall Jackson was a great hero in both the Mexican-American and the U.S. Civil Wars. In the Battle of Bull Run, all seemed hopeless for the Confederate troops, but Jackson rallied his brigade of Virginians. His biographer, R. L. Dabney, wrote, "His eye blazed with that fire which no other eye could meet; his countenance was clothed with a serene and assured smile." [1]

When his colleague Confederate General Bee reported in despairing bitterness that his own ranks had been shattered by the Federal onslaught, Jackson rose to the occasion:

> "Then," said Jackson, calm and curt, "we will give them the bayonet." Bee seemed to catch the inspiration of his determined will, and, galloping back to the broken fragments of his over-tasked command, exclaimed to them, "There is Jackson standing like a stone wall. Rally behind the Virginians. Let us determine to die here, and we will conquer. Follow me."…From that time Jackson's was known as the Stone-wall Brigade, a name henceforward immortal, and belonging to all the ages. [2]

Stonewall Jackson's legendary courage and determination didn't simply *fall from heaven*. They can profoundly be traced back to the plucky spirit of his *great grandmother*, Elizabeth Cummins, whose bravery and grit were passed on by example and instruction. Dabney describes Elizabeth as a woman of strong stature with "understanding and energies corresponding to the vigor of her bodily frame." [3]

> When the young couple (Great Grandfather John and Elizabeth) emigrated to Northwest (Virginia), the Indians were still contesting

the occupancy of its teeming valleys with the white men. The colonists were compelled to provide for their security by building stockade-forts, into which they retreated with their families and cattle at every alarm of a savage incursion. It is the tradition that, in more than one of these sieges, Elizabeth Cummins proved herself, *though a woman*, to have 'the stomach and mettle of a man,' and rendered valuable service by aiding and inspiriting the resistance of the defenders. In her industry and enterprise was realized King Lemuel's description of the ways of the virtuous woman: *'She considers a field, and buys it; with the fruit of her hands she plants a vineyard'* (Proverbs 31:16). Several patents (deeds) are still in existence, conveying to her, in her own name, lands which were afterwards the valuable possessions of her posterity. They have usually claimed that the characteristics of their race were largely inherited from her; that it was her sterling integrity, vigorous intellect, and directness of purpose which gave them their type… Hers were stamina, both of the physical and moral constitution, fitting her to rear a race that were men indeed.[4]

Oh, how desperately our generation needs "a race that are men indeed." And how desperately we need such *strong women* to rear them!

Lest you dismiss this Elizabeth Jackson as out of step with the Bible's standard of femininity and womanhood (*"a gentle and quiet spirit…a weaker vessel"*—1 Peter 3:4, 7), remember the further words of Lemuel's mother regarding her inspired blueprint of a noble woman who fears the Lord:

> *She girds herself with <u>strength</u> and makes her <u>arms strong</u>…*
> *<u>Strength</u> and dignity are her clothing, and she smiles at the future (Proverbs 31:17, 25, emphasis added).*

The false stereotype of a Christian woman being a helpless and frail mouse, who passively shades herself under the parasol of her soft femininity, and adoringly waits for her husband to do all the heavy lifting, is shattered by the Scriptures.

Yes, the godly Christian woman wears beautiful ornaments that are *"precious in the sight of God"* (1 Peter 3:4). But her jewelry is not only the necklace of *"a gentle and quiet spirit,"* but also the bracelets of *"strength and dignity."*

Charles Bridges comments on the strength of the Proverbs 31 ideal: "Christian courage and resolution lift her above appalling difficulties."[5]

Regarding her proverbial strength, George Lawson adds:

> The virtuous woman…declines not any part of her duty through aversion to toil; and by exerting her strength with a cheerful mind she improves it. Her labors give her health and vigor, and alacrity (eagerness) for new labors; so that she can with great ease and tranquility go through those duties which appear impossibilities to other women…She possesses a greatness of soul, an inward vigor and resolution of mind, which sets her above all those little and tormenting fears which keep many of her sex in perpetual uneasiness.[6]

Yes, the strong femininity of an Elizabeth Jackson is lovely in the eyes of God.

Let our sons in their youth be as grown-up plants, and our daughters as corner pillars fashioned as for a palace (Psalm 144:12, emphasis added).

But we must return from our digression into 19th century Virginia to sweltering 21st century Iowa.

Later that oppressive afternoon, Pastor Mike approached me with an idea. "I've read your book, *Manly Dominion*, and think it's great. I've begun teaching through it in a Sunday School class we've set aside for men in our church. It's been really helpful. Have you ever thought about writing a second book called *Womanly Dominion*?"

It turns out that Elizabeth, his wife, had been reading through Mike's copy of *Manly Dominion* and commented to this effect: "I sure wish there was something like this tailored for women. We face these same fundamental struggles with passivity and lethargy that men do, and could use a book to challenge us to *subdue and rule*." That conversation with Mike planted a seed in my mind.

In the introduction of *Manly Dominion* I'd written these words:

> Since the days of *The Greatest Generation* (Depression & WWII), western culture has been bathed in the putrid, lukewarm waters of

relativism, liberalism, feminism, and excuse-ism. Bold convictions on issues have been demonized as bigoted. Bold actions by leaders have been maligned as macho. Bold endeavors by individuals have been suffocated by self doubt. True, biblical, image-bearing manhood has gone into hiding.

This book is a modest attempt to rinse off and help retrain ourselves (men and women alike) to live in accordance with the scriptural commission spoken by our Almighty Maker in the beginning:

And God created man in His own image, in the image of God He created him; male and female He created them. And God blessed them; and God said to them, "Be fruitful and multiply, and fill the earth, and subdue it; and rule over the fish of the sea and over the birds of the sky, and over every living thing that moves on the earth (Genesis 1:27-28, emphasis added).[7]

And it's true. *"Men and women alike"* are both called to *subdue* and *rule* in the various spheres of their lives. Our brief introduction to the life of Elizabeth Cummins Jackson boldly underscores this practical challenge for women.

It's absolutely and wonderfully true that women are rightly designated in the Bible as the *"weaker vessel"* (1 Peter 3:7) who are to display a *"gentle and quiet spirit, which is precious in the sight of God"* (1 Peter 3:4). But such soft and tender qualities do not tell the whole story. There's much more to the challenging mission assigned to the godly woman by her Maker, Redeemer, and Lord. That's what we want to explore in *Womanly Dominion.*

Speaking of telling the whole story, I suppose you may wonder how it ended up for me on that Clear Lake, Iowa, climbing tower. Elizabeth triumphantly summitted the tower, receiving the cheers of many observers. I shouted to Nathan, "Look, Mrs. A. made it. So can we!" But after a few more minutes of battling against gravity, I fought the law, and the law won. My drained, forty-six-year old body was forced to surrender to the elements. I was gently lowered down by the rope in defeat. The Lord had used a highly competent woman to educate me in the classroom of humility.

So much for *manly* dominion! Let's now explore the challenge of the fairer sex.

CHAPTER 1:
WOMANLY DOMINION
FUNDAMENTALLY EXPLAINED

For nearly a decade and a half, I have coached our four sons' recreational soccer teams. I have found it quite a challenge to attempt to harness an undisciplined herd of testosterone-charged young males into an orderly team pulling hard toward a common goal.

Then my bride encouraged me to try something new. "Why don't you coach Abigail's soccer team this year?" Abigail is our one and only daughter. I admit that I was a bit intimidated by this new challenge. I'd grown comfortable with testosterone, but was a bit unsure about estrogen. She signed me up anyway! Before I knew it, I stood before a flock of swans which I quickly discovered must be harnessed and motivated in a different manner than horses.

Even though females are profoundly different from males, I've learned that the universal formula for coaching a successful soccer team can be digested down to training the young players to master two fundamental principles. These principles are embodied in the two common coaching slogans: "*Play your position!*" and "*Win it!*"

Let me explain.

"*Play your position!*" means, "Stay put, and don't wander away from your assigned post." If I have a defenseman who is not convinced of the importance of her guarding the goal, but instead thinks that the only important contribution is scoring goals, that roaming, undisciplined player will do great harm to the team. Imagine the damage done when a girl assigned to play goalie leaves her post to make a long and exciting run up field, only to be stripped by an opponent who's able to dribble back and make an uncontested score into a goalie-less net. The coach rightly shouts, "Jessica, you've got to stay home! You're a goalie, not a forward! You've got to *play your position*! Everyone is counting on you! *Play your position*!"

Now, let me explain "*Win it!*"

"*Win it!*" means, "Play with all of your might, in every encounter!" When the soccer ball squirts out into the open field, and my player Erica is ten yards away from the ball, while an opposing player is eight yards away, I'll shout out, "*Win it*, Erica! *Win it!*" You see, at that split second, Erica is debating whether or not to exert maximum effort to gain possession of the ball. "To try or not to try?" is the question Erica is mulling over. "Shall I passively surrender the contest, or shall I aggressively find a way to get possession of that ball?" That's when the "*Win it!*" versus the "*Surrender it!*" resolution must kick in. The final outcome of the big game is determined by the cumulative outcomes of these little contests during the game. A great player is constantly telling herself, "*Win it!*"

Here's the upshot. On the field of life, God challenges every woman to live and run *in such a way* as to *win the prize* (1 Corinthians 9:24). In whatever she puts her hand to, she's to *"do it with all her might"* (Ecclesiastes 9:10) in order to hear that blessed commendation from her Lord, *"Well done, you good and faithful servant"* (Matthew 25:21). And if she's to achieve this noble goal on the field of life, she needs to be convinced of living according to these two fundamental principles: "*Play your position!*" and "*Win it!*"

1. Dominion Commonality

Manly Dominion, this book's forerunner, is basically an exposition and application of the first words God ever spoke to mankind. In these principle-packed words, we find our mandate, our marching orders, our commission, as image-bearers of God.

> *Be fruitful and multiply, and fill the earth, and subdue it; and rule over the fish of the sea and over the birds of the sky*

and over every living thing that moves on the earth (Genesis 1:28).

Theologians call this our *"dominion mandate."*

Why am I here? What am I supposed to be doing with my time? How am I to go about my business? This Genesis *dominion mandate* charges us with a glorious assignment. Fundamentally, we are to be *subduers* and *rulers*. We're to aggressively exercise dominion over the earth and its resources.

In *Manly Dominion*, I wrote:

> Man is to aggressively *dominate* his environment, instead of allowing his environment to *dominate* him. I am not to be a passive-purple-four-ball! I am rather to be a cue stick carrying player! In the spheres of my life, I must *subdue* and *rule*, and not permit myself to be subdued and ruled. We have been commissioned by God to go out and aggressively assert ourselves as masters over every realm of our lives. I have not been assigned to stare out my bedroom, living room, or office window, passively daydreaming about what I *might* do, *if only* there weren't so many obstacles. Rather I am to get out there, so help me God, and *plan it*, and clear it, and *do it*, with all my might, to the glory of God.[8]

Now, the first book chiefly addressed the practical implications of this *dominion mandate* for the male gender. But this command was not given exclusively to the male gender. It was given to both genders— male and female. As image-bearers, men and women share the same *dominion mandate* in common.

> *And God created <u>man</u> in His <u>image</u>, in the <u>image</u> of God He created him; <u>male and female</u> He created <u>them</u>. And God blessed <u>them</u>: and God said to <u>them</u>, "Be fruitful and multiply, and fill the earth, and subdue it; and rule over the fish of the sea and over the birds of the sky and over every living thing that moves on the earth" (Genesis 1:27-28, emphasis added).*

Biblically speaking, "man" or "mankind" encompasses both genders *"male and female."* Therefore, the first book, *Manly Dominion*, only told half the story! *Womanly Dominion* tells the other half, and a crucially important half at that.

Then the LORD God said, "It is not good for man to be alone; I will make him a helper suitable for him" (Genesis 2:18).

"Why," asks a woman, "am I here?" What am I supposed to be doing with my time? How am I to go about my business?" *Womanly Dominion* seeks to provide answers—answers at a critical hour when misguided voices from both sidelines, and even from inside her own head, are shouting at her all kinds of foolishness.

2. Personal Intensity

Every day, women, just like men, are faced with intimidating challenges. A beneficial opportunity rolls within a woman's reach. "Should I go after it?" she wonders. And the shouting match begins. "No!" urges the passive Patsy within. "You probably can't get to it in time, so I recommend you don't even try. Just *surrender it*."

As a senior in high school, Leslie, an excellent student, contemplates an option that's bouncing in front of her. "Should I apply for acceptance in the University's highly competitive nursing program? They accept less than one quarter of the applicants. It would be so humiliating and discouraging to be rejected. Maybe I shouldn't even try. Maybe instead of aggressively applying, I should pass on this. I might save myself a lot of headaches and grief in the long run."

Esther is in the home stretch of her junior year in college. She's feeling the mounting pressure of semester-ending term papers, group projects, and final exams. She's overwhelmed and emotionally fraying at the edges. She finds herself lying one morning on her dorm room bed, not wanting to get up and climb this steep and daunting hill of responsibilities. "Should I surrender in the face of this intimidating challenge? I could still drop a couple of these courses. Or should I leap out of this bed, and step by step, study and write my way up that hill, and strive to pass each of these classes, so help me God?"

Rachel has gotten romantically involved with a man. At first, he seemed like a wonderful person, so caring and considerate and enjoyable. But as time has progressed, it's become evident to her that he's a man of poor character. As she strolls all alone one night near dusk, she ponders her options. "I know that the right thing to do is to end my relationship with him. My best counselors have told me I'd regret the day I walked down the aisle with him. But I just don't think I can end it. How do I know if I'll ever find anyone better? I just can't bear the idea of my someday spending Christmas Eve alone as a fifty-year-old spinster. It would be so hard to take a stand and break up."

Marcia's household is slipping toward disorder and disarray. The dishes, glasses, and silverware are piling up on the kitchen counters. Dirty towels, shirts, and pants are piling up in the laundry room. The unpaid bills are mounting up on her computer desk. "I know what I should do today, but I don't feel like doing it. Besides, it's so beautiful outside, and the children would love to spend a few hours at the park." She has a strong aversion to attacking, and a prevailing inclination to retreating, from her domestic challenges.

Lynda has become very fearful as she observes her teenage children being pulled down into the sucking vortex of the godless contemporary culture. Every day seems to bring a new threat. One day, it's immodest clothing styles. The next, it's a new Hollywood movie release. Then it's some new internet youth trap, or a peer group temptation issue, or some pairing-off romance peril. The skirmishes are never ending. She's suffering battle fatigue and is tempted to passively throw in the surrender towel just like most other parents who shrug their shoulders and leave their kids to "sink or swim" on their own. Here's where the *"Win it!"* mindset must kick in, where Lynda must resolve to fight the good fight, contest after contest, valiantly seeking to raise her children in the fear of the Lord.

Godly women, made in the image of God, must daily tell themselves: *"Win it!"* to the glory of God. Leslie's, Esther's, Rachel's, Marcia's, and Lynda's must for the long haul, for the entire game, contest after contest, resolve to put forth maximum effort to *rule* and *subdue* their daily challenges, so help them God.

Womanly dominion is a blessed virtue, as urgently needed in our day as manly dominion.

3. Positional Loyalty

But everyday, women, *unlike men*, face an additional fierce life challenge. Due to high-powered feminist social pressures, they've got to keep telling themselves, *"Play your position!"* On the field of life, women hear constant shouts from unprincipled sideline voices telling them to leave their God-assigned posts. These voices are much like the voices of misguided parents telling their goalie daughter to "Get the ball, honey, and try to dribble down field and score!"

But the coach has charged her to *"Play your position."* The Lord has created her *"in the image of God,"* and not male but *"female He has created"* her (Genesis 1:26-27), as a *"helper suitable"* (Genesis 2:18). She's been assigned a glorious and important position in this world. But the sideline voices attempt to drown out her Lord's words of instruction.

The Army recruiter at the high school tells Susan that women are as well suited for military combat as are men (See *A Woman Warrior?* in chapter 13). Her basketball coach, who encourages Susan to pump heavy iron in the off season in the weight room, echoes the recruiter's combat claims.

Cindy's college professor insists that as a gifted student, she should pursue a PhD in her field of study. Cindy then divulges that she's hoping soon to marry a fine young man, become his wife, and eventually be a stay-at-home mother. Therefore, Cindy questions the prudence of dedicating so many years to a post-graduate degree and incurring so much financial debt. Her professor reacts with disgust and disdain. "I'm really disappointed that you'd voluntarily derail your own personal potential, and choose to be demeaned and shackled by the patriarchal institutions of marriage and motherhood."

The magazines at Stacy's office shout to her loud and clear that her husband has no right to expect her to abandon her promising career to stay at home with the children. "Why should he enjoy the exhilaration of climbing the corporate ladder while you are left at home to wipe drooling faces and dirty behinds?"

Michelle's own inner voices constantly holler that her day-in-and-day-out selflessly serving her husband and her children is a thankless waste of a life. "When I see my sharply dressed, career-focused neighbor pull out of her driveway, and drive down the street in her late model SUV every morning, I just think to myself, 'That could be me. I could be heading out into the stimulating world, instead of being hand-cuffed here to this boring home life.'"

Pauleen's younger and less mature sister Pamela is an elder in her church. She constantly calls her older sister for advice as she writes occasional sermons and wrestles through her numerous pastoral counseling situations. Occasionally, Pamela will lament, "I can't believe it, Pauleen, that your church refuses to ordain women pastors! You're so gifted!" And Pauleen is left to struggle with her less-than-high profile, but God-ordained low profile, position in her church.

Godly women, made in the image of God, must repeatedly remind themselves, *"Play your position!"* They must loyally resolve to stay at their God-assigned posts, to the glory of God, despite the shouts from the misguided cultural sidelines.

Thus, the slogans *"Win it!"* and *"Play your position!"* well summarize the fundamental struggle for womanly dominion in the early 21st century.

CHAPTER 2:
WOMANLY DOMINION
THEOLOGICALLY UNPACKED

The *New York Times,* no particular friend of a biblical worldview, ran an interesting article in September of 2005. It was entitled, "Many Women at Elite Colleges Set Career Path to Motherhood." Its author, Louise Story, reported a curious societal phenomenon among women who've dared to reject the priority career focus of progressive feminism.

> Cynthia Liu is precisely the kind of high achiever Yale wants: smart (1510 SAT), disciplined (4.0 grade point average), competitive (finalist in Texas oratory competition), musical (pianist), athletic (runner) and altruistic (hospital volunteer). And at the start of her sophomore year at Yale, Ms. Liu is full of ambition, planning to go to law school.
>
> So will she join the long tradition of famous Ivy League graduates? Not likely. By the time she is 30, this accomplished 19-year-old expects to be a stay-at-home mom.
>
> "My mother's always told me you can't be the best career woman and the best mother at the same time," Ms. Liu said matter-of-factly. "You always have to choose one over the other."

At Yale and other top colleges, women are being groomed to take their place in an ever more diverse professional elite. It is almost taken for granted that, just as they make up half the students at these institutions, they will move into leadership roles on an equal basis with their male classmates.

There is just one problem with this scenario: many of these women say that is not what they want.

Many women at the nation's most elite colleges say they have already decided that they will put aside their careers in favor of raising children. Though some of these students are not planning to have children and some hope to have a family and work full time, many others, like Ms. Liu, say they will happily play a traditional female role, with motherhood as their main commitment.

Much attention has been focused on career women who leave the work force to rear children. What seems to be changing is that while many women in college two or three decades ago expected to have full-time careers, their daughters, while still in college, say they have already decided to suspend or end their careers when they have children.

"At the height of the women's movement and shortly thereafter, women were much more firm in their expectation that they could somehow combine full-time work with child rearing," said Cynthia E. Russett, a professor of American history who has taught at Yale since 1967. "The women today are, in effect, turning realistic."

Dr. Russett is among more than a dozen faculty members and administrators at the most exclusive institutions who have been on campus for decades and who said in interviews that they had noticed the changing attitude. [9]

Government statistics verify the *Times'* assertion.

According to the US Department of Labor, the proportion of mothers in the labor force has been trending downward since the turn of the century, falling to 70.5 % in 2005 from 72.3% in 2000. [10]

Attitudes are becoming realistic. Or maybe the better word is theistic. In the beginning, God provided for man and woman a basic blueprint for personal and familial prosperity and fulfillment. Progressive feminism has for decades passionately rejected those basic principles, resulting in a growing sense of disillusionment among a growing segment of women. They no longer want to fight common sense. They're turning back to the old path—God's basic blueprint.

The first words of the Creator to his image-bearing creatures provided *them* with *their* fundamental assignments.

> *And God created man in His own image, in the image of God He created him; male and female He created <u>them</u>. And God blessed <u>them</u>; and God said to <u>them</u>, "Be fruitful and multiply, and fill the earth, and subdue it; and rule over the fish of the sea and over the birds of the sky, and over every living thing that moves on the earth" (Genesis 1:27, emphasis added).*

"Man" is the collective term for the race of mankind, encompassing both man and woman, male and female. God is here addressing not only men, but women as well. "God blessed *them*, and said to *them*." Both Adam (manhood) and Eve (womanhood) are equally assigned and commissioned in this *creation mandate*.

Consider the three chief dimensions of this mandate.

1. Domination

The Scriptures declare that both man and woman were created in the "*image*" and "*likeness*" of God.

> *Then God said, "Let Us make man in Our <u>image</u>, according to Our <u>likeness</u>; and let them rule over the fish of the sea and over the birds of the sky and over the cattle and over all the earth, and over every creeping thing that creeps on the earth" (Genesis 1:26, emphasis added)*

Here is found the essence of our assignment on the earth. The Hebrew word for "image," *tselem*, springs from a root that means "to carve" or "to cut." The Hebrew word for "likeness," *demuth*, is derived from a root that means "to be like." Combining the two, we see that in man and woman, God left imprints on the earth, that are profoundly to be representative likenesses of Himself. As the castle-building child presses his hands into the wet beach sand, leaving an impression of the sculptor, in man and woman, God pressed His face to the earth, leaving an impression of the Creator. In man and woman, it was intended that we would view a mirror reflection of God's character.

Thus man and woman's basic identity unveils their fundamental duty which is *imitation*. God is saying: "Be like me. *Imitate* me. Resemble me." Anthony Hoekema underscores the initial character trait that God wants us to imitate:

> From Genesis 1:26 we may infer that <u>dominion</u> over the animals and over all the earth is one aspect of the image of God. In exercising this <u>dominion</u> man is like God, since God has supreme and ultimate <u>dominion</u> over the earth.[11]

Men and women are to exercise dominion, to employ a governing mastery over the earth. This concept is unpacked by the words *"subdue"* and *"rule."*

The word *"subdue"* in Genesis 1:28 is the translation of the Hebrew word *kabash* which means to bring something into bondage, to make it serve you by force, to dominate it:

> *And Moses said to them, "If the sons of Gad and the sons of Reuben, everyone who is armed for battle, will cross with you over the Jordan in the presence of the LORD, and the land will be <u>subdued</u> [kabash] before you, then you shall give them the land of Gilead for a possession (Numbers 32:29, emphasis added).*

God promised to *subdue* the raging nations of Canaan *under the feet* of His people Israel. An intimately related Hebrew word *kebesh* means "footstool" (see 2 Chronicles 9:18). We see this *subduing-into-a-footstool* imagery in Joshua 10:24, where Joshua symbolically depicts Israel's military triumph and resultant domination over the previously mutinous Canaanites.

> *And it came about when they brought these kings out to Joshua, that Joshua called for all the men of Israel, and said to the chiefs of the men of war who had gone with him, "Come near, <u>put your feet on the necks of these kings</u>." So they came near and <u>put their feet on their necks</u> (Joshua 10:24, emphasis added.)*

Israel flexed its military muscles, and with the help of God, *subdued* the Canaanite nations, along with their chiefs, *under their feet*.

Psalm 110:1 echoes this same theme of *"subduing"* adverse forces:

"The LORD says to my LORD: 'Sit at My right hand, until I make Thine enemies a footstool [*kebesh*] for *Thy feet*.'"

As men and women, we are to flex our abilities, and with the help of God, *subdue* the mutinous and adverse forces of the earth *under our feet*. We are to take into our hands the earth and its menagerie of operations, and through forceful and aggressive effort, compel them to do our bidding.

In doing this, we are imitating God, in whose image we are made. In the beginning, God took hold of a newly created earth which was a *"formless and void"* chaos (Genesis 1:2). God premeditatedly designed a plan for its creative development in the space of six days. Then He systematically and progressively put His plan into action. The result was an orderly world bearing witness to the genius of its Designer. And so, every image-bearing man and woman is obligated to imitate his/her Maker in his own miniature world. Each is assigned a lifelong plot of wild earth that he/she is to stake out, cut down, plow up, plant, and harvest. We must aggressively *subdue*, and not passively loiter.

Every week of our lives, we are to reflect our Heavenly Father. Six days we labor to *subdue* the earth, and on the seventh day we rest, basking in the satisfaction of a job well done, restfully praising the Lord for the work He's enabled our hands to do. The completed projects act as gratifying and comfortable *footstools* for our feet. We're able to say, "That week of work was *good, very good*" (Genesis 1:31).

This is profoundly true for women and their life endeavors. My bride of 25 years strikingly imitates her subduing God. I constantly stand in appreciative awe of her extensive and detailed calendars and to-do lists. Dianne diligently plots out her week with calculated premeditation. She synchronizes her short-term goals with the annual and monthly calendar appointments. Out of this she forges to-do lists for each day of the week. Then she relentlessly crosses out those task challenges one by one. She absolutely loves crossing things out! With this vigorous spirit, my wife *subdues* the chaos and overcomes the obstacles before her, creating order and stability in our family's otherwise disheveled world. My wife seeks to imitate her God by *dominating* her world.

> ...and God said to them, "Be fruitful and multiply, and fill the earth, and <u>subdue</u> it; and <u>rule</u> over the fish of the sea and over the birds of the sky, and over every living thing that moves on the earth" (Genesis 1:28, emphasis added).

This theme of domination is further advanced by the Lord's joining the obligation to *"rule"* with the duty to *"subdue."* The word *"rule"* in Genesis 1:28 is the translation of the Hebrew word *rada* which means to govern something, to reign or hold sway over it. Specifically, man and woman are assigned to *"rule"* over the inhabitants of the three chief spheres of the earth: *sea* (fish), *sky* (birds), and *land* (creeping things).

Psalm 8:4-8 echoes God's Edenic mandate for mankind:

> *What is man, that Thou dost take thought of him? And the son of man, that Thou dost care for him? Yet Thou hast made him a little lower than God, and dost crown him with glory and majesty! Thou dost make him to <u>rule</u> over the works of Thy hands; Thou hast put all things under his feet, all sheep and oxen, and also the <u>beasts of the field</u>, the <u>birds of the heavens</u>, and the <u>fish of the sea</u>, whatever passes through the paths of the seas (emphasis added).*

Who is the true king of the beasts? It's not the lion. It's man. And for our purposes, we identify woman as the queen of the beasts! She is to daily assert herself as a ruler over the spheres of her life.

Years ago, I visited Dutch Village here in Holland, Michigan. It's a delightfully preserved historic town depicting the conditions of the original Dutch settlers of Western Michigan back in the late 1800s. I entered a quaint cottage and was greeted by an elderly lady dressed in 19th century attire (long dress, bonnet) and rocking in a chair. To my surprise, she was not a weary-minded prop, but a spry woman of wit and wisdom with a PhD. in history. She declared that for an early West Michigan household, "A woman in an apron was more valuable than three men in boots." She went on to explain that a skilled household mistress was capable of stretching a pound of butter, a sack of flour, and a portion of meat into an unthinkable number of meals.

Our church building is located in Holland on the north side of Lake Macatawa, the river-fed harbor-lake that pours its waters into the great Lake Michigan. I imagine for myself the settler woman who *ruled* over the original farmhouse and surrounding lands a century and a half ago. I see her harnessing a horse (creeping thing) to plow, netting salmon (fish) to feed her family, and maybe even attaching a note to the leg of a homing pigeon (bird) to send a message across the lake to a woman-in-an-apron friend on the south side. She aggressively *ruled* over these three spheres to the glory of God!

Recently, I made a pastoral visit to the home of a family in our church. As I drove up that warm spring evening, there sat Larry and Jacqueline on the front porch of their country estate home. They were watching their three young sons (ages 4 ½, 3, 1 ½), jumping together on a trampoline in the front yard. As we talked, they jumped. Jacqueline's eyes sparkled as she stared at the bouncing boys. "I love boys!" she said. It was clear that this woman viewed her three testosterone-charged sons as her three God-assigned spheres for *subduing* and *ruling*.

Each son is a peculiar challenge for this stay-at-home mom. The firstborn Robert is the physical one. As demonstrated that evening by his ability to splash the basketball net, his athletic skills will need to be harnessed for God's glory.

The second born Marcos is the rhetorical one. He couldn't get the ball anywhere near the hoop, but when the quiet Robert was asked a question, it was Marcos who provided the answer in paragraphs. Now that silver tongue is a talent requiring a mother's polishing for kingdom use.

The jury is still out on the third born Lorenzo. But if he shares his father's interest in books, he may turn out to be the academic one. Scholarliness is another invaluable endowment for a dominion-minded mother's cultivating. Her college degree, whether it be from Yale or Western Michigan University, will be invaluable in educating these future leaders to impact their world for great good.

Surely, Jacqueline's God-ordained assignment here in West Michigan is an adventurous challenge, the frontiers of which know no bounds. No wonder her eyes sparkle.

In such ways, a woman is to dominate aggressively her environment, rather than allow her environment to dominate her. She needs to work and play with a *win it* instead of with a *surrender it* mindset. She must *rule* and *subdue*, rather than letting herself be ruled and subdued. God has commissioned her to assert herself aggressively as a master over the teeming spheres of her life. God has not assigned her to sit on her porch swing with a pink parasol daydreaming what she might do "if only" the obstacles weren't so complicated. No! She's to get out there and *do it* with all her might!

> *Whatever your hand finds to do, verily, <u>do it with all your might</u>; for there is no activity or planning or knowledge or wisdom in Sheol where you are going (Ecclesiastes 9:10, emphasis added).*

2. Procreation

Procreation is a second chief dimension of mankind's creation mandate. *"And God blessed them; and God said to them, 'Be fruitful and multiply, and fill the earth'"* (Genesis 1:28, emphasis added).

In these words, the Lord gives man and woman a sacred focus for their dominion activities—their offspring! Children are introduced not merely as a preferential option, but as a holy obligation.

"Be fruitful" expresses the Hebrew word *parah*. It elicits agricultural imagery. *"Your wife will be like a fruitful vine within your house; your children like olive plants around your table"* (Psalm 128:3a, emphasis added).

Fruitfulness varies in its manifestation among different plants. A fruitful grape-vine will sport many, many clusters of grapes. On the other hand, a productive pumpkin vine may only generate four or five pumpkins. A farmer is very thankful if a single cornstalk produces two ears! Fruitfulness will vary from womb to womb, family to family. Revelation, providence, liberty and wisdom must be conscientiously blended.

"Multiply" expresses the Hebrew word *ravah*. This is not a literal mathematical term, but conveys the idea of "increasing," or "becoming many." Exodus 1:7 describes the exceedingly high fertility rates enjoyed by the Israelites in Goshen. Here "multiplying" is accompanied by the concept of "swarming."

> But the sons of Israel were fruitful [parah] and increased greatly [swarmed] and multiplied [ravah], and became exceedingly mighty, so that the land was filled [mala] with them (Exodus 1:7, emphasis added).

Providentially nestled safely in the Goshen incubator, under the warming smile of the Lord's blessing, the twelve patriarchs grew into the swarming nation of the twelve tribes of Israel in only a few generations.

"Fill the earth" is carried by the Hebrew verb *mala*, which expresses the production of plenty and abundance. A jar of water may be "filled" to the brim (2 Kings 4:6). A land may be "filled" with sin (Jeremiah 16:18) or with people (Exodus 1:7).

God's procreation mandate assigns to man and woman the sacred obligation to make the earth *swarm* and *teem* with image-bearing creatures. The vast tracts of land that make up this globe, sprawled uninhabited and uncultivated by the shovel, mind, and ingenuity of mankind. It is God's magnificent design and plan that the offspring of Adam and Eve would spread throughout the whole earth resulting in countless thousands of tongues singing His praise from every land, tribe, and nation (see Revelation 7:9-10). God's fetching glory for Himself is the chief purpose for mankind and womankind. "Man's chief end is to glorify God and to enjoy Him forever," question one of the Westminster Shorter Catechism states.

Now, it's quite obvious that this procreation mandate is of peculiar relevance to womankind. Of course, men must participate. But woman was designated as the partner responsible for giving a special focus to offspring. Procreation permeates her very name. *"Now the man called his wife's name Eve, because she was the mother of all the living"* (Genesis 3:20, emphasis added).

Due to sin, the peculiar vocational focus of each partner will become snake-bitten, irksome, complicated, and cursed. Man, *the breadwinner*, will encounter cursed ground, thorny soil, and a sweaty face (Genesis 3:17-19). Woman, *the child nurturer*, will encounter pain in childbirth. *"To the woman He said, 'I will greatly multiply your pain in childbirth, in pain you shall bring forth children'"* (Genesis 3:16a, emphasis added).

The sacred procreation focus of woman's *creation mandate* is highlighted in the only two biographical references made to Eve's post-fall career.

> *Now the man had relations with his wife Eve, and she conceived and gave birth to Cain, and she said, "I have gotten a manchild with the help of the LORD." And again, she gave birth to his brother Abel (Genesis 4:1-2a, emphasis added).*

> *And Adam had relations with his wife again; and she gave birth to a son, and named him Seth, for, she said, "God has appointed me another offspring in place of Abel; for Cain killed him" (Genesis 4:25, emphasis added).*

Clearly, God presents to womankind her solemn privilege and responsibility to birth and nurture children as image-bearers who will live their lives to the glory of their Maker. And this is not at all incompatible with her acquisition of a degree from Yale or some other reputable university.

Matthew Henry summarizes the procreation mandate (*"Be fruitful, and multiply, and fill the earth"*) assigned to Adam and Eve: "Their posterity should extend to the utmost corners of the earth and continue to the utmost period of time."[12]

Some offhandedly contend that surely this procreation mandate is a *mission accomplished.* They argue that the world is certainly full, and they even groan that it's far too full. "Hey, mankind can check off that *'be fruitful and fill the earth'* box."

For decades now, we've been deluged with propaganda warning us of the devastating threat of global overpopulation. As a teenager in the early 1970's, I watched the movie "Soylent Green," starring Charlton Heston. It was a science fiction film that projected us forward fifty years to the year 2022 where the earth was packed tight with shoulder-to-shoulder people everywhere. The chief theme was "No More Room." Privacy was extinct. Poverty reigned. Food was scarce. The globe couldn't feed the hunger of the unwieldy population. Soylent Green had become the government-issued nutritional ration for the masses. The main character conducts an action-packed investigation into the production of Soylent Green. The film ends with Mr. Heston shouting out to anyone who would hear his grizzly and cannibalistic discovery that, "Soylent Green is people!"

We've now been told that we best serve the planet by depopulating rather than by procreating. This notion dovetails nicely with the "me-centered" philosophy of life marketed by modern feminism: "Children are a nuisance and an irritable obstacle to my self-actualization and personal fulfillment. They're a drag on my economic prosperity." This mindset has resulted in the teeming proliferation of "the pill" usage, abortions, and sterilizations. Applause abounds.

But there's an ominous downside to this contempt for procreation. In 1987, Ben Wattenberg wrote a perceptive book called *The Birth Dearth*, in which he warned about the coming crisis due to the dangerously low birth rates in industrialized nations. He predicted that many of the most highly developed countries would suffer because of *a lack* of people. Everyone laughed. But now, thirty years later, the laughter has stopped.

In recent years, my wife and I have traveled a number of times to Europe, and each time we've turned to each other and asked, "Where are the children?" It seems we were on to something.

Consider these excerpts from Michael Meyers' *Newsweek International* article (September 27, 2004), entitled "Birth Dearth:

Remember the population bomb?: The new threat to the planet is not too many people, but too few."

Fertility rates have dropped by half since 1972, from six children per woman to 2.9. And demographers say they're still falling, faster than ever. The world's population will continue to grow—from today's 6.4 billion to around 9 billion in 2050. But after that, it will go sharply into decline. Indeed, a phenomenon that we're destined to learn much more about—depopulation—has already begun in a number of countries... .

To reproduce itself, a society's women must each bear 2.1 children. Europe's fertility rates fall far short of that, according to the 2002 U.N. population report. France and Ireland, at 1.8, top Europe's childbearing charts. Italy and Spain, at 1.2, bring up the rear. In between are countries such as Germany, whose fertility rate of 1.4 is exactly Europe's average... .

And so it is across the Continent. Bulgaria will shrink by 38 percent, Romania by 27 percent, Estonia by 25 percent. "Parts of Eastern Europe, already sparsely populated, will just empty out," predicts Reiner Klingholz, director of the Berlin Institute for Population and Development. Russia is already losing close to 750,000 people yearly. (President Vladimir Putin calls it a "national crisis.") So is Western Europe, and that figure could grow to as much as 3 million a year by mid-century, if not more.

The potential consequences of the population implosion are enormous. Consider the global economy, as Phillip Longman describes it in another recent book, *The Empty Cradle: How Falling Birthrates Threaten World Prosperity and What to Do About It*" A population expert at the New America Foundation in Washington, he sees danger for global prosperity. Whether it's real estate or consumer spending, economic growth and population have always been closely linked. "There are people who cling to the hope that you can have a vibrant economy without a growing population, but mainstream economists are pessimistic," says Longman. You have only to look at Japan or Europe for a whiff of what the future might bring, he adds. In Italy, demographers forecast a 40 percent decline in the working-age population over the next four decades—accompanied by a commensurate drop in growth across the Continent, according to the European Commission. What happens when Europe's cohort of baby boomers begins to retire around 2020? Recent strikes and demonstrations in Germany, Italy, France, and Austria over the most modest pension reforms are only the beginning of what promises to become a major sociological battle between Europe's older and younger generations.

That will be only a skirmish compared with the conflict brewing in China. There market reforms have removed the cradle-to-grave benefits of the planned economy, while the Communist Party hasn't constructed an adequate social safety net to take their place. Less than one quarter of the population is covered by retirement pensions, according to CSIS. That puts the burden of elder care almost entirely on what is now a generation of only children. The one-child policy has led to the so-called 4-2-1 problem, in which each child will be potentially responsible for caring for two parents and four grandparents.[13]

Wattenberg's ominous predictions are coming true. Consider the Russian mathematical momentum. It is already losing 750,000 people yearly. That's a city the size of Baltimore wiped out every year. This trend will result in a 50% drop in the population of Russia by the mid-century. Jeremy Page entitled his article in *The Times* (UK) on September 24, 2005: "Mother Russia Now Sees More Abortions Than Babies Born." Christian Lowe entitled his article in *The Scotsman* on May 11, 2006: "Putin offers Russians cash to have more babies." He documents Vladimir Putin's proposal to provide monthly stipends to women willing to bear children.

Michael Medved recently stated on his radio program that 30% of German women are ending up childless—by choice. Is it any wonder why some European races are becoming an endangered species and why that continent is experiencing a Muslim inundation? A recent UK news article revealed that "Mohammed" and its most common alternative spelling "Muhammed" are now more popular babies' names in England and Wales than "George."[14] Are there any lessons for us here in the U.S.?

Joel Belz sounded striking notes in his *World Magazine* article of May 6, 2006, entitled "The New Baby Boom: Remember all the jokes about big families?" He interacts with Philip Longman's 2004 book *The Empty Cradle: Freedom and Fertility in an Aging World*. Belz' silver lining thesis is: "Conservatives will inherit the earth."

The statistics simply don't lie. Mr. Longman says that "nearly 20 percent of women born in the late 1950s are reaching the end of their reproductive lives without having had children"—and that such a proportion is nearly twice what it was a generation earlier. This "greatly expanded childless segment of contemporary society, whose members are drawn disproportionately from the feminist and countercultural movements of the 1960s and 70s, will leave no genetic legacy." The children they might have influenced, Mr. Longman says candidly, were never born (emphasis added).[15]

Ah, what a morbid curse there is on any people whose women refuse to *"play their position"* as appointed by God. Belz continues:

> Conservatives, meanwhile—typically including lots of evangelical Christians—have gone right on having babies. In doing so, they may be profoundly increasing their influence in the world at large. Nor is this impact just a fuzzy researcher's theory. Fertility rates in the states carried in 2004 by George W. Bush are 11 percent higher, Mr. Longman says, than in states won by John Kerry. In other words, conservative dominance might be expected to continue to grow where a majority has already been established, while what he calls "progressive" political influence will probably shrink.[16]

What is the mightiest strategy for influencing the world unto God-glorifying good? It was unveiled in the Garden of Eden. *"Be fruitful and multiply, and fill the earth, and subdue it."* Women of dominion who give their lives to the bearing and nurturing of God-fearing offspring are the power brokers of the earth. The hand that rocks the cradle is the hand that rules the world!

Wise women instinctively know this. A couple Mother's Days ago, I decided to switch from the "fresh flowers" motif to the "stuffed animal" motif. Our then 14-year-old daughter Abigail and I went shopping and found a beautiful brown mama bear holding in her lap a cute little pink baby bear. "That's you and Mom. Now we've got to find the four boys," I said. In another department, we found four little cubs, looking very scruffy and unkempt. Sunday morning, we arranged the stuffed animals on the kitchen table. Mama bear was holding little beauty, surrounded by the four beasts. When my bride entered the room, her eyes sparkled with the same flash that came from Jacqueline's on her front porch days earlier. Transfixed, she said, "There are so many!" She was clearly gratified with the contemplation of having given the best years of her life to the mothering of a brood of children from the ages of 12 to 22.

Procreation summons a woman to an extraordinarily God-glorifying enterprise; and godly women of dominion have a peculiar eye toward it. How can she effectively subdue and rule the earth? She can best accomplish it by taking seriously her creation mandate.

3. Position

Genesis 1:27 states, "*And God created man in His own image, in the image of God He created him; male and female He created them.*" A profound statement, this verse declares the *equality of essence* shared by men and women. We're both *"image of God."* We share an equal nature. It blasts out of the water the twisted notion that the man possesses a superior nature above the woman. It's a sharp reproof to all forms of male tyranny, especially within marriage.

The Apostle Peter extols the virtues of Sarah's submission to Abraham (1 Peter 3:5-6), yet immediately chops down at the roots any thought of chauvinistic supremacy in verse 7. He exhorts: "*You husbands likewise, live with your wives in an understanding way, as with a weaker vessel, since she is a woman; and grant her honor as a fellow heir of the grace of life, so that your prayers may not be hindered*" (emphasis added).

Husbands and wives are *"fellow heirs."* We're both equally image-bearing children of the King. "*There is neither Jew nor Greek, there is neither slave nor free man, there is neither male nor female; for you are all one in Christ Jesus*" (Galatians 3:28, emphasis added).

As Christians, regardless of our race (Jew/Gentile/Black/White/Latino), social status (freeman/slave/rich/poor), or sex (male/female), Paul insists that we all stand before God on an equal footing. In Christ, we're all *"one,"* sharing an equality of essence.

However, though men and women share a blessed *equality*, we're also endowed with a holy and wonderful *diversity*. "*Male and female He created them*" (Genesis 1:27b, emphasis added).

God's image-bearing masterpiece manifests a purposeful *diversity*. Think of the Trinity of the Godhead. There is one God (singularity and *equality*). But there are three Persons: Father, Son, Holy Spirit (plurality and *diversity*). *Equality* of essence is accompanied by *diversity* of function. The Father decrees redemption. The Son accomplishes redemption. The Spirit applies redemption. God is *equality* and *diversity*. And so in His fashioning an image-bearing race of mankind, God purposefully infuses the profound elements of *equality* and *diversity*— *"In the image of God He created him"* (equality); *"male and female He created them"* (diversity). This masterpiece reflects the glorious nature of God Himself.

But our God-defying world culture seeks to vandalize the divine masterpiece. For decades, radical feminism has staged an all-out assault on God's creation order by seeking to obliterate the blessed differences between male and female. Feminists are seeking to *feminize* our boys and *masculinize* our girls. They want to level the distinctions between male and female. It seems that the androgynous (indistinguishable as to gender) Michael Jackson, in many ways, has become the standard of excellence toward which we should strive.

To the contrary, God created male and female to be profoundly different. Yes, we certainly share an *equality of essence and nature*; but we just as certainly are given a *diversity of position and function*. God has assigned to man the *primary role of head and leader* and to woman the *auxiliary role of follower and assistant*.

Says who? Says the Bible! Notice the clear assertions of male headship and female assistantship.

First, we see that the race is named *"man"* (Genesis 1:26, 27; 5:1; 6:3, 6). This honor, reflected in our tradition of a bride's taking her husband's name, conveys the investment of primary authority in the male.

Second, we see in the stated and created order an intended priority: *"male and female He created them."* The Apostle Paul, in arguing for women's submissiveness in the church, traces his conviction of male authority and headship back to Eden's order. *"But I do not allow a woman to teach or exercise authority over a man, but to remain quiet. For it was Adam who was first created, and then Eve"* (1 Timothy 2:12, emphasis added).

Third, we see the crystal clear divine appointment of the woman to an auxiliary assistant's role to the man. *"Then the LORD God said, 'It is not good for the man to be alone; I will make him a helper suitable for him'"* (Genesis 2:18, emphasis added):

> The designation "helper suitable" or "helpmeet" gives her a distinct manward focus. "The Hebrew expression is *ezer kenegdo. Neged* means "corresponding to" or "answering to." Literally, therefore, the expression means "a help answering to him." The words imply that woman complements him, supplements him, completes him,

is strong where he may be weak, supplies his deficiencies and fills his needs.[17]

Fourth, we see man exerting his delegated authority and headship over the woman by the act of actually naming her. *"Now the man called his wife's name Eve, because she was the mother of all the living"* (Genesis 3:20, emphasis added).

Clearly, in God's created order men and women have been assigned to different positions and roles in God's world. Yes, there is *equality of essence*, but *diversity of function*, between the sexes. Generally speaking, the normal course of life results in a woman pairing up with and marrying a man. (I am aware that we live in an imperfect, sin-cursed world that doesn't always match every Eve with an Adam.) It's God's will for a married woman to assume her auxiliary position at her husband's side as his supportive *"helpmeet,"* dedicating herself to the grand project of helping her man and nurturing her children.

I realize that the Bible's view of the world doesn't conform to the feminism-saturated culture of political correctness. I realize that this declaration of gender diversity and womanly submission may sound offensive and denigrating to a 21st Century female reader. But it shouldn't.

Let's reason scripturally together. Is it denigrating for the Son of God to assume a position of submission under the authority of the Father? Did it degrade his divine Person when He said, *"For I have come down from heaven, not to do My own will, but the will of Him who sent Me"* (John 6:38)? Oh no! The Son's humble submission under the Father's authority is the essence His praiseworthy glory.

> *Have this attitude in yourselves which was also in Christ Jesus, who, although He existed in the form of God, did not regard equality with God a thing to be grasped, but emptied Himself, taking the form of a bond-servant, and being made in the likeness of men. And being found in appearance as a man, He humbled Himself by becoming obedient to the point of death, even death on a cross. Therefore also God highly exalted Him, and bestowed on Him the name which is above every name* (Philippians 2:5-9, emphasis added).

For a woman who rejects the mind of the world and puts on the mind of Christ, it is counted a great honor to follow in the submissive footsteps of the servant-hearted Son of God. For there's no more prestigious role in the world than humbly occupying the position, and performing the role assigned by one's heavenly Father. This is what it means to be Christ-like. The way of humility is the road to glory. Dear Christ-loving women of dominion, regardless of what abuse the feminists heap on you, stay at your posts. Regardless of how shrill their screams become, *play your position*.

I know. I know. It's easy for me to say. I'm a man. I know what you're thinking. "The Celestial Coach has assigned *him* to play a glamorous position!" As a man and husband, I'm like one of those golden-boy forwards on the soccer field who get to score the goals. Those offensive strikers get all the headlines and applause. But women who are positioned as servant-minded defensive guardians typically get ignored and overlooked. I know. I know.

I once coached a great soccer player in the pre-high school leagues. Jerry had all the tools: speed, strength, stamina, quickness. He was a prolific scorer and thrived on splashing the net. But when his high school coach saw his abilities, he resolved to make him the team's *sweeper*. A *sweeper* is the defensive player who stands as the last line of defense in front of the goalie. He's the super-swift and aggressive guardian who fights off the triple threat of the opponent's scoring front line. The *sweeper* sweeps up after the mess left by his teammates who've let the ball through their defenses. This coach wanted his strongest player anchoring his defense. He figured this gave his team the best chance to win.

Jerry's position reassignment from the front to the back was psychologically devastating. He became depressed about soccer. He confided in me that he'd lost his enthusiasm for the game. "All I'm doing is serving everyone else, keeping the score down, stopping the opponents' shots, and passing the ball ahead to set up my teammates so that *they* can score. They're splashing the net. They're getting all the attention and applause. I hate my position!"

Eventually, Jerry resigned himself to his supportive, servant's role. He became an outstanding *sweeper*, who *"played his position"* with all his might, with a *"win it"* mentality. He scored few, if any, goals. But at the end of the season, when the league coaches gathered to select the All-Conference honors, Jerry was the only player from his team who was draped with the medal. He was also chosen by his fellow players as the team's MVP. Jerry stayed at his post. He held his position. At the end of the day, he got the *"Well done, good and faithful servant."*

Thus the last shall be first, and the first last (Matthew 20:16).

4. Motivation

Let me become your cheerleader from the sidelines.

Dear women, you are remarkably gifted and talented souls, who've been positioned by your Lord on the field of life as *sweepers*. You've been appointed as helpmeet wives to set up your husbands for success and applause. Behind the scenes you go about the business of daily feeding *him* with opportunities to score in his vocation, in his community, and in his church. The axiom is profoundly true: "Behind every great man is an even greater woman."

You've been appointed as child-nurturing mothers whose *sweeper* labors are well epitomized by the TV commercial with the little boy sitting on the bathroom throne, swinging his bare legs in the air and shouting, "Mom, I'm done!" There he waits for your maternal wipe. I know you're tempted to despise it. But think of the Lord Jesus. He submitted to the Father's will, emptying Himself to the point of death on a cross, wiping up with his own body the immoral mess left by God's children. The goal was the salvation of their never-dying souls. So it is with you.

And remember. By rocking the cradle conscientiously, you rule the world profoundly. In his book *The Mother at Home* (1833), John S. C. Abbott quotes the mother of George Washington: "A good boy generally makes a good man."[18]

Then Abbott goes on to express our debt as a nation to her.

> George Washington had a mother who made him a good boy, and instilled into his heart those principles which raised him to be the benefactor of his country, and one of the brightest ornaments of the world. The mother of Washington is entitled to the nation's gratitude. She taught her boy the principles of obedience, and moral courage, and virtue. She in a great measure formed the character of the hero, and the statesman. It was by her own fireside that she taught her playful boy to govern himself, and thus he was prepared (to govern a nation). We are indebted to God for the gift of Washington, but we are no less indebted to God for the gift of his inestimable mother. Had she been a weak, and indulgent, and unfaithful parent, the unchecked energies of Washington might

have elevated him to the throne of a tyrant.[19]

It's interesting to note that John Abbott possibly didn't even know Mrs. Washington's first name. In his historical survey, he refers to her only as "Lady Washington." Par for the course, right, ladies?

But keep in mind the pep talk given to the greatness-vying disciples by our beloved Master and Savior and "coach." *"And sitting down, He called the twelve and said to them, "If anyone wants to be first, he shall be last of all, and servant of all"* (Mark 9:35).

And remember, it is He who will hand out the trophies in the end!

> Once the *New York Times* was asked to help a group of club women decide on the twelve greatest women in the United States. After due consideration, the editors replied, 'The twelve greatest women in the United States are women who have never been heard of outside of their own homes.... I ask you, who was greater, Thomas A. Edison or his mother? When he was a young lad his teacher sent him home with a note which said, "Your child is dumb. We can't do anything for him." Mrs. Edison wrote back, "You do not understand my boy. I will teach him myself." And she did, with results that are well known.[20]

It's generally true both maritally and maternally: "Behind every great man is an even greater woman."

Dear beloved and blessed wives and mothers, your Creator has endowed you with breathtaking gifts and positioned you in the garden. I know that some of you have been long on the field, and it's late in the game, and you're fatigued to the point of exhaustion. Though the outside world may not applaud you, and your inside flesh may scold you, I cheer you on to *"play your position."* Don't let this world squeeze you into its narcissistic, me-oriented mold. Oh, with what craft and subtlety the serpent is persuading the daughters of Eve these days. Listen to the Word of your Heavenly Father shouting to you from the sidelines: *"Honey! Play your position! Win it!"* Press on with your womanly dominion assignment. I assure you. At the end of the day, you'll not regret it. You'll be draped with the only medal that really matters. The ultimate selfless *sweeper* Himself, the Lord Jesus Christ, will personally commend you with history's highest honor: *"Well done, thou good and faithful servant."*

CHAPTER 3:
WOMANLY DOMINION
DECEITFULLY ASSAULTED

No one likes *to be duped.*

George Bailey was the firstborn son of the President of the Building & Loan in Bedford Falls. His dad had selflessly dedicated himself to facilitating Depression-era families with the honor of owning their own home—a financial impossibility for most who couldn't satisfy the loan demands of the Scrooge-like local banker, Old Man Potter. But George dreamed of far greater things for himself—like traveling the world, like building skyscrapers and bridges, like lassoing the moon. But the premature death of his father kept George grounded at home, stuck in his father's humdrum office, securing the American dream for a multitude of local neighbors. Life was good and sweet.

You know the storyline of the classic Christmas movie *It's a Wonderful Life.* Events conspired to whisper into George's good ear that he'd been *duped.* His younger brother Harry left town to become a college football hero. His enterprising friend went to New York and became wealthy. George, on the other hand, was stuck nurturing the hometown folk at the mundane Building & Loan. The soft voice hissed: "George, you're wasting your life. People are taking advantage of you. The wide-open world awaits your arrival. But you're allowing yourself *to be duped.*"

The temptation-to-leave onslaught strikes its crescendo when Potter invites George into his office and lights up a cigar for his guest.

> POTTER: George, I'm an old man, and most people hate me. But I don't like them either, so that makes it all even. You know just as well as I do that I run practically everything in this town but the Bailey Building and Loan. You know, also, that for a number of years I've been trying to get control of it...or kill it. But I haven't been able to do it. You have been stopping me. In fact, you have beaten me, George, and as anyone in this county can tell you, that takes some doing. Take during the Depression, for instance. You and I were the only ones that kept our heads. You saved the Building and Loan, and I saved all the rest.

> GEORGE: Yes. Well, most people say you stole all the rest.

> POTTER: The envious ones say that, George, the suckers. Now, I have stated my side very frankly. Now, let's look at your side. Young man, twenty-seven, twenty-eight...married, making, say...forty a week.

> GEORGE (indignantly): Forty-five!

> POTTER: Forty-five. Forty-five. Out of which, after supporting your mother, and paying your bills, you're able to keep, say, ten, if you skimp. A child or two comes along, and you won't even be able to save the ten. Now, if this young man of twenty-eight was a common, ordinary yokel, I'd say he was doing fine. But George Bailey is not a common, ordinary yokel. He's an intelligent, smart, ambitious young man—who hates his job—who hates the Building & Loan almost as much as I do. A young man who's been dying to get out on his own ever since he was born. A young man...the smartest one of the crowd, mind you, a young man who has to sit by and watch his friends go places, because he's trapped. Yes, sir, trapped into frittering his life away playing nursemaid to a lot of garlic-eaters. Do I paint a correct picture, or do I exaggerate?

Potter then goes on to entice George away from his post at the Building & Loan by offering a hefty salary along with frequent trips to New York and Europe.

This leaves George's head spinning. He thinks: "Potter's right. *I've been duped* by my foolhardy dad's vision. I'm trapped by this 'serving others' mindset. I owe it to myself to break out of this prison, and start a life worth living."

You know the rest of the story. George eventually shakes off the poisonous enticements of Potter, and is brought to the inspiring conclusion that a wonderful life is measured not by the number of dollars accumulated, the number of headlines made, or the number of trips abroad taken. A wonderful life is measured by the number of lives nobly touched.

This revelation is reached by George's eerie viewing of his hometown void of his influence. Mr. Gower, the pharmacist, without George's conscientious help, became a drunk of an ex-convict. Uncle Billy, without George's humanitarian skill, was thrown into an insane asylum. The charming and delightful town of Bedford Falls, without George's philanthropic nurturing, became the corrupt and slimy town of Pottersville. His little brother Harry, without George's heroic rescuing in the icy river, drowned at age nine and never grew up to save the transport ship full of soldiers by shooting down two Japanese Kamikaze Zeroes. Clarence, the guardian angel, said it best to George:

> CLARENCE: Every man on that transport died. Harry wasn't there to save them because you weren't there to save Harry.... Strange, isn't it? Each man's life touches so many other lives, and when he isn't around he leaves an awful hole, doesn't he?...You see, George, you really had *a wonderful life.*

Women of dominion, like George Bailey, have been appointed to undertake *a wonderful life* mission. God has called them to take on grand projects which will nobly touch lives in earth-shaking ways. Sure, they'll encounter pain and thorns and thistles in the process. Sure, they'll need to exercise Herculean discipline and self-denial. But the wonderful final-day revelation will leave them with no regrets.

But in the meantime, the serpent whispers: *"You're being duped!"* These days, all hell is endeavoring to entice women away from their dominion mandate. The enemy daily lights up slender cigarettes and tells ladies how it's far more fulfilling to *lasso the moon* their way, than to *subdue and rule* God's way.

Like Eve in the Garden of Eden, so women on the field of life, are not left alone to serve their Maker without harassment. "*Now the serpent was more crafty than any beast of the field which the* LORD *God had* *made. And he said <u>to the woman</u>, "Indeed, has God said, 'You shall not eat from any tree of the garden'?"* (Genesis 3:1, emphasis added)

Eve and her daughters are peculiarly prime targets for Satan's assaults. His fiery darts come by way of subtle suggestions.

> Why does the serpent approach Eve rather than Adam? This is a difficult question to answer, and it is well not to be dogmatic where dogmatism is out of place. There are, however, certain Scriptural statements which should be noted. In writing to Timothy, Paul says, "For it was Adam who was first created, and then Eve. And it was not Adam who was deceived, but the woman being quite deceived, fell into transgression" (1 Timothy 2:13-14). Again Paul speaks of the serpent beguiling Eve through subtlety (2 Corinthians 11:3), and in 1 Peter 3:7 the wife is spoken of as the weaker vessel.[21]

This *weaker vessel* reference may be an allusion to the woman's *constitutional sensitivity*, as she is the *deeper feeling* gender and, thus, more susceptible to passionate persuasion. In addition, it may refer to her *positional vulnerability*, as she is the subordinated gender and more susceptible to suggestions of foul play on God's part. "Well, Eve, it looks like once again you've received the short-end-of-the-stick. God has withheld from you something else that's sweet and necessary for your happiness."

Young writes, "At any rate, the serpent approached her and in this approach manifests his subtlety."[22] So, ladies, consider yourselves warned. The Liar takes a special pleasure in whispering into your pretty ears. You are darling targets for his dart-like wiles.

Nancy Leigh DeMoss, in her book, *Lies Women Believe*, confesses:

> Eve believed the lie, and we, the daughters of Eve, have followed in her steps—listening to, believing, and acting on one lie after another.... Satan poses as an "Angel of light" (2 Corinthians 11:14). He promises happiness and pretends to have our best interest at heart. But he is a deceiver and a destroyer; he is determined to dethrone God by getting us to side with him against God.[23]

The enemy is determined to get you to spurn your God-assigned *mandate*. He grinds his teeth when he sees you *playing your position* with a *"win it"* attitude. He detests a woman on a mission, *subduing and ruling* her life to the glory of God with a dominion mindset.

Such mighty women are a great threat to his dark kingdom. So he continuously slithers across your path, and with subtlety, persuades you to reject your positional loyalty and your win-it tenacity. Instead, he wants you to take up a surrender mentality and a do-your-own-thing individuality. He's bent on getting you to trade in your dominion mindset for a victimization mindset. He wants you to think: "God has given me the short-end-of-the-stick, and I'm not going to take it anymore."

Here are four contemporary lies:

1. You're a Genetic Victim

Here's a common hiss: "I know God has called you to subdue and rule your life responsibilities, but you've been dealt a bad *genetic* hand, so *you just can't* do it."

It's not your fault. It's your parents' and grandparents' fault. They gave you bad DNA, a bad chromosomal disposition. That's the source of your inability to achieve your goals.

In *Lies Women Believe*, Nancy Leigh DeMoss provides a reservoir of insight into the spiritual warfare of modern-day Eves, with actual case study quotations of lies and excuses women use to evade personal responsibility in life's challenges. She cites excerpts from personal confessions:

> The lie I believed was: "You'll be just like your parents—it's hereditary—you can't help it." [24]

> "My hormones are going crazy."[25]

> "My mother and her mother were both manic depressive—I guess it just runs in our family."[26]

A homemaker may claim that her house is a shambles, because she's just not mentally wired to be a "multi-tasker." The Bible labels sloppy slothfulness as a moral issue: *"Through indolence the rafters sag, and through slackness the house leaks"* (Ecclesiastes 10:18). But she protests it has nothing to do with a sinful laziness, only with a genetic disposition. That's why *she can't rule and subdue* in this important domestic assignment.

Another woman may say, "I know that I'm considerably overweight, but I'm a victim of a bad metabolism. It's that bad DNA inherited from my mom's side that does me in. That's why I'm not responsible for my overweight condition." A woman confessed:

> I believed I had a weight problem because my dad's family is fat. I have their body type, so I am always going to struggle. No use trying—it just comes back anyway. Therefore, I was placing blame on them for my bondage to food.[27]

A wife may plead that she just doesn't have the same drive for physical intimacy as her husband has. So she habitually withholds bedroom expressions of love.

A mother contends that during certain times of the month, she's just not responsible for controlling her hair-trigger temper.

A dear lady believes that God gave her a high-octane, less than sweet and tender personality, so she's basically exempt from cultivating a *"gentle and quiet spirit, which is precious in the sight of God"* (1 Peter 3:4).

In this way, we believe the lies and champion the excuses as to why we can't *"win it"* in many contests against the world, the flesh, and the Devil. We surrender the ground God has commissioned us to *subdue and rule*. We fail to act as men and women of dominion.

2. You're a Circumstantial Victim

Here's another hiss: "I know God has called you to *rule* the spheres of your life, but your difficult *circumstances* have made it impossible for you to succeed. That's why *you can't* do it."

Nancy Leigh DeMoss' mailbox is again helpful:

> "My mother was never a real mother to me—I've never had a model to show me how to raise my kids…"

> "I had an abusive childhood; I've never been able to trust people…"

> "My family never dealt with problems; we just stuffed everything inside and pretended like nothing was wrong. To this day *I can't* really confront issues…"[28]

And that's why my family and church relationships are in a shambles. *I can't help it.* That's why I can't keep myself pure. I can't help it. That's why I'm so distrustful, suspiciously assuming the worst of my husband and children and friends. This is so destructive. But *I can't help it.* That's why I'm so inept as a mother in the home. *I can't help it.*

My parents never forced me to discipline myself. That's why I can't get up on time in the morning. That's why I can't consistently do my devotions. That's why I can't keep my commitments. That's why I can't aggressively get out there and do well in school.

My house is so small and congested. That's why the dishes and the laundry are piled so high.

My acquaintances are so selfish. That's why I leave behind me a trail of broken relationships wherever I go.

My church is so cliquey. That's why I shy away from social activities and harbor bitterness toward so many women there.

> Marcia traces her present obesity back to the summer afternoon during her early teen years when her uncle took her behind the barn and sexually abused her. "Because of what he did to me, I just can't control what I eat. I use my extra pounds as a defense mechanism. Food makes me feel secure. I'm a victim, and that's why I can't get mastery over this area of my life."
>
> Please understand that I am not unsympathetic regarding the painful scars left behind by sinful abuses done to dear souls by ignorant and evil people. I ache and grieve about such abuses. We need to *weep with those who weep* (Romans 12:15).
>
> However, I don't believe that I'm being a true friend to people by encouraging them, in the name of sympathy, to abdicate their holy obligations toward God. Simply being a victim determines nothing. Millions of verbally abused children grow up to be successful students, businessmen, and pastors. Innumerable carnage-viewing Vietnam vets have returned home to become mighty pillars in our nation. Thousands of fatherless boys have grown up to become mighty-men dads in their homes. Countless sexually-abused teen girls have grown to be well adjusted and physically fit women. [29]

In this regard, Dr. Laura Schlessinger's book, *Bad Childhood—Good Life: How to Blossom and Thrive in Spite of an Unhappy Childhood* contains some solid horse sense for abused souls. Her thesis in a nutshell: Growing up in an abusive or broken home doesn't mean that your future is shattered, too! More importantly, God's Word tells us that redemption in Christ makes us new creatures who *can* put behind us the things of a futile and abusive past.

> *Knowing that you were not redeemed with perishable things like silver or gold from your futile way of life inherited from your forefathers (1 Peter 1:18, emphasis added).*

> *But one thing I do: forgetting what lies behind and reaching forward to what lies ahead, I press on toward the goal for the prize of the upward call of God in Christ Jesus (Philippians 3:13-14, emphasis added).*

Again, simply being a victim determines nothing. Victims have the solemn obligation to respond to their abuse in a God-honoring way. The call away from the excuse-making of *victimology* is not cruel, but very kind and liberating!

What a blessing it is to know that by the grace of God I can break these shackles, stand up on my own two feet, and *subdue* this sphere of my life to the glory of God!

Nancy Leigh DeMoss says it well:

> If our circumstances make us what we are, then we are all victims. And that's just what the Enemy wants us to believe. Because if we are victims, then we aren't responsible—we can't help the way we are. But God says we are responsible—not for the failures of others, but for our own responses and lives.[30]

Women of *dominion* trample serpents under their feet (Psalm 91:13).

3. You're a Marital Victim

Let's consider another hiss. "I know God's called you to be a *helper suitable* to your mate, but with that creep of a husband, He's got to be kidding!"

Brooke traces her ever-present piles of wash in the laundry room and piles of dishes in the sink back to the insensitivity of her husband. "He's always criticizing my housekeeping. He's never satisfied with my cooking. He hardly ever tells me that I'm doing a great job. I can't remember the last time he encouraged me. In this non-affirming climate, I'm just not very motivated to enthusiastically dive into my tasks. How can I be blamed for my argumentative bitterness toward a guy who treats me this way? How am I supposed to be inspired to serve and submit to such a creep?"

I understand Brooke's plight. I'm a husband, who can sometimes act like a creep. If this were a book on manly dominion, I'd grab husbands by the lapels and get right in their faces. Here's a sampling from *Manly Dominion* of what husbands need to hear and do:

The Lord Jesus is the model husband.

Husbands, love your wives, just as Christ also loved the church and <u>gave Himself up for her</u>; that He might sanctify her, having cleansed her by the washing of water with the word, that He might present to Himself the church in all her glory, having no spot or wrinkle or any such thing; but that she should be holy and blameless (Ephesians 5:25-27, emphasis added).

Yes, He is the head and lord of his bride. But these crucial roles were exercised with the tenderest of self-sacrificial love.
Did our Savior come down to his earthly bride and recline on a sofa, expecting her to fetch His slippers and newspaper? To the contrary, He came and emptied Himself out for her good.

For even the Son of Man did not come to be served, but to serve, and to give His life a ransom for many (Mark 10:45)

For His bride, He left heaven's glory. For His bride, He was willing to wiggle in Bethlehem's manger and work in Nazareth's workshop. For His bride, he was numbered with the transgressors in His baptism. For His bride, He endured near starvation and Satanic temptation in the wilderness. For His bride, He absorbed years of public ministry abuse by a wicked and adulterous generation. For His bride, he had no place to lay his head. For His bride, he marched fearlessly toward the Jerusalem slaughterhouse. For His bride, He broke the bread in the upper room. For His bride, He was drenched in blood-like sweat. For His bride, He said, "Not my will, but Thine be done." For His Bride, He handed Himself over to a kangaroo court. For His bride, He was again and again spat upon and struck in the head. For His bride, he stood bare-backed at a pillar absorbing scourge after scourge. For His bride, he was mocked while holding a reed scepter. For His bride, He carried and collapsed under the crossbeam. For His bride, He was stripped naked. For His bride, He absorbed the spikes into His hands and feet. For His bride, he was lifted up between heaven and earth as an accursed spectacle. For His bride, He hung before head wagging scoffers. For His Bride, he gasped for breath and cried out "My God, My God, why hast Thou forsaken me?" For His bride, He finished it and died.

This is an overwhelming model for husbands. We wouldn't have dared to put it before ourselves. We would have considered it profanity to join together two things so far apart: sinful men and the sinless Savior! But with this very ideal, the Holy Spirit has charged us.

D. Martyn Lloyd-Jones asks: "How many of us have realized that we are always to think of the married state in terms of the doctrine of the atonement?"

I must tend to her with an attitude of self sacrifice. I can't be content to sit back and observe with appreciation her selflessness toward me, as she rises early, labors long, and works late into the night for my family. I've been given the charge of sacrificing myself for her good. I've got to lead her instead of being mothered by her. I've got to serve her instead of being satisfied with being served by her. I need to beat down my love of leisure and my right to watch the NCAA Basketball Tournament. What about her and the benefit she'd receive from a couple solid hours away from the children? I need to assertively subdue and rule in the lives of those children instead of acting as a passive spectator to her mothering. I've got to take the initiative to romance her, pray with her, and complete her "honey-do" lists. I need to make the advancement of her personal and spiritual prosperity the chief project of my earthly life.[31]

But this is not a book on manly dominion. It's on womanly dominion. And so, I must speak directly to wives of husbands who fall far short of heroic Christ-likeness. It's not time to fixate on a husband's duties, but on a wife's. The Serpent points fingers at others, blaming them. The Savior presses us each with our own personal responsibility. *"Peter therefore seeing him said to Jesus, 'Lord, and what about this man?' Jesus said to him, 'If I want him to remain until I come, <u>what is</u> that <u>to you?</u>*

You follow Me!'" (John 21:21-22, emphasis added)

Consider the excellent wife of Proverbs 31. Her most striking trait is the fact that she is so utterly selfless. *"She does him* (her husband) *good and not evil all the days of her life"* (Proverbs 31:12). She *"works with her hands in delight... brings food from afar... rises while it's still night... looks well to the ways of her household, and does not eat the bread of idleness"* (31:13, 14, 15, 27).

And what does such selfless, servant-hearted, help-meeting get her? Is she oppressed and abused? To the contrary, her husband is crazy about her! He's convinced she's one in a million, *"... worth is far above jewels. The heart of her husband trusts in her."* And he tells her so: *"Her husband...praises her..."* (31:28). He brags about her to his friends, *"... her works praise her in the gates"* (31:31). His children honor and praise her, *"Her children rise up and bless her"* (31:28).

To Proverbs 31, Nancy Leigh DeMoss responds:

> Doesn't sound like an oppressed woman to me! In fact, what woman wouldn't be overjoyed to have the same rewards? But how did she get all those "benefits"? Not by insisting that her husband roll up his sleeves and help out with the household chores (although there's certainly nothing wrong with men doing so), but by choosing the pathway of servanthood—by making it her number one priority (after her relationship with God) to meet the needs of her family.
>
> "Vicki" describes how God set her free from the deception that she was to expect her husband to serve her:
>
> "Several years ago, I was set free from a big lie. I always expected my husband to serve me by helping me with household chores and children. I resented it if he did not do so or if he didn't do it well enough; I resented picking up after him or doing things to help or serve him. I had always known that Eve was created as Adam's helpmate, but one day the Holy Spirit personalized this for me and showed me that I had not embraced the role of being a 'helper' to my husband.
>
> "Now I pick up my husband's socks or newspapers and remind myself that I am 'helping' him. I am grateful for all the help he does give me (which really is a lot), and I look for ways to help him accomplish his agenda (free him from jobs around the house, keep kids out of his way, etc), instead of expecting him to help me accomplish my agenda. It has really helped our marriage."[32]

I read that above extended quotation to Dianne, my own bride of 25 years, and mother of our five children. She was doing her hair. I wondered what she'd think of it. I wondered if she'd be offended by the way it sounded. She put down her curling iron and brush and stared at me for a moment. Then she said, "That is so huge! That strikes at the root. That's why I struggled terribly during the early years of marriage. I didn't get it."

She went on to describe how helpful and reinforcing our trip in 1995 to Birmingham, England, had been for her. We stayed a few days with Bob and Anne. Bob was working long and tedious hours for an American company that was relying on him to establish a satellite base in the UK. Dianne watched Anne, the mother of four highly testosterone-charged boys ages one to seven and a newborn girl, "doing it all"—the wash, the housework, garage cleanup, auto maintenance, meal preparation, even a second hot meal for Bob when he came home late. Anne did it all without a sigh of discontent. When Dianne asked, "Why Anne?" she responded, "He works so hard for us. I'm so grateful. I'd never want the boys to hear me complaining about their father. This is the job God gave me. I'm his helper."

I know what some of you may be thinking, ladies. "If I had such a husband, I could be such a wife." But I wonder which came first—the chicken or the egg? As a pastor for over 20 years, I've experientially found it true that behind every great man is typically an even greater woman. Usually, the man who is highly esteemed at the city gates (Proverbs 31:23), has behind him a bride who *"does him good and not evil all the days of her life"* (Proverbs 31:12).

Here's some biblical advice contrary to the serpent's hissing. **Stop blaming your man, and start helping him!**

You may, on the other hand, be a woman who wishes you had a husband, period. "Yes, I'm a marital victim. Marriage has passed me by!"

Nancy Leigh DeMoss provides us with insight. She herself is nearly fifty and has never been married.

> Lie #21. I have to have a husband to be happy.
> The truth is that the ultimate purpose of marriage is not to make us happy. Women who get married for the purpose of finding happiness are setting themselves up for almost certain disappointment; they seldom find what they are looking for…
> The truth is that happiness is not found in (or out of) marriage; it

is not found in any human relationship. True joy can only be found through Christ.[33]

> *I have learned to be <u>content in whatever circumstances I am</u>... And my God shall supply all your needs according to His riches in glory in Christ Jesus (Philippians 4:11b, 19 emphasis added).*

The truth is that the serpent will always suggest that the grass is greener on the other side, that God has given you the short-end-of-the-stick. When you're not married, the Enemy will tell you that you're unfairly victimized by your *singleness*. And when you are married, he'll tell you that you're unfairly victimized by your *attachedness*. The snake slithers and hisses on both sides of the fence.

4. You're a Maternal Victim

Here's a final hiss: "I know God's called you to give yourself to childbearing and nurturing, but that old patriarchalism degrades and belittles women. Surely this is just another example of your getting the short-end-of-the-stick. Who can blame you for seeking self-affirmation in a personally fulfilling career? Look! It's good for the ego, a delight to the eyes, and desirable to make you wise. You go, girl! Get out there and score for yourself."

Linda Hirshman has written a book entitled, *Get to Work: A Manifesto for Women of the World.*

Here's an excerpt from the February 22 and 23, 2006, editions of ABC's *Good Morning America*:

> DIANE SAWYER (host): Well, as we said, the "mommy wars" are back and raging again big-time, but with a brand new gladiator. Professor Linda Hirshman wrote an article, called "Homeward Bound" last year for *The American Prospect* magazine. And it began a ballistic debate and here's why: the number of college-educated women who are leaving the workforce to go home with the kids. In fact, census figures show 54 percent of mothers with a graduate or professional degree are no longer working full-time. And Hirshman says this is a big mistake, that women will pay a large price for it with no measurable gain for their kids... Law professor Linda Hirshman, a mother herself, who says women who choose

their children over an independent career life are simply wrong.

> HIRSHMAN: There are no reliable statistics showing that the children of working mothers do worse than the children of stay-at-home mothers… I think it's a mistake for these highly educated and capable women to make that choice… <u>I think that one could argue that these women are letting down the team</u>. Consider a society in which the entire Supreme Court is male. We may actually experience that in our lifetime. What would it feel like if all—the entire Congress were male?[34]

That's the kind of breezy thinking behind Shelley's dropping off her three-month-old and two-year-old at 7:30 AM in the daycare lobby. "I've got too much education and ability to waste it wiping noses and bottoms all day. Besides, I've read studies that show that kids develop better in a more structured and socially stimulating environment like this."

But the likes of Linda Hirshman sense a threatening shift in the prevailing feminist wind. Though being offered profitable careers outside of the home, many degreed women are reverting back to a more traditional role—"choosing the cradle over the corporate ladder, bedtime stories over boardroom meetings."[35]

Many eyes are opening to the fact that the unbiblical feminist mantra of careerism is a primary source of much female denigration today. Hirshman-style feminism has actually deflowered and violated the very women it claimed to defend and protect. It has trampled their beautiful and God-endowed femininity and imposed in its place a macho perversion. The courteous and chivalrous treatment enjoyed by June Cleaver in the fifties has been replaced by the crude and coarse treatment paid to Murphy Brown in the nineties. And in presently growing numbers, educated women are concluding that true, lasting fulfillment is not found in shuffling papers or downloading e-mails in an office building, but in nurturing their own children in their own homes.

On May 3, 2006, Jeanne Sahadi, *CNNMoney.com* senior staff writer, penned an interesting article entitled *"Being a Mom Could be a 6-Figure Job."* She summarized research done by *Salary.com* which calculated that a stay-at-home mother might be paid as much as $134,121 per year for her 91.6 hours/week job equivalent blended functions as a housekeeper, chef, teacher, CEO, facilities manager, chauffeur, janitor, psychologist, and computer technician.[36] Running a fast-paced household, managing a domestic budget, scheduling a complex calendar, educating a diversified student body, and acting as a consultant to a successful husband all combine to create a daunting job description. It's a profession of diversified adventures and borderless frontiers. Stay-at-home mothers may be underpaid, but they're certainly not underchallenged!

In response, an exhausted mother may say, "That's it! I'm over-challenged. I'm in way over my head! I'm underequipped for this overwhelming task. My swarming responsibilities sometimes paralyze me. Sometimes I just retreat to my bedroom and surrender the field. I concede defeat and don't even fight to *win it* back. How am I supposed to *subdue and rule*?

"You should see this peculiarly difficult hand I've been dealt, with the blend of my children. One of them is really moody. Another wears an I-don't-care-attitude. A third is a poster boy for a Ritalin distributor. The last has symptoms of dyslexia. And they all seem so ungrateful for my mothering. The whole bad brew depresses me. I've basically given up *winning* over these problems. I'm really tempted to *wimp out* and *run away* to some neat package of an office job. Why is my lot so much more difficult than other mothers'?"

"The snake is right."

"I'm a maternal victim."

"I'm a marital victim."

"I'm a circumstantial victim."

"I'm a genetic victim."

"For these reasons, *I just can't*, and I will never be a woman of dominion. *I just can't* subdue and rule in my God-assigned spheres of life."

CHAPTER 4:
WOMANLY DOMINION
IN THE OLD TESTAMENT

Pilgrim's Progress, the classic allegory of the Christian life tracing the adventures of "Christian" in his travels from "The City of Destruction" to "The Celestial City," is history's second most-read book. It is second only to the Bible. It was penned by John Bunyan, the pastor of Bedford, England, during his dozen years of imprisonment in the Bedford jail. At any time he could have returned to his fireside, surrounded by his second wife Elizabeth and his four children. He needed simply to soil his conscience by agreeing *not* to preach. He chose prison and a clear conscience over freedom and family happiness. But this decision often tormented him. From the jail, he wrote:

> The parting with my wife and poor children hath often been to me in this place as the pulling of the flesh from my bones; [37]

But it was not only John Bunyan who valiantly endured hardship. His new bride Elizabeth was made of the same courageous stuff. Though dealt a very bad hand, and given a very challenging lot in life, she handled it as a woman of dominion.

Ten years after he was married, when Bunyan was 30, his wife died in 1658, leaving him with four children under ten, one of them blind. A year later, he married Elizabeth who was a remarkable woman. The year after their marriage, Bunyan was arrested and put in prison. She was pregnant with their firstborn and miscarried in the crisis. Then she cared for the children as stepmother for 12 years alone, and bore Bunyan two more children, Sarah and Joseph.

She deserves at least one story here about her valor in the way she went to the authorities in August of 1661, a year after John's imprisonment. She had already been to London with one petition. Now she met with one stiff question:

"Would he stop preaching?"

"My lord, he dares not leave off preaching as long as he can speak."

"What is the need of talking?"

"There is need for this, my lord, for I have four small children that cannot help themselves, of which one is blind, and we have nothing to live upon but the charity of good people."

Matthew Hale with pity asked if she really had four children being so young.

"My lord, I am but mother-in-law to them, having not been married to him yet full two years. Indeed, I was with child when my husband was first apprehended; but being young and unaccustomed to such things, I being dismayed at the news, fell into labor, and so continued for eight days, and then was delivered; but my child died."

Hale was moved, but other judges were hardened and spoke against him. "He is a mere tinker!"

"Yes, and because he is a tinker and a poor man, therefore he is despised and cannot have justice."

One Mr. Chester was enraged and said that Bunyan will preach and do as he wishes.

"He preaches nothing but the word of God!" said Elizabeth.

Mr. Twisden, in a rage: "He runs up and down and does harm."

"No, my lord, it is not so; God hath owned him and done much good by him."

The angry man: "His doctrine is the doctrine of the devil."

She: "My lord, when the righteous Judge shall appear, it will be known that his doctrine is not the doctrine of the devil!"

Bunyan's biographer comments, "Elizabeth Bunyan was simply an English peasant woman. Could she have spoken with more dignity had she been a crowned queen?"[38]

Elizabeth Bunyan was *more than a gentle and quiet spirit*. In the face of intimidating circumstances, she refused to curl up into a ball of victimized despair. She's an example to any 21st-century woman encountering great difficulties. She *"quit herself as a man"* (1 Corinthians 16:13, KJV), demonstrating that courageous spirit which resolves to boldly *subdue* and *rule* in stressful situations.

The Bible is teeming with such women who refused to give excuses, play the victim, listen to lies, and passively use them to exempt themselves from the responsibilities which God, in His providence, had dealt them. *"Whatever your hand finds to do, verily, <u>do it with all your might</u>"* (Ecclesiastes 9:10, emphasis added).

The Bible is full of examples of women who *just did it*. They didn't make excuses. They aggressively faced their challenges head on. They *subdued* and *ruled* as *women of dominion*. Let's examine the lives of a few of these women.

1. Sarah

The wife of Abraham was a *"very beautiful"* woman whose striking external appearance turned heads wherever she went (Genesis 12:11-14; 20:2). But Sarah's true beauty was found in her *womanly dominion*. The Apostle Peter pays her great tribute in lifting up her internal *makeup* as a model for all Christian women.

> *And let not your adornment be merely <u>external</u>—braiding the hair, and wearing gold jewelry, or putting on dresses; but let it be the hidden person of the heart, with the imperishable quality of <u>a gentle and quiet spirit</u>, which is precious in the sight of God. For in this way in former times the holy women also, <u>who hoped in God</u>, used to adorn themselves, being submissive to their own husbands. Thus Sarah obeyed Abraham, calling him lord, and you have become her children if you <u>do what is right without being frightened by any fear</u> (1 Peter 3:3-6, emphasis added).*

In extolling Sarah's internal beauty, "Peter does not seem to be referring to any specific incident here, for the main verb and both participles in verse 5 all indicate a continuing pattern of conduct during one's life."[39] But Peter does highlight a specific strength in Sarah namely, her *subduing* and *ruling* over her fears. This is a fundamental battle for any woman. Panic attacks are a common affliction in stressful times. Sarah is a heroine worthy of imitation, for instead of fretting and surrendering, she managed to *"hope in God"* and *"do what is right without being frightened by fear."*

We're introduced to Sarah immediately after God called her husband to uproot and move from the familiar hometown surroundings of Ur, across the howling Arabian Desert, to set up house in the alien land of Canaan (Genesis12:5). She subdued any fears she may have faced, and courageously went, humbly acquiescing to her husband's conscience convictions.

Nancy Hasseltine was a true *daughter* of Sarah. In 1810, Adoniram Judson was packing for Burma to become the first American-sent missionary to the heathen. Smitten with Nancy, he asked John Hasseltine for his daughter's hand in marriage with this eye-popping letter:

> I have now to ask, whether you can consent to part with your daughter early next spring, to see her no more in this world; whether you can consent to her departure, and her subjection to the hardships and sufferings of a missionary life; whether you can consent to her exposure to the dangers of the ocean; to the fatal influence of the southern climate of India; to every kind of want and distress; to degradation, insult, persecution, and perhaps violent death. Can you consent to all this, for the sake of him who left his heavenly home, and died for her and for you; for the sake of perishing, immortal souls; for the sake of Zion, and the glory of God? Can you consent to all this, in hope of soon meeting your daughter in the world of glory, with the crown of righteousness, brightened with the acclamations of praise which shall redound to her Saviour from heathens saved, through her means, from eternal woe and despair?[40]

Though a friend stoutly declared he'd "tie his own daughter to the bedpost rather than let her go on such a hair-brained adventure,"[41] John Hasseltine left the decision to Nancy, who chose to go, writing:

Jesus is faithful; his promises are precious. Were it not for these considerations, I should, with my present prospects, sink down in despair, especially as no female has, to my knowledge, ever left the shores of America to spend her life among the heathen; nor do I yet know, that I shall have a single female companion. [42]

Here is tonic for the devastated high school-aged daughter whose father's job transfer to another state will painfully uproot her from precious friends and activities. Providence brings to women all manner of causes for *fear* and trembling.

Sarah bravely coped with the prospects of bearing a child (Isaac) at the age of 90 (see Genesis 18:12, an occasion for calling Abraham "lord"). Imagine that, dear forty- something reader, who may find yourself unexpectedly pregnant! Then upon birthing this specially loved boy and nurturing him toward manhood, providence conspired to brutally snatch him from Sarah's embrace. God called father Abraham to sacrifice their son on Mount Moriah (Genesis 22:1-8).

Mary, our Lord's biological mother, also had to watch her specially born Boy be escorted by His Father up a hill in the region of Moriah (Golgotha) to be crucified there (Luke 2:35, John 19:26).

> *And Simeon blessed them, and said to Mary His mother, "Behold, this Child is appointed for the fall and rise of many.... and a sword will pierce even your own soul—"(Luke 2:34a, 35a, emphasis added).*

> *Therefore the soldiers did these things. But there were standing by the cross of Jesus His mother, and His mother's sister, Mary the wife of Clopas, and Mary Magdalene (John 19:25, emphasis added).*

What fearful heart piercings loving mothers must endure! They pour their hearts into their children. Then they must helplessly watch, sometimes from tear-drenched pillows, their darlings run the gauntlet of a wicked and cruel world. Godly mothering isn't for cowards!

The same is true for godly wifing. Mighty women of God must be anchored by an inward trust in Him as of old, *"holy women...hoped in God"* (1 Peter 3:5). Peter's commendation of Sarah in 1 Peter 3 particularly emphasizes her courage in being submissive to the marital authority of her husband (*"thus Sarah obeyed Abraham,"* 3:6a). Such a policy makes a woman vulnerable to potential mishandling. Husbands can seemingly be such insensitive blockheads. "Honey, I know your doubts and hesitations, but after much counsel and prayer, I've come to the conclusion that God would have us move from California to Michigan." Wayne Grudem summarizes Sarah's excellence in this:

> Quiet confidence in God produces in a woman the imperishable beauty of a gentle and quiet spirit, but it also enables her to submit to her husband's authority without fear that it will ultimately be harmful to her well being or her personhood.[43]

Sarah was a beautiful *woman of dominion, subduing* and *ruling* over her fears. She was much more than *a gentle and quiet spirit.*

2. Zelophehad's Daughters

> *Then the <u>daughters of Zelophehad</u>, the son of Hepher, the son of Gilead, the son of Machir, the son of Manasseh, of the families of Manasseh the son of Joseph, came near; and these are the names of his daughters: Mahlah, Noah and Hoglah and Milcah and Tirzah. And <u>they stood before Moses and before Eleazar the priest and before the leaders and all the congregation, at the doorway of the tent of meeting,</u> saying, "Our father died in the wilderness, yet he was not among the company of those who gathered themselves together against the LORD in the company of Korah; but he died in his own sin, and he had no sons. Why should the name of our father be withdrawn from among his family because he had no son? <u>Give us a possession among our father's brothers</u>" (Numbers 27:1-4, emphasis added).*

Here we meet five *women of dominion*: Mahlah, Noah, Hoglah, Milcah, and Tirzah. They were the daughters of Zelophehad, from the tribe of Manasseh, all unmarried women (Numbers 36:2-6). Sonless father Zelophehad had died in the wilderness before he could stake his real estate claim in the Promised Land of Canaan. These fatherless women rightly anticipated their own upcoming bankruptcy upon entering Canaan. They would have no land or assets.

In the Middle East, a father's property was divided between his sons after his death (Deuteronomy 21:15-17). Daughters usually received a substantial gift from their fathers, called a dowry, consisting of clothes, jewelry, money, etc. By this system, land was kept within a family and passed on to the next generation through its sons. But in the case of Zelophehad, his family's estate would be wiped out.

These five daughters deftly spied an unjust loophole in the Israelite civil law code. What did they do? Did they passively and sheepishly sit in their tent poisonously murmuring to one another about the perceived abuse? No way! They fashioned a compelling legal argument, marched unitedly through the tent city, and *"stood before Moses and before Eleazar the priest and before the leaders of all the congregation, at the doorway of the tent of meeting"* (Numbers 27:2). Reading between the lines, a flabbergasted hush came over the crowd. They then spoke with the utmost dignity, respect, and eloquence. I really like these five ladies!

Consider Lynn who graduated from her high school with outstanding academic credentials. Many colleges and universities sought her enrollment in their four-year BS nursing programs. She accepted the package offered by a state university and excelled in the classroom during her freshman year. But when she pursued early registration for her sophomore classes, she was informed by the registrar that due to an enrollment overload, certain essential sequential classes wouldn't be available to her in the upcoming semester, resulting in her need to recalibrate her plans into a five-year format. Lynn viewed this as an unconscionable injustice. Due to the university's miscalculation, they were asking her to put her life on hold for a year. Was this more appropriate than asking professors to increase their class sizes for a semester? Instead of brewing up a stew of bitter resentment, she crafted a series of arguments and made an appointment with an administrator. Lynn is again on the four-year plan.

Or reflect on Nancy Hasseltine Judson who did indeed experience distress, degradation, and insult among the heathens of Burma. In 1824, her husband Adoniram was caught in the crossfire of the brewing war between Burma and England, and was imprisoned along with other teachers for nearly two years in a sweltering "Death Camp." During this time, though pregnant and eventually nursing her newborn Maria, Nancy labored fiercely as her husband's relentless defense attorney and political advocate. She crafted an appeal and personally presented it to Bandula, the acting king of Burma.

> With fear and trembling Nancy took it to the great man through the surrounding crowd of courtiers. A secretary read it aloud.

Bandula actually listened, and rather pleasantly asked her several questions about the teachers. Her answers seemed to satisfy him. He promised to think about the subject. She should come again and he would give her a decision.[44]

Adoniram survived the withering imprisonment on death row and was eventually released to press on with his epic missionary labors chiefly because of his helpmeet's bold and tireless efforts to secure special favors and political cover for him. Nancy's heroics gave to Burma its Bible, and to countless souls, eternal life. Nancy was the great woman behind the great man.

Back to Zelophehad's daughters and their example. Moses was not offended by the *assertive daring* of these five ladies. To the contrary, he was duly impressed by their bold initiative. He *"brought the case before the Lord"* (Numbers 27:5). And lo and behold, the five girls *win it*!

> *Then the* LORD *spoke to Moses, saying, "The daughters of Zelophehad are right in their statements. You shall surely give them a hereditary possession among their father's brothers, and you shall transfer the inheritance of their father to them. Further, you shall speak to the sons of Israel, saying, 'If a man dies and has no son, then you shall transfer his inheritance to his daughter'"* (Numbers 27:6-8, emphasis added).

Surely *"a gentle and quiet spirit, which is precious in the sight of God"* (1 Peter 3:4b) does not mean that a woman is obligated to act like a *passive doormat* who is willing to be trampled upon by unjust circumstances. The Lord loves to see *women of dominion* courageously step forward in the name of truth and justice.

3. Deborah

Sometimes when men are hiding in the dugout, women need to step up to the plate and *win it*.

Sometimes women's bold bravery must make up for men's craven cowardice.

On a *familial* scale, we see Zipporah aggressively stepping up when her husband Moses was passively hiding. In this case, Moses' passive negligence almost cost him his life.

Now it came about at the lodging place on the way that the
LORD met him and sought to put him to death. Then Zipporah
took a flint and cut off her son's foreskin and threw it at Moses'
feet, and she said, "You are indeed a bridegroom of blood to
me." So He let him alone. At that time she said, "You are a
bridegroom of blood"—because of the circumcision (Exodus
4:24-26, emphasis added).

It seemed that Moses had neglected his fatherly obligation to
circumcise his son (probably Gershom), according to God's requirement
handed down to all Jews, through Abraham (Genesis 17:10-14). Maybe
he didn't want to offend the sensitivities of his Midianite bride with the
bloody ritual.

Walt Kaiser comments: "Thus for one small neglect, apparently out
of deference for his wife's wishes, or perhaps to keep peace in the home,
Moses almost forfeited his opportunity to serve God and wasted eighty
years of preparation and training!"[45]

The LORD wasn't going to put up with a national leader who was a
domestic coward. Due to Moses' cowardly abdication of his fatherly
duty, Zipporah was pressed to bravely take matters into her own hands.
This woman of dominion saved the life of her negligent man.

What Zipporah did on a *familial* scale, Deborah did on a *national*
scale.

During the period of the Judges, Israel was in a backslidden state.
"In those days there was no king in Israel; every man did what was right
in his own eyes" (Judges 17:6). Personal preferences and feelings ruled.
God's Word and Law were trampled. The fourth chapter opens up with:
"And the sons of Israel again did evil in the sight of the Lord... And the
Lord sold them into the hand of Jabin king of Canaan" (4:1-2). At this
time, Israel was under the rod of God's discipline. God has His ways of
chastening His people.

Woe to the wicked! It will go badly with him, for what he
deserves will be done to him. O My people! Their oppressors
are children, and women rule over them, O My people! Those
who guide you lead you astray, and confuse the direction of
your paths (Isaiah 3:11-12, emphasis added).

Now Deborah, a prophetess, the wife of Lappidoth, was judging
Israel at that time (Judges 4:4, emphasis added).

Is it any surprise that *Israel's only female leader* stepped up at *Israel's morally darkest hour*? Quite clearly, her divine appointment as a female leader was a divine rebuke to male dereliction.

Our home, just fifteen miles from Lake Michigan, has a driveway nearly a football field long. The "lake effect" snow machine typically dumps many feet of snow per winter. When our four boys have displayed a lack of inspiration for snow removal, I've watched my bride don her arctic gear and begin shoveling. Pretty soon, they're out there, too. The lady shames them out of their negligence!

Deborah's valiant labors were a shameful indictment of male irresponsibility .

Look at the leading male actor of the chapter. The Lord commanded Barak, through Deborah, to lead 10,000 men to defeat the Canaanites at Mt. Tabor. Listen to his spineless response to the lady: *"Then Barak said to her, 'If you will go with me, then I will go; but if you will not go with me, I will not go'"* (Judges 4:8, emphasis added).

Shame on you, Barak! Act like a man! Thomas Scott comments: "He was *culpably afraid and not honoring God as he ought to have done."*[46]

> *And she (Deborah) said, "I will surely go with you; <u>nevertheless, the honor shall not be yours</u> on the journey that you are about to take, <u>for the LORD will sell Sisera into the hands of a woman</u>." Then Deborah arose and went with Barak to Kedesh (Judges 4:9, emphasis added).*

That's right! Another woman named Jael was enlisted to the shame of the faint-hearted Barak, to finish off the Canaanite commander Sisera, by driving a tent peg through his temple and into the ground (4:21). Once again, a woman was compelled to bloody her hands because of a man's abdicating his leadership duty.

Here's the upshot. At times, when men are passive and inattentive, their women need to step up and become aggressive and decisive.

Karl is a Christian who had backslidden into a state of deep spiritual despondency. His job situation had become irritating, his financial condition frustrating, his devotional life languishing, his exercise habits vanishing, his waistline expanding, his spiritual condition backsliding. Samantha, his bride, sought to arrest his freefall with verbal encouragement and prayer. Her maternal heart ached as she saw night after night Karl's refusal to lead her and their three boys in family devotions, and Lord's Day after Lord's Day, his refusal to get out of bed and lead the family to church. Pastors and churchmen strongly exhorted Karl with little improvement.

But then something happened. Samantha concluded that she needed to be *"more than a gentle and quiet spirit."* She needed to be an aggressive and decisive Deborah. That Sunday evening, while Karl was lounging in front of the TV, Samantha got the boys ready, piled them into the van, and led her little platoon into the sanctuary, in full view of the watching and exhilarated congregation. That night was the turning point for lounging Karl. Samantha's stepping up to the plate, while he hid in the dugout, arrested his spiritual nosedive. The outcome has been blessed. Karl was awakened to the urgency of the battle and now stands as a mighty man leading his platoon in fighting the good fight.

I've heard of women in Samantha's predicament who claim that quietly knitting a sweater is more godly than decisively leading to church services or leading family devotions. They claim it's their obligation to *passively* and submissively seek to win their husbands *"without a word"* (1 Peter 3:1). But God has commissioned parents to bring up their children *"in the discipline and instruction of the Lord"* (Ephesians 6:4; Deuteronomy 6:7; 2 Timothy 1:5). In such circumstances, discreetly, women *"must obey God rather than men"* (Acts 5:29).

In the long run, such a Deborah's rising to the occasion as *"a mother in Israel"* (Judges 5:7) will bring her praise at the gate from her husband, should the Lord Jesus put him in his right mind.

A few minutes after I concluded a sermon commending this woman of dominion Judge in Israel, Charles met me earnestly and emotionally in the church lobby with a little son in one hand and a little daughter in another. Charles had recently been baptized in our church. He had been raised in a Christian home, but for the first years of his marriage, he was spiritually AWOL. During this time, his gifted and intelligent wife Rebecca was saved and discreetly nudged him to get right with God and take up the mantle as a man of God. He too was marvelously saved and has taken hold of the reins of his young family. That evening, Charles got his moist eyes right in my face and joyfully said, "Pastor, Rebecca is my Deborah!"

Just like Deborah, Rebecca helped her husband and nurtured her flock with all her might, doing whatever it would take to *"win it"* to the glory of God.

4. Ruth

During this same time of the judges, we meet another *woman of dominion*. "*So Naomi returned, and with her <u>Ruth</u> the Moabitess, her daughter-in-law, who returned from the land of Moab. And they came to Bethlehem at the beginning of the barley harvest*" (Ruth 1:22).

Here is this Ruth, the Moabitess, a Gentile social outcast in the Israelite town of Bethlehem. No ethnic group in world history was more *exclusive* than the ancient Jewish nation. To add insult to injury, Ruth was *a widow* in this foreign land. Now, left to her fears and insecurities, surely she would have curled up into a ball of self-pity and barely eked out a miserable existence for herself and her mother-in-law. But that's not how the story reads.

Instead, Ruth aggressively pursued a respectable income by gleaning the grain left behind by the harvesters, "*Please let me go to the field and glean among the ears of grain after one in whose sight I may find favor*" (2:2). She clearly saw her duty and stepped forward trusting in her new-found Lord ("*Your people shall be my people, and your God, my God*"—1:16b) to establish the work of her hands. The Lord crowned her bold efforts with success by her "chance meeting" ("*she <u>happened</u> to come to the portion of the field belonging to Boaz*"—2:3, emphasis added) with the godly and dignified Boaz.

Ruth's mother-in-law, in seeking out provision for the future, counseled Ruth to make a bold attempt at securing the wealthy and dashing Boaz as her husband: "*Wash yourself therefore, and anoint yourself and put on your best clothes, and go down to the threshing floor...*" (Ruth 3:3).

What did this Gentile widow do? Did she succumb to her feelings of *inferiority* and *insecurity*? Did she say: "No, Mother-in-law, *I can't* do that. I'm a widow. I'm a Gentile. He won't have anything to do with me"? No. She trampled these obvious fears under her feet and tactfully made herself available for a marriage proposal. Again, the Lord crowned her aggressive efforts with great blessing. Ruth the Moabitess eventually became the great grandmother of King David (4:17-22).

By the way, there's a lesson here for young ladies who desire that the Lord would give them a godly husband. Many "desperate" women make sad moral compromises in order to attract a man. I've seen ladies depart from small, but biblically faithful, churches, to attend large, but spiritually shallow, churches, with the justification: "But I'll never meet anyone back there!" Look at Ruth. Duty led her away from Moab where beaus were plentiful, toward Bethlehem where few would show interest in a Gentile maiden. But Ruth was directed by moral principle and not romantic pragmatism. She kept the fifth commandment and honored her mother-in-law. *"Seek first His kingdom and His righteousness; and all these things will be added unto you"* (Matthew 6:33). Ruth's priority was to honor God through Naomi, and thus God provided for Ruth through Boaz, probably the godliest man on the face of the earth during this dark period of the Judges.

Realize also that Ruth's discreet and deliberate *"hankie dropping"* overture is a far cry from the bawdy and brassy female *"stalking"* that takes place in our day. High school and college girls *"hit on"* boys in the hallways and parking lots, constantly telephone males seeking their attention, forwardly *"ask out"* young men on dates, and physically force their seductively attired bodies into male laps. This is an unfortunate perversion of the lovely *"weaker vessel,"* and a sad forecast of manly passivity in marriages.

Nevertheless, Ruth's discreet efforts provide us with a refreshing and emboldening example.

We, too, must never allow our fears make our decisions. Fear is the most strangling emotion known to man or woman. Who of us can't think back on all the things we failed even to attempt because of unfounded but paralyzing fear? Many young men have disqualified themselves from pursuing relationships with extraordinary young women because they were afraid she might say, "Sorry, I'm not interested."

Back in 1979, I was diligently studying in the college library when I felt a tap on my shoulder. I looked up to behold an absolutely delightful looking, blue-eyed swan of a young woman. "Whoa!" I shouted on the inside, but stayed calm on the outside. Sweetly, she asked if she might be able to borrow my yellow high-liter that was sitting on the table near my books. Her name was Dianne, and she's been my wife now for 25 years. She discreetly, yet deliberately, "dropped her hankie," and I've been blessed ever since.

Many capable young basketball players prematurely end their basketball careers in their freshman year by refusing to even try out for the team for fear that they might be cut. What if Michael Jordan had been cowed into hanging up his sneakers after being cut from his high school junior varsity basketball team? As we survey our lives, many of us ache regarding friends we never made, classes we never took, teams we never played on, experiences we never enjoyed—all because we were intimidated by fears which held us down under their feet.

Shakespeare poetically put it:

Our doubts are traitors
and make us lose the good we oft might win
by fearing to attempt.
(*Measure for Measure*, 1, 4)

Our daughter Abigail broke her leg (tibia) in May. Due to slower than normal healing, she didn't get the green light to run until the last week of August. She wanted to try out as a freshman for the high school cross country team, but feared limping through races and finishing dead last. She went out anyway. Watching her hobble through early races was painful. But by the end of the year, she shattered the school record by 47 seconds and placed 50th at the state meet—and this as a freshman!

Theodore Roosevelt wisely said, "There is no disgrace in failure, only in a failure to try."[47]

Elsewhere, Roosevelt declared:

Far better it is to dare mighty things, to win glorious triumphs, even though checkered by failure, than to take rank with those poor spirits who neither enjoy much nor suffer much because they live in the gray twilight that knows neither victory nor defeat. [48]

Solomon put it this way: "*The wicked flee when no one is pursuing, but the righteous are bold as a lion*" (Proverbs 28:1).

We must be men and women of dominion, boldly making decisions on the basis of our duty, obligation, and opportunity, not on the basis of our fears and insecurities.

5. Abigail

We have four sons, but only one daughter. We named her "Abigail" with the great hope that she'd grow up to be like her biblical namesake.

a. Abigail had an intelligent mind.

Now the man's name was Nabal, and his wife's name was Abigail. And the woman was <u>intelligent</u>*...(1 Samuel 25:3a, emphasis added).*

b. Abigail had a beautiful appearance.

And the woman was intelligent and <u>beautiful in appearance</u>,... (1 Samuel 25:3b, emphasis added).

c. Abigail had a servant's heart.

And she arose and bowed with her face to the ground and said, "Behold, <u>your maidservant is a maid to wash the feet of my lord's servant</u>" (1 Samuel 25:41, emphasis added).

d. Abigail had a dominion attitude.

Then <u>Abigail hurried and took</u> two hundred loaves of bread and two jugs of wine and five sheep already prepared and five measures of roasted grain and a hundred clusters of raisins and two hundred cakes of figs, and <u>loaded them on donkeys</u>. And she said to her young men, "<u>Go on before me</u>; behold, I am coming after you." But she did not tell her husband Nabal. And it came about as she was riding on her donkey and coming down by the hidden part of the mountain, that behold, David and his men were coming down toward her; so she met them. Now David had said, "Surely in vain I have guarded all that this man has in the wilderness, so that nothing was missed of all that belonged to him; and he has returned me evil for good. "May God do so to the enemies of David, and more also, if by morning I leave as much as one male of any who belong to him." When <u>Abigail saw David, she hurried and dismounted from her donkey</u>, and fell on her face before David, and bowed herself to the ground. And she fell at his feet and said, "On me alone, my lord, be the blame. And please <u>let your maidservant speak to you, and listen to the words of your maidservant</u> (1 Samuel 25:18-24, emphasis added).

You probably know the story. Abigail was married to a rich, but evil and harsh, man named Nabal. David's mighty men had acted as security guards protecting Nabal's flocks from harm, but Nabal insultingly scorned David's diplomatic request for compensation. David was furious. He ordered four hundred of his warriors to strap on their swords and follow him down the mountainside to slaughter every male in Nabal's household. That's when Abigail got the word that David was offended and was on the war path.

Abigail needed to *get to the ball* before David did! There was no time for passive hesitation. She acted brilliantly, with decisive bravery and discretion. W. G. Blaikie swoons over her excellence:

> With the quickness and instinctive certainty of a clever woman's judgment, Abigail, Nabal's wife, saw at once how things were going. With more than the calmness and self possession of many a clever woman, she arranged and dispatched the remedy almost instantaneously after the infliction of the wrong. How so superior a woman should have got yoked to so worthless a man we can scarcely conjecture,…Her promptness and her prudence all must admire; her commissariat skill was wonderful in its way; and the exquisite tact and cleverness with which she showed and checked the intended crime of David—all the while seeming to pay him a compliment—could not have been surpassed.[49]

I've heard some argue that Abigail was in the wrong here—that she should have kept on knitting with a *gentle and quiet spirit*, that she had no business to act so decisively without first submissively consulting with her husband Nabal. I strongly disagree. There are times when it's a subordinate's duty to act contrary to an authority's wishes. Should a woman submit to an abortion simply because her evil husband requests it? When a woman's inaction will result in the breaking of God's Law and Word, she must move.

Matthew Henry hits the mark:

> We have here an account of Abigail's prudent management for the preservation of her husband and family from the destruction that was just coming upon them;…Abigail not only lawfully, but laudably, disposed of all these goods of her husband's without his knowledge (even when she had reason to think that if he had known what she did he would not have consented to it), because it was not to gratify her own pride or vanity, but for the necessary defense of him and his family, which otherwise would have been inevitably ruined.[50]

Such a praiseworthy interpretation of Abigail's actions is vindicated by David's commendation of this magnificent lady of dominion. "*Then*

David said to Abigail, 'Blessed be the LORD God of Israel, who sent you this day to meet me, and blessed be your discernment, and blessed be you, who have kept me this day from bloodshed, and from avenging myself by my own hand'" (1 Samuel 25:32-33, emphasis added).

There's a time for a woman to resignedly sit back and wait for the Lord to change her husband's mind. And there's a time for a woman to assertively rise up and take matters into her own hands. Abigail knew how to tell time.

Joe proudly parks his brand new four-wheel drive muscle truck in the driveway and excitedly asks his wife to come out and take a look. "I know we talked about our buying a less expensive older model, but having spent most of the day in the showroom with the salesmen, I'm convinced that *new* is the way to go."

Though the truck is a sleek and handsome black, Rachel sees red, especially when she reads the sticker price taped to the window—nearly $14,000 more than Joe planned to spend. Rachel pays the bills and knows that this "mortgage payment" on the truck will send the whole family into a financial tailspin. It's not time for Rachel to smile and affirm her husband's folly by gently and quietly returning to prepare dinner. It's time for her to discuss with her man the implications of this impulsive purchase and to suggest that he seriously consider returning the vehicle within the "24-hour no-questions-asked return policy."

Abigails know how to tell time.

Abigail also knew how to remain sweet. A besetting sin of many women is sharp-tongued argumentativeness. *"It is better to live in a corner of a roof, than in a house shared with a contentious woman"* (Proverbs 21:9; see also 21:19, 25:24). This was not Abigail's style. She was not arrogant and shrill, but assumed a humble posture and enlisted soft, self-effacing words: *"Abigail…hurried and dismounted from her donkey, and fell on her face before David, and bowed herself to the ground. She fell at his feet and said, 'On me alone, my lord, be the blame.'"* She even called herself David's *"maidservant"* (1 Samuel 25:23-24). Abigail wonderfully combined bold assertiveness with humble sweetness. Such a woman of dominion "wins" the hearts of men, as in the end, David actually proposed to the freshly widowed Abigail (25:39).

This *"Abigail Principle"* of tactful boldness is especially crucial in today's 21st century society of unequally yoked marriages and grievously dysfunctional homes. Christian women are married to Nabal's wallowing in sins of drunkenness, extramarital affairs, incest, physical abuse, etc. In keeping with biblical wisdom, spiritual insight, and sound counsel, many such mistreated women are called to rise up off a sofa of helplessness. They're called to take bold, and even drastic, measures to secure the safety of their children and families.

Julia called late one evening. "Pastor, my husband is drunk. He's told me I'm not to tell anyone, but I desperately need you to come over and confront him with this ongoing problem." I did, and the Spirit has used it wonderfully unto years of repentance and sobriety. The *subduing and ruling* of Julia diverted her husband and family from disaster.

A similarly blessed outcome resulted when Melissa requested a pastoral visit and tearfully reported—in her living room, in front of her husband whom she'd previously confronted—that she'd found footprints of pornography on his computer hard drive.

Lucy's husband had moved out of the house and into an apartment in the next town. He said he "needed some space" away from his wife and kids so he could "get his head together." He claimed he was not doing anything worthy of her biblically divorcing him, like abandonment (1 Corinthians 7:15) or adultery (Matthew 5:31-32; 19:9). He returned home occasionally, sent her a portion of every paycheck, and assured her there was no one else. But Lucy suspected there was another woman involved. Some of her friends had counseled her to quietly and submissively "wait on God." But Lucy used the *"Abigail Principle"* and instead hired a private investigator to find out what was really going on. Maybe she did have biblical grounds and warrant for divorce.

Some women, afraid of being left abandoned and all alone in the world, wrongly *put up with* all manner of physically abusive and even incestuous household behavior on the part of their husbands. The godly *woman of dominion* knows how to tell time. Such is not the time for waiting on God, but for taking action in the Name of God. She must protect her children and her family.

Furthermore, understand that it's not only Nabals who need Abigails. Davids need them, too. Men *"after God's own heart"* often need their women to step in front of them when they're charging down a mountainside to do something they may later regret. One day, I caught wind of something foolish that our college-aged son had done. I *saw red*. I strapped on my sword and headed down the stairs to *deal with it*. After 25 years, my bride knows how my footsteps pound when my invisible sword is strapped on. She said, "Honey, what are you going to do?" I stopped on the fifth step, climbed back up, and walked into a fifteen-minute closed door discussion in our bedroom where she tactfully and sweetly explained why she believed it was not the time for me to exercise *the nuclear option.*

I desperately need this Abigail in my life! She's not always right. But usually she is. Blessed be the Lord who sent her to me; and blessed be her and her discernment in family matters, church matters, financial matters, relational matters, educational matters, and all manner of matters.

You may ask, "But doesn't such initiative on the part of a wife classify her as unsubmissive?" It may, if she communicates stridently, argumentatively, and insubordinately and then makes his life miserable should he choose not to take her counsel. But she's not unsubmissive if she extends her advice discreetly, tender-heartedly, and humbly and then supports his leadership should he decide to take a contrary course. A godly wife owes her husband the love of tactfully sharing her advice with him. In the context of marriage, all the biblical principles of giving and receiving counsel are in play.

> *The way of a fool is right in his own eyes, but a wise man is he who listens to counsel (Proverbs 12:15).*

> *A gentle answer turns away wrath, but a harsh word stirs up anger. The tongue of the wise makes knowledge acceptable,....A soothing tongue is a tree of life, but perversion in it crushes the spirit (Proverbs 15:1. 2a, 4).*

> *Prepare plans by consultation, and make war by wise guidance (Proverbs 20:18).*

> *Faithful are the wounds of a friend, but deceitful are the kisses of an enemy (Proverbs 27:6).*

> *Oil and perfume make the heart glad, so a man's counsel is sweet to his friend (Proverbs 27:9).*

It's a blessed man who can sincerely say of his helpmeet, "She is my best friend." Faithful and loving counsel is a stock element of a God-honoring marriage. An Abigail-like wife is woman enough to deliver it. A David-like husband is man enough to receive it.

I tell our sons regarding their lovely, bright, discerning, perceptive, kind, tactful, and initiative-taking mother: "This is the kind of a woman you want and need—not some mere dizzy blond who looks pretty, but can't think clearly, and act decisively, and confront sweetly. You want a *woman of dominion.*"

That's why our only daughter's name is Abigail.

6. The Excellent Wife of Proverbs

Jody was pursuing a master's degree in education, when she took a multi-week trip to far-east Asia to work with missionaries involved in church planting, orphan rescuing, and literature publishing. She thought maybe the Lord wanted her to serve as an overseas missionary there. But the Lord had other plans for Jody. She returned to the States and landed a special education position in a public school where she brought *"salt and light"* into the lives of many unbelieving students and their families. Then one Sunday the Lord brought to our church, for a brief visit, Captain Trevor from the Air Force base in San Antonio, Texas. He sat in his burgundy chair, in the same row as the stunningly beautiful Jody, and eventually whisked her away as his bride.

Jody's rough-and-tumble spirit of adventure and her Spartan outlook on life convinced Trevor that she'd make an outstanding military wife on whom would be placed many unnatural demands. She didn't pamper herself with idealistic dreams of upper-middle-class suburban living in the conservative Midwest. Shortly after the honeymoon, the soon-to-be promoted to Major Trevor's orders sent him and his bride off to Japan, where Jody labored as a helpmeet to Trevor, and as a missionary for the gospel.

Just last week, I spoke to Jody on the phone. They are now living near Washington, DC, as now Lieutenant Colonel Trevor's skills have brought his family to the Capital. They now have four boys, ages five years, two years, and twins of four months. Trevor has been in Afghanistan for two months as a strategic communication advisor for the fledgling government there. He'll be gone for six months. His recently sent e-mail reads:

> *Warm greetings from sunny Kabul! Thank you so much for your note—an encouragement to me from across the world (Prov. 25:25). Jody, too, mentioned her good phone call with you. <u>I am so thankful for a capable wife who is handling a busy household while I'm gone.</u> I long to be there as her head and father to our boys... .*

Trevor's words from Afghanistan reminded me of the Excellent Wife of Proverbs 31. *"An excellent wife, who can find? For her worth is far above jewels. The heart of her husband trusts in her, and he will have no lack of gain"* (Proverbs 31:10-11).

This "excellent wife" of Proverbs 31 is the Bible's chief poster-girl for *womanly dominion.* Here we find the sketch of a woman who pursues her creation mandate with all of her might. Note a few highlights:

She's a *subduing* woman. She subdues her fleshly love of ease and her challenging daily schedule: *"She rises also while it is still night,…Her lamp does not go out at night"* (31:15a, 18b). She *subdues* the forces of the marketplace: *"She is like merchant ships; she brings her food from afar… She considers a field and buys it; from her earnings she plants a vineyard"* (31:14, 16). She *subdues* her tongue: *"She opens her mouth in wisdom"* (31:26a).

She's a *ruling* woman. She *rules* her household which she views as her headquarters and chief sphere of responsibility: *"She looks well to the ways of her household, and does not eat the bread of idleness… She is not afraid of snow for her household, for all her household are clothed with scarlet"* (31:27, 21b). She *rules* with foresight over her long-term annual calendar. Winter coats are economically procured and hanging in the closets well before the first December blizzard hits. Hers is not haphazard crisis management. *"Strength and dignity are her clothing, and she smiles at the future"* (31:25). Most importantly, she *rules* over her own sinful heart as she is *"a woman who fears the Lord"* (31:30b).

She's a *multiplying* woman. She not only gives physical birth to a number of children, but she sacrificially nurtures them in such a way that *"Her children rise up and bless her"* (31:28a). This is *"the product* [literally, fruit] *of her hands"* (31:31a)—not the bitter fruit of obviously neglected children, but the sweet fruit of conscientiously cultivated children. They've been clothed, not only outwardly with scarlet, but inwardly with wisdom: *"The teaching of kindness is on her tongue"* (31:26b).

She's a *helpmeeting* woman. Like Lt. Colonel Trevor, *"Her husband trusts in her, and he will have no lack of gain"* (31:11). She sees her priority of bringing success and fulfillment, not to herself, but to her husband: *"She does good and not evil to him all the days of her life"* (31:12). Though her duties are swarming and exhausting, she makes sure that she remains visually and stylishly attractive in his eyes: *"Her clothing is fine linen and purple"* (31:22b). And her efforts to please him do not go unnoticed: *"Her husband also, and he praises her"* (31:28b).

The mission of China was not the Lord's plan for Jody. Instead, it was the adventure of Trevor. Providentially, she was not called to labor in the hinterlands of the Far East, but in the "homelands" of an American warrior. In the most challenging of circumstances, she's "making a home"—and an extraordinary one at that, for Trevor and their boys.

As I spoke with Jody, she talked of the almost daily telephone calls she's able to share with Trevor, as his particular position has given him this special communication access. She relishes her advisory role to her man. Though she'd never acknowledge it, she's having an effect on international affairs. She also told of her need to move out of her domestic comfort zone, as she was forced to handle malfunctions in their van's electrical system during a snow storm, and to even play carpenter by hanging a door in their new house.

She seized on the opportunity of my calling to pass the phone to first-born Andrew whom she thought would be bolstered and invigorated by my reminding him that now he is *the man of the house* while Dad's gone. When I heard small children crying in the background, Jody laughed and announced, "Duty calls." I hung up with a sense that this is a special *woman of dominion* who absolutely loves the challenging mission to which her Heavenly Father has assigned her.

Ladies, do you long for a life of challenging fulfillment? What mission could be more meaningful than being an excellent wife alongside a mighty man of God?

Derek Kidner summarizes this role of the wonder woman described in Proverbs 31: "Here is scope for formidable powers and great achievements."[51]

1. Mary, the Lord's Biological Mother

Three days ago, after the Lord's Day morning worship service, I was greeting God's people as they exited the auditorium. Up stepped 20ish-year-old Sarah, with a beaming face and an extended left hand. She had something she wanted to show me on her ring finger. It was a diamond. The sparkle in her young eyes spoke volumes. Her dreams are coming true. A godly man is committing his life to her. She'll be married, swept away on his white horse, and live happily ever after.

Mary, a lovely teenage virgin woman from Nazareth, was living that same dream. She was engaged to a *"righteous man"* named Joseph. He probably didn't have a white horse, but maybe a donkey, which would do just fine in sweeping her off her feet. She was living her dream.

But the appearance of the angel Gabriel made for a rude awakening. *"And behold, <u>you will conceive in your womb</u>, and bear a son, and you shall name Him Jesus. He will be great, and will be called the Son of the Most High"* (Luke 1:31-32a, emphasis added).

Though this news was exciting, it was also disturbing. Surely there must be some mistake. It's not supposed to work that way. It's not normal. And certainly it's not proper. So Mary, a bit bewildered and flustered, begs for clarification.

And Mary said to the angel, "<u>How can this be, since I am a virgin?</u>" And the angel answered and said to her, "The Holy Spirit will come upon you, and the power of the Most High will overshadow you; and for that reason the holy offspring shall be called the Son of God" (Luke 1:34-35, emphasis added).

Yes, just as she feared, this announced errand for the Lord was both exciting and disturbing. It shattered her young womanly dreams of living happily ever.

> Mary knew that becoming pregnant at this particular time, before her marriage to Joseph had been consummated, would expose her to painful criticism and ridicule; perhaps to something even worse (see Deuteronomy 22:23f, stoning; also Matthew 1:18f divorcing). But she made a complete surrender. She placed herself, body and soul, at the disposal of her God who loved her.[52]

And so it happens to many a woman of God whose teenage eyes once sparkled with idealism regarding a life of happily-ever-after personal fulfillment. They wake up one day and are faced with the realization that their idealism was a misguided fantasy. "God's errand for me is disturbingly difficult. My storybook marriage is plagued with aggravating difficulties. My idyllic motherly expectations have been smashed under the relentless crush of day-after-day selfless serving." She looks with appalling disappointment into the black hole of decades of self-sacrifice—just as Mary stared at the assignment announced by Gabriel. "*And Mary said, 'Behold, <u>the bondslave of the Lord</u>; be it done to me according to your word'*" (Luke 1:38, emphasis added).

Marvel at the anti-Eve attitude of Mary. Our first mother was made discontent with God's restrictive assignment, by listening to the serpent's propaganda, and gazing on the sparkling forbidden fruit he advertised. "Come on baby! What a lady wants, a lady should have!" Elisabeth Elliot concisely identifies Mary's greatness:

> Eve refused what was given, usurped what was not given, and said, in effect, "My will be done." Consequently, sin entered into the world and death by sin. Thanks be to God, there is redemption. A humble village girl in Nazareth was visited by an angel, who delivered a startling message. Mary was to become the mother of the Son of God. Although she was greatly troubled, she received

the message. "I am the Lord's bondservant," she responded. "Be it done to me according to your word."[53]

This is *womanly dominion*. Mary, faced with an intimidating legion of fears, difficulties, unknown dangers, and challenges, *subdues* them under her feet. She expressly resolves to take her stand at her assigned post as a bond servant of the Lord. "Lord, it's not about what seems *good* to me, is a *delight* to my eyes, and is *desirable* to make me happy. It's about my living *according to Your word*."

J. C. Ryle exhorts us all with Mary's example:

> Let us seek in our daily practical Christianity to exercise the same blessed spirit of faith which we see in the virgin Mary. Let us be willing to go anywhere and do anything and be anything, whatever the present and immediate inconvenience, so long as God's will is clear and the path of duty is plain. The words of Bishop Hall on this passage are worth remembering: "All disputes with God after His will is known arise from infidelity. There is not a more noble proof of faith than to captivate all the powers of our understanding and will to our Creator, and without any questionings to *go blindfolded wherever He will lead us*."[54]

Yes, and Mary not only promised to live as the Lord's bond servant, though her assignment grew more daunting over the years, she delivered on her promise and finished her errand.

She bore the social reproach of her irregular pregnancy. She stood her ground in the Temple when Simeon, holding her child, prophesied to her, *"and a sword will pierce your own soul"* (Luke 2:35). She didn't collapse under the overwhelming maternal responsibility of nurturing *"Immanuel…God with us"* (Matthew 1:23). Do you think faithfully mothering through the teen years is confusing and bewildering? Imagine fielding these questions: *"Why is it that you were looking for me? Did you not know that I had to be in My Father's house?"* (Luke 2:49). And, oh, how agonizing it is for a loving mother, who's given the best years of her life to nurture a child, to be forced to helplessly stand by sorrowfully watching him endure horrible pain or injustice.

> *The soldiers, therefore, when they had crucified Jesus, took His outer garments and made four parts, a part to every soldier and also the tunic; now the tunic was seamless, woven in one piece.*

They said therefore to one another, "Let us not tear it, but cast lots for it, to decide whose it shall be"; that the Scripture might be fulfilled, "THEY DIVIDED MY OUTER GARMENTS AMONG THEM, AND FOR MY CLOTHING THEY CAST LOTS." Therefore the soldiers did these things. <u>But there were standing by the cross of Jesus His mother</u>,...(John 19:23-25, emphasis added).

She lived by the motto of her Son: *"My Father,...not as I will, but... Thy will be done"* (Matthew 26:39-41). She stayed at her post till her errand was *"finished"* (John 19:30).

Such a momentous assignment is not for the starry-eyed, the self-centered, the soft-minded, or the faint-hearted. It's for the strong-spirited lady of *womanly dominion*.

2. Mary, the Sister of Martha

Now as they were traveling along, He entered a certain village; and a woman named Martha welcomed Him into her home. And she had a sister called <u>Mary, who moreover was listening to the Lord's word, seated at His feet</u>. But Martha was distracted with all her preparations; and she came up to Him, and said, "Lord, do You not care that my sister has left me to do all the serving alone? Then tell her to help me." But the Lord answered and said to her, "Martha, Martha, you are worried and bothered about so many things; but only a few things are necessary, really only one, for <u>Mary has chosen the good part</u>, which shall not be taken away from her " (Luke 10:38-42, emphasis added).

Regarding *womanly dominion*, we could certainly highlight sister Martha and her praiseworthy, energetic, and selfless feats in the field of domestic hospitality. Her commendable virtue is underscored in John 12:2, where six days before Jesus' death, He receives a refreshing welcome in the home of Lazarus: *"So they made Him supper there, and Martha was serving."* But such a focus would be to retrace the themes presented in connection with the woman of Proverbs 31.

Instead, let's focus in on the other sister Mary. Note this sister's decisive resolve and choice to concentrate on the chief priority of life, the *one thing* necessary—the drawing of her soul near to her Savior. There she is, *"seated at His feet... listening to His words."* Surely, the swarming household duties needed attention, but Mary wisely set them aside for the purpose of cultivating her spiritual relationship with the Lord Jesus. And for this, the Master commends her, *"Mary has chosen the good part."*

Mary refused to be pushed around and bullied by the *"so many things"* that cried out for her attention. In the crucial area of keeping her heart, Mary refused to permit her environment to dominate her; instead, she chose to dominate her environment. She manhandled her schedule in such a way as to make time with the Lord Jesus a non-negotiable priority.

A 21st century woman of dominion will imitate Mary. Yes, she'll labor diligently to develop a fellow-man-loving servant's heart and life like Martha's. But more importantly, she'll not forget to cultivate a Lord-and-Savior-loving devotional heart and devotional life like Mary's. She'll *manhandle* her schedule to make it happen.

J. C. Ryle again weighs in:

> Martha's excessive zeal for temporal provisions made her forget for a time the things of her soul... The words of high commendation our Lord Jesus pronounced on Mary's choice...were meant to encourage all true Christians to be single-eyed and whole-hearted, to follow the Lord fully and to walk closely with God, to make soul business immeasurably their first business and to think comparatively little for the things of the world.[55]

John Angell James gives perspective:

> The design of our Lord's language is not so much to form a comparison between two courses of life, so separate and distinct as not to allow the mixture of one with the other, as to administer a rebuke to a person who pursuing one course had too much neglected the other. Not to prevent Mary from attending at all to temporal matters, but to engage Martha's anxiety about them, and to a stricter regard to things unseen and eternal.[56]

In Nancy Leigh DeMoss' book, *Lies Women Believe*, Lie #19 reads: "I can make it without consistent time in the word and prayer." She then warns: "Satan knows that if he succeeds in getting us to live independently of the Word of God, we become more vulnerable to deception in every area of our lives."[57] When we throw ourselves into important projects without consulting the Lord, we're acting arrogantly. Practical *womanly dominion* without devotional *womanly dominion* can easily deteriorate into *atheistic enterprising.*

> *Come now, you who say, "Today or tomorrow, we shall go to such and such a city, and spend a year there and engage in business and make a profit." Yet you do not know what your life will be like tomorrow. You are just a vapor that appears for a little while and then vanishes away. Instead, you ought to say, "If the Lord wills, we shall live and also do this or that." But as it is, you boast in your arrogance; all such boasting is evil (James 4:13-16, emphasis added).*

Such *atheistic enterprising* is the very thing we do if we put our hands to the daily plow without taking time to pray and plead for the help of God to establish the work of our hands. "*In the morning, O LORD, Thou wilt hear my voice; in the morning I will order my prayer to Thee and eagerly watch*" (Psalm 5:3).

Nancy Leigh DeMoss confesses:

> Sometimes I get the sense that God may be saying to me, "You want to handle this day by yourself? Go ahead." The result? At best, an empty, fruitless day lived by and for myself. At worst, oh, what a mess I end up making of things… The truth is, it is impossible for me to be the woman God wants me to be apart from my spending consistent time cultivating a relationship with Him in the Word and prayer. [58]

Devotional consistency requires practical creativity.

> Anita is the mother of three very young boys. She resolved to make her devotional life a priority. She set the early morning as the time. Her boys had other ideas. When they'd hear her moving about the house in the early morning, they'd wake up and sabotage her Bible reading and prayer time. Instead of being harassed by untimely rambunctiousness, she drew a line in the sand. "You boys don't get out of bed until 8 o'clock." This would give her time to shower, groom, read, and pray before her horses were let loose. Logan, her three-year-old youngest, pleaded ignorance. "I can't tell time,

Mommy." Anita then purchased for Logan's room a digital clock and established *The Law of the Snowman.* "You, sir, don't get out of bed until you see that the first number is a *snowman.*"[59]

Now, that's a *woman of dominion.*

3. Phoebe

It has been my pleasure on occasion to visit sister churches in distant places. Often, after I've preached on a Lord's Day morning, a pastor has escorted me to the back of the church building and stood alongside me while the parade of saints leaves the auditorium. He takes it on himself to personally introduce to me each of his precious flock. And what a joy it has been to sense the pulsing love and affection as a humorous story is told of Mr. Smith here, a high compliment is given to Mrs. Jones there, and a bear hug embrace is shared with Mr. Brown, a warm anecdote is told of Miss Black, a roar of laughter comes from Mr. Blue, a boasting comment is made about Deacon Green, and a tender word of appreciation is spoken for the selflessness of Secretary Gray. Such an experience makes me think of David and his fond attachment to his parade of heroic *"mighty men"* with whom the Lord had blessed him (2 Samuel 23).

In Romans 16, it's our privilege to spend some time at the door of the church in Rome with the Apostle Paul where he commends and greets the parade of twenty-nine mighty men and women as they pour out of the chapter. It's interesting to note that the first two individuals publicly commended here are women—Phoebe and Prisca (elsewhere called Priscilla).

> *I commend to you our <u>sister Phoebe</u>, who is a servant of the church which is at Cenchrea; that you receive her in the Lord in a manner worthy of the saints, and that you help her in whatever matter she may have need of you; for she herself has also been a helper of many, and of myself as well. Greet <u>Prisca</u> and Aquila, my fellow workers in Christ Jesus, who for my life risked their own necks, to whom not only do I give thanks, but also all the churches of the Gentiles (Romans 16:1-4, emphasis added).*

These two women are commended first, before all of the others. I believe that there is significance and priority in this order, underscoring the peculiarly noteworthy heroism demonstrated in the lives of these *women of dominion*.

Phoebe is first. She was probably the courier carrying Paul's Epistle to the Romans, traveling from Corinth to Rome. She's named after the pagan moon goddess (Phoebe: bright or *radiant*), indicating her almost certain pagan upbringing in the vicinity of the notoriously immoral city of Corinth, of which Cenchrea is a suburb. She'd apparently been a hell-bound idolater, but now Paul commends her as "our sister." Her adoption into the family of God was a *radiant* exhibition of Christ's saving power.

Many think that Phoebe was a wealthy woman traveling to Rome on business, as the phrase "that you *help her in whatever matter* she may have need," was often used in trade and law court contexts. Geoffrey Wilson comments: "It would appear that Phoebe, like Lydia (*'the seller of purple fabrics'*, Acts 16:14-15, 40), was a woman whose wealth and position enabled her to render such service to others." [60]

Paul introduces her as a bright star in the church: *"... a servant of the church which is at Cenchrea... for she herself has also been a helper of many, and of myself as well"* (16:1b, 2b). Probably, like Lydia (the seller of purple fabrics from Thyatira, Acts 16:14f), Phoebe had provided Paul and the saints with lodging, hospitality, and economic shelter, seemingly choosing to use her wealth to extend the kingdom.

Phoebe reminds me of the influential Englishwoman, Lady Selina, Countess of Huntingdon (1707-1791). In a day when there was an appalling spiritual barrenness in England, itinerant preachers like the Wesleys and George Whitefield began preaching to large crowds in the open air, having been banished by the indifferent clergy from using established church buildings. Through this movement, Selina's soul was saved. After the death of her husband, the Earl of Huntingdon, in 1746, she devoted her remaining decades to gospel spreading and kingdom building. A local newspaper in Savannah, Georgia, honored her memory by publishing a biographical sketch:

> Appointing Rev. George Whitefield as one of her chaplains, she established sixty-four meeting houses in England and provided seminaries for the education of ministers to supply them.
>
> While the Wesleys, Whitefield and other powerful preachers were reaching the proletariat (common people), Selina worked valiantly to save the souls of the nobility. Sometimes her letters

received indignant replies. The Duchess of Buckingham wrote: "I thank your Ladyship for information on the Methodist preaching. Their doctrines are strongly tinctured with impertinence toward their superiors... It is monstrous to be told you have a heart as sinful as the common wretches who crawl the earth."

Lady Huntingdon reproved the Archbishop of Canterbury for the worldly behavior unbecoming to his position as church leader. When he laughed her to scorn, Selina arranged an audience with Queen Charlotte and King George II who sharply rebuked the Bishop.

George Whitefield founded the Bethesda orphanage in Georgia about 1740. It is the country's oldest home for boys. Selina inherited Bethesda and upon receipt of it, set aside a day of prayer and fasting, then began long range plans for making Bethesda the launching base for a great missionary movement among the settlers and Indians, using missionaries from Trevecka College in Wales which she had already established for educating ministers.

Selina appointed William Piercy of St. Pauls Charleston, Bethesda's president, and sent over her own housekeeper. Before the missionaries set sail, she laid down strict rules for prayers and services during the crossing to America. Upon arrival, the missionaries dispersed and began preaching.

Wishing to prove faithful to Whitefield, she obtained advice from Governor James Wright of Georgia, who told her to give full power to the law firm of Tattnall and Hall, and to call the resident at Bethesda to account, which she did. Lady Huntingdon never received a penny from her Georgia estates; instead she spent thousands of pounds of her own paying bills. She rejoiced that no lives were lost in a Bethesda fire caused by lightning, and sold her jewelry for funds to help restore the buildings. Then the American Revolution interrupted her good works. [61]

Phoebe, like Selina, was a mighty kingdom force in her day. But take note of her role. Paul does not acclaim her as a pastor, elder, overseer, or evangelist. These are positions deemed only for men. Paul identifies her as a *"servant of the church."* This term identifies her as a "helper," "attendant," "one who waits on tables." Was this term used by the apostle as an expression of chauvinistic degradation toward this precious female saint? To the contrary, this term was selected to give Phoebe the ultimate commendation! *"Servant"* placed Phoebe on a plane with

Him who laid aside his garments, took up the towel and basin (John 13:4-5), and laid aside his glory, taking for Himself *the form of a bond-servant,* Thus He fetched for Himself *"the Name which is above every name"* (Philippians 2:5-11).

> *Jesus said to them, "But it is not so among you, but whoever wishes to become great among you shall be your servant; and whoever wishes to be first among you shall be slave of all. For even the Son of Man did not come to be served, but to serve, and to give His life a ransom for many" (Mark 10:42a, 43-45, emphasis added).*

Dear ladies, beware of worldly feminism and its perversions which brazenly shout into the doors and windows of the modern church that biblical church order is abusive to women and that any restrictions from leadership are demeaning.

Wayne Mack laments in his book, *Life in the Father's House, A Member's Guide to the Local Church*: "Our sinful society (and perhaps our sinful hearts) have convinced many of us that it is more blessed *to lead than it is to follow.*" [62]

Dear ladies, peculiarly gifted by God as *helpers suitable*, heroically play your God-appointed positions in the church. You weren't assigned to be corporately leading and publicly preaching, but supportively helping and humbly serving. In our local church, our mighty women are dedicatedly "sweeping" as hospitality extenders, Sunday School teachers, event planners, meal preparers, piano players, Solomon-like counselors, emotional shock absorbers, nursery laborers, building maintainers, interior designers, community witnesses, administrative assistants, visitor greeters, musical administrators, women's Bible study leaders, etc. They may not be getting the notoriety and the headlines, but due to their selfless service, the church is *"winning"* souls for Christ.

The church of Christ desperately needs Phoebe-like women of dominion.

4. Priscilla

Next after Phoebe in the Romans 16 parade of the saints, comes Prisca, elsewhere called Priscilla. Note how Priscilla's name is mentioned before her husband's. *"Greet Prisca and Aquila, my fellow workers in Christ Jesus, who for my life risked their own necks, to whom not only do I give thanks, but also all the churches of the Gentiles"* (Romans 16:3-4).

For the Apostle Paul, Priscilla, along with her husband Aquila, constitute another Corinthian connection. According to Acts 18:1-3, Priscilla and Aquila were banished from Rome due to the decree of Emperor Claudius, who sent all Jews packing from the capital city. This was probably the result of intramural Jewish tensions which had flared up in Rome regarding the claim of Jewish Christians that Jesus was the Messiah. This tent-making, probably Jewish-Christian couple thus journeyed across the Adriatic Sea and set up a leather-works shop in the cosmopolitan town of Corinth. Paul himself, having delivered his sermon to the Athenians on Mars Hill, traveled alone down to Corinth where he found self-supporting employment. In this environment of edifying spiritual fellowship, Paul enjoyed a supportive base for weeks of effective ministry in the Corinthian synagogue (18:4).

After an extended ministry in Corinth, Paul boarded an Ephesus-bound ship accompanied by *"Priscilla and Aquila"* (Acts 18:18; note again the wife-before-the-husband name order). Having settled into Ephesus, Priscilla and Aquila soon bid farewell to Paul who headed off to touch base at his home church in Antioch (Acts 18:21).

Meanwhile, back in Ephesus, an Alexandrian Jew named Apollos who was *"mighty in the Scriptures,"* appeared in the Ephesian synagogue and began to boldly preach Christ. *"But when Priscilla and Aquila heard him, they took him aside and explained to him the way of God more accurately"* (Acts 18:26b, emphasis added).

Note again the *wife-before-the-husband* name order, which also appears in 1 Corinthians 16:19 and 1 Timothy 4:19. Why this repeated sequential priority of the wife Priscilla before her husband Aquila? Jacob Kapp writes: "The fact that Priscilla's name is mentioned several times before that of her husband has called forth a number of conjectures. The best explanation seems to be that she was the stronger character."[63]

Alexander Maclaren comments: "Did you ever notice that in the majority of the places where these two are named,...Priscilla's name comes first? She seems to have been the *'the better man of the two'"*[64]

Charles Spurgeon reasons:

> I do not know why Paul in this case wrote "Priscilla and Aquila," thus placing the wife first, for in the Acts we read of them as

Aquila and Priscilla. I should not wonder but he put them in order according to quality rather than according to the rule of sex. He named Priscilla first because she was first in energy of character and attainments in grace. There is a precedence which, in Christ, is due to the woman when she becomes the leader in devotion, and manifests the stronger mind in the things of God. It is well when nature and grace both authorize our saying "Aquila and Priscilla," but it is not amiss when grace outruns nature and we hear of "Priscilla and Aquila."[65]

Regarding the couple's encounter with the *mighty man* Apollos, we may with due warrant suppose that they *"took him aside"* (Acts 18:26) privately by inviting him to their home after a synagogue public meeting. There, possibly at table over a late evening dinner, do we see the wise Aquila deferring to his more theologically astute and verbally skilled helpmate? Do we see her holding the *"mighty in the Scriptures"* Apollos spellbound with her across-the-table unpacking of the Apostle Paul's liberating doctrine of justification by faith in Christ? It seems quite clear that the *wife-before-the-husband* name order intimates that it was Priscilla who took the verbal lead in sharpening Apollos' sword.

This Priscilla is a wonderful and amazing woman. The Apostle Paul, who instructs women to *"keep silent in the churches"* (1 Corinthians 14:34), and to *"be subject to your own husbands"* (Ephesians 5:22), commendably recognizes her rich deposit of grace, wisdom, and gift by granting her priority treatment over her husband in the Romans 16 parade of the saints.

Clearly it is unbiblical and inaccurate to conclude that the *"weaker vessel"* is the "less competent vessel." Years ago, I preached on Romans 16 to my own precious congregation. I said in the sermon: "Gentlemen, I hate to burst any of your bubbles, but in some of your cases, I value your wives' opinions above yours!"

Such a well-endowed, highly competent, scripturally wise woman does not bring shame to her husband's face, but constitutes a crown for his head (Proverbs 12:4). We've already seen that the excellent wife *"opens her mouth in wisdom"* (Proverbs 31:26).

My own father was *a mighty man of God.* He was a rock of integrity just as Aquila apparently was—*"risking his own neck"* for the Apostle (Romans 16:3b). Dad will forever remain my spiritual hero, as a self-sacrificing saint who fought the good fight, faithful in character to the end, clinging to the sword till his last breath, and getting the swift sweet chariot home via a massive heart attack as a healthy and undiminished 71-year-old. When he would say to me, "Step into my office," Dad's figurative and portable counseling room, I knew I'd receive the faithful and invaluable blows of a straight-talking, wise friend. There was never any question as to who was the head of Dad's house. I desperately miss him.

My dad was a high-octane version of Aquila, but Mom was Priscilla. Dad was the rock, but Mom was the tutor. Mom was the reader, the book buyer, the Bible study attender, the sermon tape listener, the magazine article sender, the late night counselor, the doctrinal debater, the verbally agile persuader, the ladies' book study leader, the telephone advisor, the Priscilla. For every word Dad spoke, Mom spoke five.

My mother is a blessed Priscilla, who still in her early 70's remains an invaluable gift to the church and her family. Though she never has, and never will, preach a single public sermon in the church, her private sermons have been uncountable and invaluable. Two of her sons are pastors, and the other two are deacons. Her lone daughter is a young Priscilla-like wife and mother. Mom is now remarried and has resumed her helpmeet ministry to a widower pastor with a well-known pulpit ministry.

The Old Covenant people of God enjoyed the gifted ministry of the Prophetess Huldah (2 Kings 22:14-20). The first-century New Covenant people benefited greatly from the gifted prophetess daughters of Philip (Acts 21:8-9). And every generation of the church has been incalculably enriched by the ministries of its contemporary Priscillas—*women of dominion* who know how to *subdue* and *rule* in their feminine spheres of influence. They *"play their positions"* with a *"win it"* mindset for the glory of God and the advancement of His kingdom.

CHAPTER 6:

WOMANLY DOMINION

IN SCRIPTURAL MOTHERHOOD

It was an advertisement for Mother's Day.

Spread out before me on a yellowing newspaper page from May of 1992, two large, dueling black and white silhouettes, one on each side of the page, catch the reader's eyes.

On the left side is the rendition of the traditional mother. She's sitting in a straight back chair, wearing a bonnet and an ankle-length dress, resting her feet on a stool with her hands in her lap. She's obviously staying home. At her feet sits her toddler daughter with a wrapped gift.

On the right side is the rendition of the contemporary mother. She's dressed in a stylishly fitting blazer and skirt, high heels, and matching jewelry. Tucked under one arm is her compact purse, and her opposite hand holds her sleek briefcase. She's obviously off to work, full time. Her toddler daughter holds a bottle and stands on tiptoes to reach her mommy with a good-bye kiss.

The dueling silhouettes are intended to make us laugh—as when we see an Amish horse-and-buggy passed on the Indiana highway by a sleek new SUV—the absurd and obsolete replaced by the modern and sophisticated. But this motherly contrast should instead make us weep.

News America Media commissioned Bendixen & Associates to conduct an extensive survey of California young people ages 16-22. These are the infants and toddlers who were left behind while their 1990ish mommies sought self-actualization in the workplace rather than in the home. They've grown up now. The report, "California Dreamers," was published in 2007. When asked "What do you consider the most pressing issue facing your generation in the world today?" The most frequent answer was not global warming, community violence, poverty, racism, war, or terrorism. The most pressing concern, registered by 24% of those surveyed, was "the breakdown of the family." *The Washington Times'* Cheryl Wetzstein summarized this survey in her article, "Youths Fear Decay of Family" (April 27, 2007). She quotes Sandy Close, director of News America Media, who concludes that young people have a *"fear of winding up alone."*

Is it any wonder this generation fears *"winding up alone"*? They were *"left alone"* by their mommies in the day care centers. These are the "latch-key" kids who were "left home alone" for hours after school, wandering aimlessly in their empty, motherless homes. These are the teens who've been wholesale "left alone" as their parents divorced in unprecedented numbers due, in no small part, to mommies' workforce distractions and relationships. These young people see the family breakdown rubble of their own lives, courtesy of their parents' self-indulgent domestic philosophy, and are hopefully registering their determination to do it differently.

The point is that the traditional and biblical role of motherhood is not something to be cavalierly laughed about, but something to be conscientiously aimed at. This will be a driving focus of the true *woman of dominion* who has children. She'll disregard the foolish cultural sideline shouts, and she will give herself fully to her dignified, God-ordained assignment as a mother.

By definition, *motherhood is that dignified and strenuous life vocation taken up by a woman who has resolved to give herself fully to the task of nurturing godly children from a godly home environment.* Women who dedicate the best years of their lives to this challenging endeavor are not to be laughed at and pitied, but highly esteemed and even envied.

For decades now, the voice of feminism has called women away from their children, telling them that they're wasting their lives.

When Bill Clinton was running for president in 1992, his wife Hillary was asked why she still worked as a lawyer after becoming a mother. She answered, *"I suppose I could have stayed home and baked*

cookies and had teas, but what I decided to do was fulfill my profession.[66]
Her message came through loud and clear: Stay-at-home mothers are
dupes—brainwashed by cultural patriarchalism—that need to "get a life."

But the fact is that stay-at-home mothering did not culturally evolve
from the influence of heavy-handed men; it was sovereignly ordained
by the decree of our good heavenly Father.

1. Saved Through Child Bearing (1 Timothy 2:15)

> But <u>women shall be preserved through the bearing of children</u> if
> *they continue in faith and love and sanctity with self-restraint*
> *(1 Timothy 2:15, emphasis added).*

The phrase underlined above is an interesting one. It literally says,
"*saved through the bearing of children.*" What does that mean? Surely
it's not saying that physically birthing children *earns* a woman heaven.
The context sheds much light:

> *Let a woman quietly receive instruction with entire submissive-*
> *ness. But I do not allow a woman to teach or exercise authority*
> *over a man, but to remain quiet. For it was Adam who was first*
> *created, and then Eve. And it was not Adam who was deceived,*
> *but the woman being quite deceived, fell into transgression*
> *(1 Timothy 2:11-14).*

Paul is engaged in a discussion on the woman's role (function, task,
assignment) in the church. He encourages her to *play her position.*
And it's here that the apostle unveils the authority on which he asserts
the role diversity between women and men. Diversity of function is
not due to cultural evolution or societal tradition, but rather divine
declaration. Paul appeals to Genesis 1, where God's creating man first
strategically endowed him with the authority to lead (2:13). Paul then
reminds us of the debacle of Genesis 3, where Adam abdicated his role
as spiritual leader. He left Eve to assume it, and that resulted in her
gullibly leading the human race over the precipice of error into the
cursed canyon of the fall. This passage makes it clear that God did not
design women to spiritually lead, because they are more vulnerable to
the deceptive strategies of the enemy than are their male counterparts
(2:14). Therefore, women are not to be the public teachers and leaders
of the church (2:11-12).

Here Paul anticipates the loud sigh of a dear sister: "Well, if women can't teach, what in the world can we do?!" Here's where verse 15 fits in. Women can persevere in the faith by giving themselves fully to their divinely-given assignment—*"the bearing of children,"* which is a figurative reference to the great work of "mothering." James Hurley well summarizes: "Eve, and women in general, will be saved, or kept safe, from wrongly seizing men's roles by embracing a woman's role."[67]

William Hendriksen comments: "Not by way of preaching to adults but by way of bearing children does a woman attain to real happiness,… It is God's will that the woman should influence mankind 'from the bottom up' (that is, by way of the child), not 'from the top down.'" [68]

Generally speaking, when a woman gives herself wholeheartedly to her God-ordained occupation of mothering, she is *saved* from many spiritual dangers. She is *kept safe* from arrogantly taking on a ministry to which she was never called and for which she was never equipped (see 1 Timothy 4:16). She is *kept safe* from destructive idleness and Satanic temptations by occupying herself with her all-consuming assignment.

2. A Reputation for Good Works (1 Timothy 5:9-15)

> *Let a widow be put on the list only if she is not less than sixty years old, having been the wife of one man, having a reputation for good works; and if she has <u>brought up children</u>, if she has shown hospitality to strangers, if she has washed the saints' feet, if she has assisted those in distress, and if she has devoted herself to every good work. But refuse to put younger widows on the list, for when they <u>feel sensual desires</u> in disregard of Christ, they want to get married, thus incurring condemnation, because they have set aside their previous pledge. And at the same time they also <u>learn to be idle, as they go around from house to house; and not merely idle, but also gossips and busybodies, talking about things not proper to mention</u>. Therefore, I want younger widows to <u>get married, bear children, keep house, and give the enemy no occasion for reproach</u>; for some have already <u>turned aside to follow Satan</u> (1 Timothy 5:9-15, emphasis added).*

What conscientious mother has too much time on her hands? If more mothers were at home focusing full time on their children, rather than out in the work force focusing on their colleagues, divorce rates would be lower, family breakdowns would be rarer, and spiritual shipwrecks (1 Timothy 1:19) would be fewer. Mothering is a profoundly sanctifying vocation which cultivates the graces of love, patience, kindness, gentleness, faithfulness, self control, selflessness, humility, dependence, prayerfulness, and joy as none other.

Paul views the married mother as a blessed woman, as a train on her tracks, streaking along smoothly on her God-appointed rails. These maternal rails don't bring her into abusive oppression; rather they provide her wonderful liberation to run freely according to her Maker's design. Here, she finds God-glorifying satisfaction and fulfillment.

A. T. Robertson writes: "Childbearing, not public teaching, is the peculiar function of women with a glory and dignity all its own." [69]

Hurley perceptively adds:

> Public opinion is increasingly against the bearing of children. Both men and women often look upon children as a problem and a burden. In some circles the bearing and raising of children is viewed as a prime means of reducing women into bondage. This sentiment is sometimes expressed in the remark "*keep 'em barefoot and pregnant.*" It is easy to see that Paul's remarks here will be abrasive if received from such a perspective... The bearing and raising of children (in biblical times) were considered by women and men alike to be activities of surpassing personal and social worth. The bearing of children was a central element in the definition of womanhood and in the fulfilling of God's calling to mankind. The enjoyment of pleasures undercut the financial and personal obligations entailed in raising a family, was not common in the first century. In his day the bearing of children which Paul selected as *a part to represent the* whole of the high calling of women was a valued activity which women embraced with joy and with pride and for which they were deeply respected.[70]

Motherhood is an honorable and sacred vocation. The King of Heaven has specially appointed the mother to accomplish a noble and lofty mission. Though some shrill voices in our dimwitted society may belittle her occupation, she should press on in her duties with her head held high. She's about the King's business.

The King of Heaven has clearly expressed in His Word the kind of service He highly esteems. Regarding married women with children,

His will for their life priorities comes through loud and clear.

> Let a widow be put on the list only if she is not less than sixty years old, having been the wife of one man, having a <u>reputation</u> for <u>good works; and if she has brought up children,</u> if she has shown hospitality to strangers, if she has washed the saints' feet, if she has assisted those in distress, and if she has devoted herself to every good work… . Therefore,<u> I want younger widows to get married, bear children, keep house,</u> and give the enemy no occasion for reproach (1 Timothy 5:9-10, 14, emphasis added).

How does a married woman with children forge a noble reputation in God's eyes? She hammers it out on the anvil of sacrificial mothering. She gives herself wholly to the sacred mission of nurturing God-fearing children, from a spiritually healthy home environment.

3. Older Women Teaching Younger (Titus 2:3-5)

> <u>Older women</u> likewise are to be reverent in their behavior, not malicious gossips, nor enslaved to much wine, teaching what is good, that they may <u>encourage the young women</u> to <u>love their husbands</u>, to <u>love their children</u>, to be sensible, pure, <u>workers at home</u>, <u>kind</u>, being subject to their own husbands, that the word of God may not be dishonored (Titus 2:3-5, emphasis added).

I recently heard a woman speaking about a get-together of single college ladies in her home for an evening of discussion. Initially, they went around the room and each divulged her academic major and career goals. But as the night went on, they grew more comfortable with each other and more transparent. By the end of the evening, every last woman admitted that what she really wanted was to marry a good man and give herself to raising their children. This is what their hearts deeply yearned for.

Is this really any surprise? These young women simply bear the image of the King who made them. Instinctively, His priorities are theirs. Sadly, our God-defying culture seeks to vandalize that wholesome conscience imprint by twisting a woman's priorities.

We may hear a young woman say, "Oh, I plan on marrying and having children. But my real passion is law. I want to make my mark in this world as an attorney. This is my chief priority and ambition in life." But a godly and biblical response to such an expressed aspiration would be, "Your priorities for your life are at odds with God's priorities for your life. The King hasn't assigned married women with children to be consumed with becoming excellent professionals, but with becoming excellent wives and mothers, whose headquarters is their *home*. For Christ's sake, you need to change your ambitions." In Titus 2, Paul tells older women *in every generation* that they are solemnly obligated to *communicate this important perspective to younger women*.

I understand that young women are wise to plan for the possibility of never marrying. Career training is wise. I also believe that it is not necessarily wrong for a wife and mother to have a job outside of the home. We'll discuss this issue more fully in a later chapter (See a *Woman Worker?* in chapter 13). *But it is wrong for her to view and treat such a job as her chief priority and calling in life. The cream, and not the dregs, of her energies and time are to be poured into her loving her husband and children from her household headquarters.*

4. A Stupid Ostrich (Job 39:13-17)

Here the Scriptures help us to draw common-sense wisdom from the encyclopedia of general revelation. We learn by observing the folly of a peculiarly stupid bird and her breathtaking maternal negligence.

> *The ostriches' wings flap joyously with the pinion and plumage of love, for she abandons her eggs to the earth, and warms them in the dust, and she forgets that a foot may crush them, or that a wild beast may trample them. She treats her young cruelly, as if they were not hers; though her labor be in vain, she is unconcerned; because God has made her forget wisdom, and has not given her a share of understanding (Job 39:13-17, emphasis added).*

Early one morning, I was walking from the church parking lot to the building. As I passed by the long row of large, thick evergreen bushes, I noticed two beady eyes staring at me from the shadows. It was a mother robin patiently sitting on her nest. For many days following, there she was, at her post. One day there were six tiny beady eyes staring back at me, and mom was protectively shrieking and darting over my head.

Now that's a good and wise mother, lovingly spending herself for her young.

But an ostrich is not so wise. Instead of laying and guarding her eggs, the ostrich lays and abandons her eggs. She figures the sun can do the warming work in the sand or dirt for her. "Why should I be bothered? I've got more important things to do with my life." Her eggs are notoriously vulnerable to being crushed by beasts, eaten by reptiles, or snatched by men. In ancient times, she was a proverbial symbol for maternal neglect, a representation of cruelty and dimwittedness, due to God's withholding wisdom and understanding.

Tragically, many modern mothers resemble not the robin, but the ostrich. They birth their children, and instead of personally and tenderly nurturing their young treasures in the nest of their homes, they cruelly *dump them off* in places that make them vulnerable to being trampled by strangers. "Why should I be bothered? I've got more important things to do with my life." Why would an otherwise sensible woman do such a thing? Romans 1 speaks of the dreadful judgment of God in "giving over" sinners to a darkened mind. *"And just as they did not see fit to acknowledge God any longer, God gave them over to a depraved mind, to do things which are not proper,…without understanding, untrustworthy, <u>unloving</u>* (also translated as *without natural affection*)" (Romans 1:28, 31, emphasis added).

Many little ones who cry aloud at the crack of dawn as they watch from the day-care center window their briefcase-carrying moms running off to work, and many older ones who return home after school to an empty, motherless house, can only dream of a robin-like mama who stays at her post.

Some readers may blow the whistle here and call a foul. "Why can't we just view this child-nurturing project as a unisex thing? Let women off the hook as the *child nurturer*! Why should mothers, and not fathers, be equally pressed with this sacrificial duty?" These are good questions, especially since modern women have across the board let their husbands off the *hook* regarding their masculine duty as *bread winner*. "But in this economy he can't do it all by himself!" But God's *hooks* and assignments haven't changed since the beginning.

Man's God-appointed vocation is *bread winning*, amidst thorns and thistles, by the sweat of his brow (Genesis 3:17-19). I wonder if some of us men have forgotten how to really sweat. That's a *"Manly Dominion"* issue of great importance. I also wonder if many men's wives have made it too easy on them by *enabling* their husbands' lack of dominion (inappropriately bailing them out) when their men should be resourcefully *finding a way* to bail themselves out. Necessity is the mother of invention.

A married mother's God-appointed vocation is *child nurturing*, through much pain (Genesis 3:16). Regardless of how many "*Mr. Mom*" articles we may read, the gender roles are *not* interchangeable. The Bible is clear on this. Common sense verifies this. Women gestate their children for nine months in their wombs. Physiologically, men are distant bystanders. Women nurse their infants at their breasts. Men are not equipped for such a wonderful thing. Mothers caress with their smooth faces and sing to them with their soft voices and nurture with their sensitive emotions. Men are constitutionally rough on all three counts. A woman's instinctive mother-love is kindled at conception, roars into a raging bonfire at birth, and is brutishly beaten down when she returns to the office. Common sense screams out the fact that separating a mother from her young child is simply fighting against nature.

I realize that some women are in emergency mode. Due to the curse and sin, there are single mothers who can't rely on responsible fathers. In such cases, these dear ladies may well be morally obligated to become both *child nurturer* and *breadwinner*. But emergency and cruelty are as unmistakably different as a robin and an ostrich. *Women of dominion* know this.

A homemaking mother is not merely a conservative and anachronistic option, but a God-ordained and sacredly instituted vocation. It's the scriptural pattern and lifestyle prescribed for the woman who is married and has children.

CHAPTER 7:
WOMANLY DOMINION
AND MOTHERLY GREATNESS

Three days ago, I was standing on the sidelines of my daughter's high school district championship soccer game. A clipboard-carrying coach from another team came up alongside me. He told me he was helping to decide what players would make the "all district team." I asked him if he'd figured out our team's best and most valuable player. He pointed out an offensive player. I said, "She's really good, but our best, our most skilled and valuable player is number 16." He hadn't yet noticed her. I was pointing to Brittany, the senior defensive sweeper, who hadn't scored a single goal, but was the chief reason for her team's winning the tournament. She verbally directed the traffic of her younger teammates like a mother hen and made heroic saves in fighting off opponents' efforts to score. Brittany's soon-to-be college coach, who'd granted her a scholarship, stood a few yards away watching her with a satisfied smile. The clipboard-carrying coach wrote down the number 16 in his notes. *It takes knowledge to recognize greatness.*

Though our spectating culture may be blind to true greatness, let me encourage mothers regarding the inestimable value of their vocation.

1. Her Elite Mission

Homemaking motherhood is no refuge for the inept woman who can't *cut it* in the real world. Rather, stay-at-home mothering is the ultimate profession for the elite of her gender.

Her skill set must be highly diversified. She's no mere babysitting caretaker. She realizes she's raising thoroughbreds for the kingdom, and so she studies and reads and prepares meals with the inspiration of a *dietician* and a *nutritionist*. Her health care duties summon her often to rise to the level of *nurse* and *physician*. Domestic *engineer* is a suitable title for her who exercises dominion over her household headquarters by subduing swarming details into workable order. She is an *economist* in keeping the budget, holding the purse strings as the *accountant*, and acting as the *purchasing agent* for the family corporation, averting bankruptcy and maintaining solvency. She's a *psychologist* in analyzing the peculiarities of each temperament, tracing the development of each child, and bringing the apt word as a *counselor* in every situation. She's a *personal trainer* and *disciplinarian* as she cultivates obedience and self-control in her natively wild herd. She's a *teacher* and *professor* in instructing her students in reading, spelling, grammar, mathematics, history, science, and art. This is exceptionally and overwhelmingly true of a homeschooling mother. She's a *pastor* and *theologian* as she educates her children in the lofty themes of morality, spirituality, and eternity.

With a job description like that, I advise young women to get all the education they can. Any liberal arts or professional university degree will provide *money in the bank* knowledge from which a mother will daily make heavy withdrawals.

I know that some jobs don't really count, don't make much of a difference, don't actually matter that much, don't have much lasting significance. Not so with mothering. I know that in some jobs the worker is only handling cleaning equipment, or car parts, or computer keyboards, or insurance policies, or court cases, or political legislation, or stockholders' funds. Not so with mothering. A mother is handling things of a far greater magnitude. She's handling never-dying souls. She's daily conducting heart surgery on eternal spirits whose forever destinies are influenced most profoundly by the hands that rock their cradles, wipe their noses, spank their fannies, open their Bibles, prepare their after-school snacks, and turn off their bedroom lights. Those motherly hands are molding characters which will become men and women who will turn the world upside down either for good or for evil. Now that's a job that counts.

I know that children whose mothers have an *ostrich* view of nurturing typically grow into the full height of adulthood. I know that children generally do survive being dropped off at day care all day, spending multiple daily hours in front of the TV or the X-Box, surfing the internet endlessly without supervision, and living under the same roof as parents who are clueless about their teenage struggles. But I also know the difference between a water tower and a hot air balloon. Though both may be the same height, one was built with steel, and the other was not. One will bear great burdens, and the other will not. One stands firm in a storm, and the other does not.

2. Her Priority Focus

Part-time mothering just won't cut it.

Mike brought a wonderful young woman home from college for a weekend to meet his parents. Avery was attractive in appearance, kind in personality, tender in spirituality, and outstanding in academic achievement. In fact, she was pre-med, studying to be a surgeon. Her ability to focus on a task and discipline herself toward accomplishing a goal was impressive. When the sunny Saturday summoned her out to frolic and play, Avery stayed put in the guest room for hours mastering physiology terms and concepts for an upcoming Wednesday test. Subsequent visits made her legendary for the late-night *sliver of light* that glowed from the bottom of the guest room door where she diligently pored over her pre-med studies. Avery was on a mission, and she knew how to work hard toward fulfilling it.

But Mike's wise mother pulled him aside, first commending him for his discretion in selecting such an accomplished and competent woman as a potential mate. Then she counseled, "But you realize that being an MD is typically an all-consuming profession. I question the idea that it's something that one can do *'on the side.'* I hope that the woman *you* marry will be committed to harnessing her abilities toward her priority mission in life of being a helpmeet to you and a mother to your children. This *great vocation* is an all-consuming profession, as well. Unless Avery holds a deep conviction on these biblical womanhood priorities, I fear that you, Mike, will for decades be haunted by the *sliver of light* that will glow from the bottom of her medical office door."

Mike's mother continued: "When you come home exhausted from

your work in the demanding field of your profession, you may be met *not* with the affectionate open door of her wifely support, but with the *do-not-disturb* shut door of her medical preoccupation. And more importantly, when over the years your needy children look toward her to find that special sparkle of motherly focus in her eyes, they may be habitually disappointed to find only that dull sliver of light glowing from the bottom of her office door. That, my dear son, would be a tragedy that would tear out both your heart and mine."

Why is Mike's mother so concerned? It's *because she gets it*, and *he doesn't*. She's a seasoned mom of many who comprehends the magnitude of a mother's mission. The mother is the hub of the home, holding all the spokes in place. Without her being at her post, the family spins out of control and falls apart. When her husband hears the predawn alarm clock, she knows he's emotionally emboldened by her tenderly squeezing his arm in appreciation.

From then on, she's the nucleus of the day's family activity. She needs to nurse feed one, rouse out of bed another, review a spelling list with yet another, change a diaper, prepare a breakfast, pray God's blessing on the day, tie shoes, write out a check for a class trip, pack a lunch, check on progress regarding an upcoming book report, read and comment on a verse from Proverbs, discuss a peer conflict while chauffeuring to school, pick up Dad's suit at the dry cleaners, shop for groceries and household items at the store, sign up for soccer at the Recreational Department, read a story before putting one down for a nap, teach one phonics sounds and letters, make beds and clean up the kitchen, show how to sweep properly, search the internet for good pictures of frogs, deal with a lying problem by spanking, talking, and praying, and prepare lunch.

That's just the morning.

Then in the afternoon, she's called to teach lyrics of a song about a pirate named Patch, take a field trip to the park down the street, talk about sharing apple slices with others, explain to her child why he's not permitted to throw tantrums like others in the park, catch and analyze a grasshopper's physiological structure and functions, return home for a naptime preceded by a storybook, sit down for personal devotions and prayer, call an appliance repairman about a strange-sounding washing machine, drive to school and talk with a teacher about a child's performance in math class, talk about the day on the drive home, purchase a well-fitting pair of soccer cleats, assign and supervise the weeding of the flower garden, give out popsicles to the handful of neighborhood children playing in the yard, prepare dinner, embrace her husband and briefly share mutual experiences of the day, enjoy a nutritional supper and discussion together as a family, sit and listen to her husband lead in family worship, direct the clean-up after dinner, help with math homework, bake a batch of sweet-smelling chocolate chip cookies, wash bodies in the bathtub while singing about a pirate and a Savior, rock a little one in a chair, rub a back in bed while giving advice about an argument that took place during recess, pay bills on the internet, wash, fold, and iron shirts, counsel her husband about a relational conflict at work, and enjoy her husband rubbing her arm in bed.

With this, I've just skimmed the surface of her day. Remove the hub of her tireless labors, and her family flies apart, her husband is a frazzled wreck, and her children are greatly diminished individuals.

Over the years, my wife has occasionally departed from the home for well-deserved multi-day retreats away from us. It's during such times that we learn to deeply appreciate her incalculable contribution to our home. Usually, we're fine for the first few hours. But I, the father, have got to give consuming attention to my pastoral labors of sermon preparation and counseling interaction, leaving the children to "*do their own things*" without anyone supervising, directing, or advising them.

I appear at mealtime, help with getting the predetermined menu on the table, and make sure everyone is seated. But I've been out of touch and barely have a clue of their day's activities. The food is on the table, but there are no napkins. The children get ready for bed, but there's no cookie smelling or song singing. They're all put down to sleep, but there's not the same chair rocking and day reviewing and back rubbing. Our Technicolor family life has become a black and white movie. Our house has a roof and walls and floors, but it's missing its soul.

We ache for her return. We keep looking out the window hoping to see her coming up the driveway. I suppose it's a lot like staring at a *sliver of light* at the bottom of a door. Her return is like the sunrise. We all crawl out of our grey caves and bask in the warmth of her animating love.

"Oh," but one might say, "This is the case only with mothers of young children. When they're older and all off to school, the mother's role in the home is no longer all that crucial." Such a notion is sorely mistaken. I contend that a mother's most intense and demanding efforts are required during the teen years. Frog and grasshopper preoccupations have graduated into boy and girl infatuations. Rocking a little one in a chair early in the night has advanced to counseling a big one in the master bedroom well past midnight.

During the summer of 2006, we had everybody home for the last time. Twenty-two-year-old Jared was home from architectural school and working for a design firm. Twenty-year-old Calvin was doing an internship with a local brokerage firm and working a second job in the evenings. Eighteen-year-old Austin was working almost full time delivering truck tires. Fourteen-year-old Abigail and twelve-year-old Nathan were busy with swarming summer activities. An ignorant onlooker might have suggested, "Surely there's no need here for a *stay-at-home mother*." Oh so wrong!

These were Dianne's most demanding hours, as each child was passing through a crucial season of life involving a new girlfriend, or a complicated situation with an old girlfriend, or a vocational selection crisis, or an academic preparation issue, or a health problem like a broken leg and an emergency appendectomy with its related recovery time, or a peculiar spiritual/emotional trial. Dianne would make sure to rise early in the morning in order to be in the kitchen when each one ate breakfast and gathered their things to head out into the world. She'd ask them questions about where they were last night and with whom, and to whom they talked on their cell phones, and what their plans were during the day, all the while taking their spiritual pulses and administering words of wisdom in season.

She'd inform me of the development of each, seeking my counsel. Then, she'd often have follow-up contact with them during lunch, or later in the afternoon when they'd return from work and be off to some other social or work activity. She was a maternal air traffic controller, directing and nurturing the lives of her offspring who were now making crucial decisions that would determine the courses of the rest of their lives. Both the stakes and the stress levels were higher than they'd ever been.

She would talk to me in the evenings. I'd follow up sometimes with long late-night walks and talks with them about themes on which I'd been briefed by my *helpmeet* informant. Without her maternal perceptions and observations, I'd have been clueless. With them, our parenting labors were on the stretch as never before. We spent many nights crying out to God in prayer for their long-term prosperity. It was my wife's finest hour as a mother. I shudder to think of the present condition of our children's lives had their mother's summer input been basically reduced to a dim *sliver of light* at the bottom of a door.

I remember when a young lady friend of our son spent a weekend in our home. She sat in the living room talking with Dianne most of Saturday afternoon. There, Dianne delegated jobs, ironed shirts, folded wash, and did scheduling. Child after child (sometimes visitor after visitor) would enter the room, sit down, and talk for a few minutes. Discussions ranged from sports to theology, from psychology to modesty, from financial budgeting to beach suntanning. Dianne held court all afternoon and rarely was an important trial *not* taking place in her courtroom. I think the young lady was overwhelmed with the unspeakable influence of an available mother in the lives of her older children. I know I was.

Many years ago, my German-born mother-in-law shook her finger at me after our fifth child was born in the twelfth year of our marriage, and said, "Just remember, young man, the thick end is still coming!" By that she was forewarning me that the early years of parenting are not the most demanding, as some think. It's the later years that will bring the most labor pains and demand the most energy output. We just celebrated our 25th anniversary. She was a prophetess.

A *sliver of light* at the bottom of a door is a sorry substitute for a biblically devoted mother.

Such a conviction is not the conclusion *only* of the person steeped in biblical teaching. It's also the conviction of a multitude steeped in mere common sense.

Read this excerpt from Dr. Laura Schlessinger's popular book, *The Proper Care and Feeding of Husbands*. It reveals the heartbroken plight of a man who's discovered that he married a *stupid ostrich*:

> Finally, one husband sent me a copy of a letter to his wife he'd been up until two o'clock in the morning writing. He considered it a significant coincidence considering the announced subject of this book.
>
> Evidently, he'd been trying to communicate to his wife his feelings and thoughts about the texture and direction of their marriage. Her quickie solution to their problems, it seems, was to suggest a two-week visit to Disneyland. He did not feel that trip would be a miracle to improve the marriage.
>
> This man's letter, I believe, represents a universal truth that has been denied and largely lost by a culture hell-bent on measuring human value through power and money. That truth is that the

family needs a woman and a man, a husband and a wife, a father and a mother, much more than it needs the equal power of two career-oriented people.

He writes to his wife:

I'm learning more as the years go by that you are a career-oriented person who doesn't have a clue or understand the essence of what it means to be a wife and a mother. Call me traditional if you like, but I firmly believe that mothers need to spend more time at home, perhaps 100 percent of their time at home, to nurture a family and develop a home.

Far too often, there are too many things that get overlooked by you as a wife and mother as it pertains to this family. Our kids lack focus, training, and discipline. They have no routine and there's no order about anything that they do. Mothers, in my opinion, are nurturers and teachers who ought to spend as much time with their kids to teach them things, skills that they will use to cope with life. To put it bluntly, you haven't been a mother. Our kids have been left too often to cope and figure out things for themselves.

When it comes to being a wife, you put no effort. And I think you don't love me anymore. Making love is not high on your agenda of things to do, and showing any intimate interest in me isn't either.

I'm feeling less and less interested in you and less and less motivated to keep this family together. I'm feeling like you are married to your job and that you are more committed to it than to us as a wife and mother.

I'm not claiming that I'm the perfect husband and father. You and I both work too many hours, but I believe you underestimate the importance of the mother in a family. Mothers and fathers play different roles in a family. I've never discouraged you from pursuing a Ph.D., but I don't think it's high on the list of priorities of what I think is best for us and a family right now.

I want to love you, be with you, and support you, but I must confess that I'm feeling like we are losing each other and our kids. I don't know what the complete answer is, but I believe it has to start with us spending more time at home to grow, develop, and nurture our family relationships. [71]

All this is to say that biblical motherhood is not a periphery project that can be adequately fulfilled in one's spare time. It needs to be a woman's priority focus. It's an all-consuming life mission that requires full-time dedication, concentration, and devotion. A *woman of dominion's* eyes will sparkle with delight at the great challenge. She'll *"play her position,"* stay at her domestic post, and push hard, all the way to the end, with a *"win it"* mindset.

3. Some Historical Models

On the soccer field, young players draw inspiration to greatness by watching film of great Brazilian players like Pele or Renaldo. On the basketball court, it's the inspiration of Larry Bird or Michael Jordan. In the political realm, it's Abraham Lincoln or Winston Churchill. *Greats* of the past inspire us in the present.

Let me inspire to *greatness* in mothering by reminiscing about heroic mothers of bygone eras.

John Newton's Mother

Consider the mother of John Newton. John Newton (1725-1807) was the author of the hymn, "Amazing Grace," and an influential minister for 43 years in England. We owe much of his eventual greatness to the hand that rocked his cradle. Mrs. Newton died when John was only six. His famous autobiography, *Out of the Depths*, reveals that at the age of eleven, he took to sea with his ship captain father, where he eventually earned a reputation as a vile, debauched, immoral, money-hungry, slave-trading, blaspheming man who even shocked many hardened sailors by his evil behavior. But on March 21, 1748, at the age of 22, Newton's ship sailed into a fierce storm that threatened to sink the vessel. Too exhausted to man the pumps any longer, Newton lashed himself to the helm hoping to at least keep the ship on course in the raging sea. It was there, anticipating his any-moment death and eternal doom that his mother's voice, many years gone, resurrected in his conscience.

> My mother...was a pious, experienced Christian...I was her only child;...Almost her whole employment was the care of my education. I have some faint remembrance of her care and instructions. At not more than three years of age, she herself taught me English. When I was four years old I could read with propriety in any common book. She stored my memory, which was then very retentive, with many valuable pieces, chapters, and portions of Scripture, catechisms, hymns, and poems.

At that time, I had little inclination to the noisy sports of children, but was best pleased when in mother's company, and always as willing to learn as she was to teach. How far the best education may fall short of reaching the heart will strongly appear in the sequel (*upcoming narrative*); yet I think, for the encouragement of godly parents to go on in the good way of doing their part faithfully, I may properly propose myself as an example. Though in process of time I sinned away all the advantages of these early impressions, yet they were for a great while a restraint upon me. They returned again and again, and it was very long before I could wholly shake them off. When the Lord at length opened my eyes, I found a great benefit from the recollection of them. My dear mother, besides the pains she took with me, often commended me with many prayers and tears to God.

My mother observed my early progress with peculiar pleasure, and intended from the first to bring me up with a view to the ministry, if the Lord should so incline my heart. In my sixth year I began to learn Latin. Before I had time to know much about it, the intended plan of my education was broken. The Lord's designs were far beyond the views of an earthly parent. He was pleased to reserve me for an unusual proof of His patience, providence, and grace; therefore overruled the purpose of my friends, by depriving me of my mother when I was under seven years of age... When I was eleven years old my father took me to sea with him. A man of remarkable good sense, and great knowledge of the world, he took great care of my morals. But he could not supply my mother's part.[72]

Little did Mrs. Newton know that she didn't have much time for her *great* life's work. She wasted none of it and poured herself wholeheartedly into it, and the whole world remains her debtor for it. Well done, good and faithful Mrs. Newton! Your motherly influence, brief as it was, so tirelessly stored up in your boy's conscience, was used by God to bring the prodigal home and edify the church for centuries. May our young mothers be inspired by your heroic labors!

Thomas Edison's Mother

Consider the mother of Thomas Edison. Thomas Edison (1847-1931) was an indefatigable inventor whose relentless diligence brought to us such blessings as the incandescent light bulb, the phonograph, and motion pictures.

Early on, Edison was perceived by his teachers as a poor student of inferior abilities. When a schoolmaster called Edison "addled" (muddled and confused), his furious mother took him out of the school and proceeded to teach him at home. Edison said many years later, "My mother was the making of me. She was so true, so sure of me, and I felt that I had someone to live for, someone I must not disappoint."[73]

It was during these early years, under his mother's eyes, that Edison showed a fascination for mechanical things and for chemical experiments. It's no wonder he developed his stubborn mottos of persistence: "I will never quit until I get what I'm after" and "Genius is 1% inspiration and 99% perspiration." Edison was quoted as saying that it would take only a matter of a few weeks to invent the light bulb. But in reality, it took him almost two years of failed attempts, new discoveries, and prototypes before he would succeed. It is said that he tried over 6000 different carbonized plant fibers, looking for just the right carbon filament.

Who forged such steel into this man's backbone? His mother did! Modernized America thanks you, Nancy Edison, for your devoted and inspiring motherhood.

Susanna Wesley

Consider the mother of John and Charles Wesley. John, the preacher (1703-1791), and Charles, the hymn-writer (1707-1788), were used by God to set their nation ablaze with the fires of revival during the Great Awakening in England. They are profoundly the polished products of their mother Susanna's sacrificial and devoted mothering. Susanna gave birth to nineteen children, six in the first eight years of her marriage. Only ten survived into adulthood. Her husband, who was habitually "out of town" during the years of the children's upbringing, provided a relatively low income. Under such conditions, one might expect a household of anarchy. But Susanna was a *woman* of true *dominion*.

In his book, *Susanna Wesley*, Arnold Dallimore writes:

> She seldom left her house, and she devoted all her time and strength to her children. She later explained her chief purpose in doing so and how she concentrated all her efforts to achieve it, saying, "*I have lived such a retired life for so many years... No one can, without renouncing the world in the most literal sense, observe my method; and there are few, if any, that would entirely devote above twenty*

years of the prime of life in hopes to save the souls of their children."

In fulfillment of this design Susanna set up a school in her own home... Classes were conducted six days a week, from nine to twelve and then from two till five. "There was no such thing as loud talking or playing allowed," stated Susanna, "but everyone was kept close to business for the six hours of school.'" They had been disciplined since birth. Susanna reported that "the children were always put into a regular method of living, in such things as they were capable of, from their birth; as in dressing and undressing, changing their linen, etc... When turned a year old (and some before) they were taught to fear the rod and cry softly, by which means they escaped abundance of correction... and that most odious noise of crying of children rarely heard in the house... "

Certainly the idea of conquering the will of a child contradicts much that is taught today about educating children. Yet it is evident that what Susanna meant by this was simply a question of teaching a child that it is under authority and that it is required to obey. It has been suggested that this principle would make children spineless automatons, yet the Wesley children grew up to be men and women who showed great strength of character, one of them (John) to a degree superior to almost all others of his time. Susanna trained her children to obey and in doing so she richly molded their characters.[74]

In "devoting above twenty years of the prime of her life in hopes to save the souls of her children," she not only set aflame her offspring for the kingdom of God, but her nation, and even the entire Western World for the same.

Sarah Edwards

Consider the wife of Jonathan Edwards. Jonathan Edwards (1703-1758) is arguably the greatest theologian in American history. His sermons (including the famous "Sinners in the Hands of an Angry God") and writings continue to profoundly influence the worldwide remnant of serious Christianity to this day.

As is typical, *behind every great man is an even greater woman.* Jonathan's wife, Sarah Edwards, epitomized this axiom. In Edna Gerstner's *Jonathan and Sarah—An_Uncommon Union*, we find this pithy summary:

Edwards, known for his keen intellect, expert logic, and analytical precision was twenty-three when his life with Sarah began. Theirs was a marriage of mutual respect and admiration—"a rare and beautiful relationship." Sarah promoted the wise building of her home by respecting her husband's nearly thirteen hours a day of study time and managing her eight children through the running of a disciplined household.[75]

And what was the effect of Sarah Edwards' investing the best years of her life and strength into these eight children? Let's chronicle the traceable contribution of her mothering through the subsequent generations. From her little brood and its offspring can be traced:

- 11 College Presidents
- 65 Professors
- 100 Lawyers (including the dean of a law school)
- 30 Judges
- 66 Physicians (including the dean of a medical school)
- 80 Holders of Public Office
- 3 Mayors of large cities
- 3 State Governors
- 1 Controller of the U.S. Treasury
- 3 US Senators
- 1 Vice President of the U.S.

Surely it's true: *The hand that rocks the cradle is the hand that rules the world.*

In fact, Sarah's grandson, Timothy Dwight, who became the president of Yale University, was the son of their third daughter Mary. About his own mother, Mary Edwards Dwight, Timothy wrote: "All that I am and all that I shall be, I owe to my mother."

This passionate commendation opens up our minds to the vast and sacred challenge of a mother's solemn obligation to nurture her daughters to become *great mothers*! What a magnificent mission in itself—molding a *mighty mother* who will, in turn, rock her cradles with a world-*ruling* mindset. In this wonderfully influential daughter-directed project, surely modeling is the mightiest molder and motivator.

A man who was an All-American football wide receiver at Louisiana State University, an NFL athlete, and a pastor, is now in his sixth decade and has left all to labor together with his wife as missionaries in far-east Asia. He was recently speaking at a missions conference in Kentucky. When it was suggested to him that he needed a vacation from his strenuous, high stress schedule, he responded: "That's what heaven's for."

During one session he emphasized the necessary personal, emotional, and spiritual steel essential in missionary men and women to hold up under the strains of overseas mission work. He went on to lament the broken-down condition of U.S. culture and its increasingly dysfunctional families which sadly produce a bumper crop of damaged souls with high counts of emotional scars, personality quirks, and character deficiencies.

Then he sighed aloud, longing for workers of extraordinary character built from the ground up to bear the crushing weight of overseas missions and cried, "Oh, Lord, from where are we going to get such men and women?" The answer is—*from the church*, which encourages *women of dominion* to get a vision for the *greatness* of their building work. Godly Christian families are the training grounds for steel-backed, lion-faced, mighty kingdom warriors. Mothers, who are *women of dominion*, are the God-appointed drill sergeants. Upcoming generations are depending on them and their cradle-rocking vision.

4. Her Christ-like Sacrifice

A few weeks ago, the hands on my wristwatch stopped. I took it to a jeweler who replaced the old battery with a new one. The battery is the mainspring power source that keeps my watch running day and night.

But what is it that keeps a dedicated mother running day and night, year after year, even decade after decade? Inspirational historical models may provide a temporary enthusiasm, but a mother of dominion needs something more. Otherwise, the grueling day and night demands of crying infants, filthy bottoms, vomit-soaked blankets, strong-willed naughtiness, physical exhaustion, heart-rending grief, dull routine, deferred gratification, lack of recognition, cultural criticism, and personal disillusionment will bring the *work of her hands* (Proverbs 3:13, 19, 20, 31) to a grinding halt.

There she sits exhausted on the edge of her bed, her face in her hands, wondering, "Where's the glory in this?"

She needs something more *empowering* to keep her going.

She needs to gain and maintain the deep conviction of the glory, honor, and nobility of *selfless service*. This she finds at the foot of the cross, looking up to One who earned for Himself *"the name which is above every name"* (Philippians 2:9), by *"emptying Himself, taking the form of a bond servant"* (2:7), humbling *"Himself by becoming obedient to the point of death, even death on a cross"* (2:8). There she beholds her Savior who mopped up the damning vomit of her own sin with the precious sponge of His perfect life and atoning death. The love of Christ *constrains* and *compels* her to press on (2 Corinthians 5:14). The Spirit of Christ *empowers* her.

John Flavel writes about the powerful, invigorating effect of a Christian's continually looking upon and remembering her Lord Jesus hanging on that cross to save her soul from Hell:

> Are you staggered at your sufferings, and hard things you must endure for Christ in this world? Does the flesh shrink back from these things, and cry, "spare yourself"? What is there in the world more likely to steel and fortify your spirit with resolution and courage, than such a sight as this? Did Christ face the wrath of men, and the wrath of God too? Did he stand as a pillar of brass, ... till death beat the last breath out of his nostrils? And shall I shrink (back) for a trifle? Ah, He did not serve me so! I will arm myself with the like mind.[76]

The writer of Hebrews puts it this way:

> *Fixing our eyes on Jesus, the author and perfecter of faith, who for the joy set before Him endured the cross, despising the shame, and has sat down at the right hand of the throne of God. For consider Him who has endured such hostility by sinners against Himself, so that you may not grow weary and lose heart* (Hebrews 12:2-3, emphasis added).

There's the glory in a self-sacrificing vocation like motherhood! A woman, who takes up this assigned cross is walking in the footsteps of the One who is now glorified at the right hand of the Majesty on high. He said: *"If anyone wants to be first, he shall be last of all, and servant of all"* (Mark 9:35).

Dear faithful mothers, though you may not receive the immediate gratification of the applause you deserve now, on the day of glorification, when the Master's *"well dones"* are handed out, you'll not regret your Christ-like service. Each child is a talent of gold. Good and faithful servants invest their full energies into each one. Ostrich-like lazy ones wrap them up in napkins and bury them in the sand (Matthew z25:23-25).

Walter Chantry writes regarding the contrasting inheritances of the carnal career-minded mother and the selfless child-focused mother:

> Some day the glamour girls who leave their children in a nursery (day care), will reap their reward. They will sit in their plush houses, holding fat bank accounts, and will look with envy at a godly seed. [77]

What could bring more joy to an aging woman than to have her children rise up and call her blessed by their walking in the faith? What could bring more joy to a glorified woman than seeing around the heavenly throne a multigenerational crowd of her maternal influence? Look, Mom, you've fetched a thousand tongues to sing His praise!

I know that self-sacrificial, servant-hearted mothering is no air-tight guarantee of the salvation of all of our offspring. But J. C. Ryle is correct:

> The path of obedience is the way to blessing. We have only to do as the *servants* were commanded at the marriage feast in Cana, to fill the water-pots with water, and we may safely leave it to the Lord to turn that water into wine. [78]

So in the meantime, good and faithful Mommy, who's taking the rugged path of selfless obedience, walk with your head held high, for you are stepping in His noble footprints. Be assured. They lead to rich joy and everlasting glory.

CHAPTER 8:
WOMANLY DOMINION
IN CHILD REARING—PART 1

Victor Hugo's final novel, *Ninety-Three*, depicts the appalling upheaval of life during the Reign of Terror in 1793 France. Food shortages and unthinkable brutality abounded. Hugo describes two soldiers observing a heroic mother in action, fending for her children:

> She broke the bread into two fragments and gave them to her children, who ate with avidity (*eagerness*).
> "She hath kept none for herself," grumbled the sergeant.
> "Because she is not hungry," said a soldier.
> "No," said the sergeant, "because she is a mother."[79]

Hugo understood the greatness of loving motherhood.

It requires great courage, strength, resourcefulness, savvy, wisdom, and heroism to rear up children to the glory of God. It requires *women of dominion*. It requires mighty souls resolved to *stand their ground* and *fight with all their might* for the welfare of their offspring who look to Mom for provision, stability, and guidance.

1. Resisting the Propaganda

Back when I preached my first Mother's Day sermon in the mid-1980's, societal consensus begrudgingly conceded that a child was probably best off when raised by its mother in the home. Nevertheless, the feminists urged that a woman must *look out for herself*, and so seek a stimulating and fulfilling career outside the home.

But years later, the propaganda was ratcheted up. Guilt-ridden career women were delighted to read *"new studies"* revealing that the *"absent mother"* and the *"day- care alternative"* do not *"harm children."* University of Massachusetts psychologist Elis Harvey concluded: "Children whose mothers worked during the first three years of life after giving birth were not significantly different from those with *'unemployed'* mothers."[80]

As Dr. Laura Schlessinger, who calls the use of day care *"kid dumping,"* said in response to Harvey's study: "You can always find one shrink to say what you want to hear."[81]

But now, the propaganda has been ratcheted up even further. A stay-at-home-mom calling into a recent radio talk show said, "I can't believe what's happening today. I took my child into the pediatrician, and the doctor scolded and accused me of selfishness for keeping my one-year-old and three-year-old at home with me. He claims I'm stunting their development. He says that if I really loved them, I'd put them in day care! Even *my own mother nags* me about the same thing."

Our culture is more and more being given over to a darkened mind (Romans 1:21f) at a breathtaking pace. Not only is the unborn child the most unprotected and endangered species on earth, but our born children are suffering gross neglect upon their arrival into the world.

Many years ago, Theodore Roosevelt wrote:

> The good mother, the wise mother...is more important to the community than even the ablest man; her career is more worthy of honor and is more useful to the community than the career of any man, no matter how successful.[82]

Because of a dedicated mother's exceeding value to the good of society and the kingdom of God, the forces of darkness have aimed their big guns against her. During World War II, Hitler's thirsty military machine was fed by the rich oil fields and refineries of Ploesti in

Eastern Romania. The allies knew that if they could destroy the Ploesti refineries, they could bring down the German military. Squadrons of American B-24 Flying Fortresses, with bellies full of bombs, daily flew sorties from Italy to Ploesti, seeking to bomb out of existence the strategic fuel source. Likewise, committed motherhood is right in the crosshairs of our children's diabolical adversary. As in the Garden of Eden, his bombs are not explosive shells and shrapnel, but are words and ideas and propaganda. *Women of dominion* must heroically hunker down.

Patricia Holland has said: "If I wanted to destroy society, I would launch an all-out blitz on women."[83] She was referring to the cultural cohesiveness that mothers have provided to society.

> Like mortar that keeps a brick wall from toppling over, women have held together our most precious relationships—our marriages and child-parent ties. But now we're seeing cracks in that mortar, which reveal some things we have too long taken for granted.[84]

Consider this picture from decades ago:

> A salesman walked down a street past a group of boys playing baseball. No one answered the door at the house where he was to call. Through a side door, he saw a boy the age of those playing in the street, dutifully practicing the piano. Baseball gear leaned against the wall.
>
> He called, "Excuse me, sonny, is your mother home?"
>
> The boy glanced at his baseball gear and said glumly from the keyboard, "What do you think?"[85]

But over the last 30 years, dedicated mothers have taken it on the jaw. Heroic women who've given their lives to the welfare and education of their children have been systematically devalued and made to feel stupid and second rate because they took seriously the biblical mission of motherhood. Remove the mortar from society, and the bricks collapse.

Back in the early 1970's, Joe lived about four blocks away from my boyhood home. His mom's lifestyle was rare back then. She worked— full time. During the day, Joe's house was the site of absolute chaos and anarchy. Disgusting things took place there. I still remember my uneasy conscience when I visited the local "Animal House." But at quarter to five, the wildness had to be tamed. The house had to be rearranged and cleaned, so that Joe's mom would return and think her angels and their friends had just innocently played board games and watched *Leave it to Beaver* and *The Andy Griffith Show* all day.

An old Spanish proverb reads: "An ounce of mother is worth a ton of priest."

A dedicated mother at her post is health-infusing to the lives of her children and to society. Hour by hour, she nurses them with *"the milk of human kindness."* The story is told of a man being held up at knifepoint. He pled with his executioner who held the blade to his throat, "Please have mercy on me and spare my life!" When the would-be murderer softened and released his victim, the relieved man said to him, "You had a mother, didn't you?" The thief wept.

Shakespeare gave to us the phrase, *"the milk of human kindness,"* in *Macbeth*. Lady Macbeth is persuading her husband to murder the king and take his throne. Macbeth hesitates. His wife sneers:

Thy nature is too full o'th'milk of human kindness.

Then in a haunting passage, Lady Macbeth pleads with the evil forces of the underworld to take away her own milk of human kindness, her life-giving, nurturing female nature:

Come, you spirits that tend on mortal thoughts, unsex me here,
And fill me from the crown to the toe topful of direst cruelty!
Come to my breasts,
And take my milk for gall, you murth'ring ministers.
Come, thick night. (*Macbeth* 1, 5)

Take my woman's milk for gall! Unsex me here! This is the very project the evil one is pursuing in the 21st century. On a massive scale, he's performing psychological and emotional mastectomies on womankind. By the multitudes, tender-hearted American females are being duped and then butchered into becoming heartless Lady Macbeths.

We see them shouting with placards and shrill voices in city squares, "It's my body and it's *my right to choose* to have an abortion if I please!" But we may also hear them cooing over a cup of Starbucks, "I just know that I have too much ability and ambition to waste my whole life staying at home with my kids."

A *Rochester Times Union Newspaper* writer reported on the widespread phenomenon of working mothers' leaving *"home alone"* all day, very young (age seven and up) children, who are too ill to go to school. "You probably think it's terrible," a recent divorcee told me with a shrug, "but I have no choice but to leave my son home by himself. I can't get any help. I did stay home a couple of days and people at work were quite understanding, but now I sense my boss' patience is running out and I just can't jeopardize my job." [86]

I ache for single mothers who are in emergency mode and must work full time to put food on the table. I ache for married women whose less-than-ambitious husbands pressure their wives to become breadwinners. I ache regarding financial screws that are being tightened on families due to the increasing cost-of-living and falling wages. But I also recognize such broken situations as additional dimensions of the handiwork of the adversary who is busy launching his all-out blitz on women and their offspring.

Practically speaking, homes are becoming motherless. The maternal mortar is being sucked out of a society which is crumbling before our eyes.

Resist the 21st century pressure and propaganda. Don't let it unsex you into a heartless Lady Macbeth.

2. Evangelizing Your Offspring

Your mission, dear mother, is *not* to make your children *happy*, but to prepare them for *eternity*.

In the mid-1800's an older woman wrote to a younger woman:

> If the existence of your children were limited to a few years and then the soul and body were to expire together, maternal tenderness would impel you to make the life, which was to be so short, as happy as possible. With a mother's vigilance you would seek to render this brief period a season of uninterrupted sunshine... . Yet the unutterable interests of the soul, in that boundless immortality, are suspended upon the manner in which this fleeting little moment (of life) is spent. Upon its wise improvement or abuse depends your children's eternal possession of joys which eye hath not seen, nor ear heard, nor the heart of man conceived, or their irrevocable doom to the prison of (eternal) despair.[87]

You must labor with a *"win it"* mindset to get them right with God.

You must relentlessly evangelize their never-dying souls. You were instrumental in their condemnation at birth. *"Behold, I was brought forth in iniquity, and in sin my mother conceived me"* (Psalm 51:5, emphasis added). You must be earnest in seeking their justification in Christ.

You must daily tell them the *bad news* truth about themselves—that they are sinners whose crimes against God doom them to be punished forever by His just wrath in hell, and that there is nothing they can do by themselves to clean up their morally filthy condition.

> *For all have sinned and fall short of the glory of God (Romans 3:23).*

> *He will by no means leave the guilty unpunished (Exodus 34:7b).*

> *For all of us have become like one who is unclean, and all our righteous deeds are like a filthy garment (Isaiah 64:6, emphasis added).*

You must daily tell them the *good news* truth about Jesus Christ. He came as the Lamb of God to offer up himself as a substitutionary atonement in the place of sinners. Whoever smears Jesus' blood on the doorpost of his soul by believing in Him will have God's lethal wrath harmlessly pass over his soul on judgment day.

> *But He was pierced through for our transgressions, he was crushed for our iniquities; the chastening for our wellbeing fell upon Him, and by His scourging we are healed. All we like sheep have gone astray, each of us has turned to his own way; but the Lord has caused the iniquities of us all to fall on Him (Isaiah 53:5-6).*

> *By grace you have been saved through faith; and that not of yourselves, it is a gift of God; not as a result of works, that no one should boast (Ephesians 2:8-9).*

> *For God so loved the world, that He gave His only begotten Son, that whoever believes in Him should not perish, but have*

eternal life (John 3:16).

One sharp winter's day, a poor woman stood at the window of a king's greenhouse looking at a cluster of grapes, which she longed to have for her sick child. She went home to her spinning wheel, *earned* half a crown, and offered it to the gardener for the grapes. He waved his hand and ordered her away. She returned to her cottage, snatched the blanket from her bed, pawned it, and once more asked the gardener to *sell* her the grapes, offering him five shillings. He spoke furiously to her, and was leading her out when the princess came in, heard the gardener's anger, saw the woman's tears, and asked what was wrong. When the story was told the princess said, "My dear woman, you have made a mistake. My father is not a merchant, but a king; his business is not to *sell*, but to *give*." Upon saying this, she plucked the cluster from the vine and dropped it into the woman's apron.[88]

God is not a bartering merchant, but a *gift*-giving King. Eternal life cannot be *earned* by good works, deeds of holiness, or acts of religion. God detests such proud attempts to *buy* salvation. Only the empty hand of faith can receive the salvation which was purchased by Christ's *work* on the cross. "*But to the one who does not <u>work</u>, but <u>believes</u> in Him who justifies the ungodly, his <u>faith</u> is reckoned as righteousness*" (Romans 4:5, emphasis added).

Daily nurse and feed your little ones on these great gospel truths. A *woman of dominion* commits herself to this relentless work of Christian nurture. When the child sins, Mom exposes the transgression, disciplines for the crime, points to the Savior, demands repentance, trains in obedience, and requires daily Bible reading and prayer. And, God willing, at a given moment in time, that child will be given the new birth, believe, be justified, and saved.

But wise parents often painfully wrestle with this very theme. They ask: "When can I reasonably conclude that my child is actually saved?" Simply *praying the sinner's prayer* in the middle of a thunderstorm or around a summer-camp bonfire doesn't necessarily settle the matter. Many such *decisions* are merely temporary spasms of spiritual interest, but not authentic experiences of saving conversion. Wise parents look for solid evidences of the new birth.

For there is no good tree which produces bad fruit; nor, on the

*other hand, a bad tree which produces good fruit. For each tree
is known by its own fruit. For men do not gather figs from thorns,
nor do they pick grapes from a briar bush (Luke 6:43-44).*

After hearing in Sunday School the dramatic testimony of a man
saved out of a pagan lifestyle, a dedicated Christian mother confided
that she wished she could observe in her children such a radical life
change. But in reality her children were kept from the *"far country"*
by the fences of her Christian nurture. Though *"sinful and guilty,"* they
were never *"wild and immoral."* With one son, she'd sensed with great
hope a spiritual dawning at the age of seven. His interest in the Bible
increased. His prayers displayed depth. His conscience became more
sensitive. His kindness to his siblings surged. She cautiously hoped
he'd been born again. But after a few weeks, these fruits dried up. His
spiritual pulse went back to its previous flat line. Over the next few
years this same ebb and flow was repeated.

She lamented, "It's often so hard to know when kids raised in
Christian homes are really saved! A dramatic conversion experience
would be so wonderful. Though my son professes to be a Christian,
sometimes I don't know whether to treat him as a believer or as an
unbeliever."

Her dilemma is a common one for godly Christian mothers. Her
child has no dramatic Philippian jailer-like conversion experience
(Acts 16) as a reference point. Instead, her child is Timothy-like, *"from
childhood,"* having *"known the sacred writings which are able to give
you the wisdom that leads to salvation through faith in Christ Jesus"* (2
Timothy 3:15). As Timothy was nursed and trained by his godly mother
Eunice and grandmother Lois, the privileged child has been raised in
a home of faithful Christian nurture. Often in such circumstances,
the recognition of the new birth doesn't come instantaneously, like a
dramatic lightning strike, but gradually, as a subtle dawning of a new
day.

What's a godly mother to do? How is she to handle this delicate
matter? Should she maintain the Christian nurture mode by habitually
telling him to repent, obey, and daily read his Bible and pray? Or
should she leave him to himself to discover whether or not he's saved
and inwardly empowered by the Holy Spirit?

Rev. Albert N. Martin, in his lectures entitled, "Dealing with your
Spiritually-Awakened Children," gives very perceptive counsel regarding the common procedure used by the Spirit in converting a child

raised in the atmosphere of faithful Christian nurture. He persuasively argues that though the new birth takes place at a pinpoint moment in time, we must counterbalance this truth by this seasoned observation: in a nurturing Christian home, typically that specific moment will *not* be marked by a crisis experience. We may not know the exact date of conversion.

Martin states it this way: "The precise time when Christian nurture becomes implanted nature will most likely be known neither to the parent nor the child."[89] He then drives home the point with a brilliant illustration. I'm paraphrasing:

The early propeller planes needed to be started manually. The pilot would watch a mechanic crank the blade by hand resulting in sparking, sputtering, then dying. This sequence would be repeated until finally there would be cranking, sparking, sputtering, then roaring! You always knew the precise moment when ignition occurred by the roaring of the engine.

Later jet engines were started differently. It was first necessary to get the engine's main shaft spinning by an external source of power. Out the window a passenger could watch a truck, equipped with an electric motor, pull up and be connected to the plane's jet engine. The passenger could feel and hear the shaft begin to turn and whirr and spin. But the passenger could never be sure that external propulsion had been exchanged for internal ignition until the truck was disconnected and drove away, leaving the plane independently roaring with jet engine power. When the passenger was gliding down the runway at 150 mph and lifting off the ground, he knew the plane was self-propelled!

As long as a child remains in a Christian home, the parents are solemnly obligated to keep turning the engine shaft of his soul. Don't expect some *crisis experience* to assure you that he's saved. Continue to press him to confess his sins, believe, repent, obey, read, and pray. As long as he's under your roof, keep him connected to the umbilical cord of Christian nurture. Then, when he's disconnected by adult independence, such as, going off to a challenging job, to college, or to marriage, you'll be able to observe him picking up speed, gaining altitude, and flying in the ways of godliness. "Look at him! He's propelled by the Spirit. Man, he's cruising! Praise God!"

But, dear mother of *womanly dominion*, until then keep cranking and turning his spiritual shaft. Though your shoulder gets sore and your soul gets weary, keep nurturing. God willing, you'll enjoy increasingly surging hopes along the way. God willing, you'll hear holy roaring from his soul. But your motherly duty remains the same. Keep cranking. Don't gratify your hankering to prematurely *"get it settled right now"* regarding his salvation. Press on in your nurturing project of bringing him up in the discipline and instruction of the Lord (Ephesians 6:4; Proverbs 1:8).

Relentlessly evangelize their never-dying souls.

3. Defending Your Culturally-Threatened Brood

The May 18, 2007, news article was entitled: "Australian Mother Says She Fought Shark off with Camera to Save Children."

> A woman who was attacked by a shark on a West Australian reef says all she could think of was fighting it off before it could savage her teenage son wading alongside, or the 3-year-old on her hip. Mother-of-five Becky Cooke, 38, had her heel and calf lacerated by the 2.5 meter shark as she waded across a coral reef with two of her sons at remote Warra beach, south of Coral Bay, on Wednesday. From her bed in Royal Perth Hospital Friday she described how scared she had been when she realized she had been bitten and more sharks could be attracted by her spreading blood. "All I could think of was getting it off my leg so I could get to shore because I did not know if it was alone, or if there were other sharks out there," Cooke said.
>
> Flanked by her husband Peter and sons, Brandon (13), Hayden (10), Jacob (7), James (6), and Ethan (3), Cooke explained she had been wading in shallow water with Ethan and Brandon when the shark struck on day four of their nine-day holiday. "It just felt like something had hit me, at first, I turned around and I saw all this thrashing and the water just turned red.
>
> "My son was with me, we were walking together. I just think, 'Thank goodness it bit me, not Brandon.' I had my camera in my hand and Ethan on my hip, I started hitting it with my camera and shaking my leg trying to get it off. It let go, I took a couple of steps and fell into the water because my leg was pretty bad. As I fell into the water the sea just turned to blood. It was pretty scary, I wasn't sure if it had gone, or if it was going to come back."

Cooke said her main worry was that the unidentified shark might attack her children.

"Brandon came running over, and I said to him 'take Ethan' and he grabbed Ethan and ran back to shore."

She said she did not feel the pain until she reached the shore where she was given first aid, helped by her husband, family friends and two volunteer conservation officers who turned up at the beach just moments before the attack.

She will have an operation tonight on her severe calf wounds, knowing she could face two years of treatment. "I could still lose my foot, I would like to try and save my foot," she said. [90]

Now *this* mother is a true *woman of dominion*. She's *"more than a gentle and quiet spirit."* She stood her ground and fought a good fight, risking life and limb, all for the sake of her children.

We desperately need *subduing* and *ruling* women like Becky Cooke, because the waters of our 21st century culture are shark-infested cesspools of immorality, and our vulnerable children are hunted day and night. The role of maternal guardian is not for the faint-hearted.

Rebecca Hagelin is the author of *Home Invasion: Protecting Your Family in a Culture that's Gone Stark Raving Mad*. She tells of driving her child-filled family van from Virginia to Disney World. Due to business commitments, her husband would fly to Orlando. She was the guardian.

The Interstate 95 roadside was filled with tacky billboards screaming, "Topless! We Dare, We Bare!" Eventually they pulled into a gas station for ice cream. Upon returning from the ladies' room, there stood two of her girls licking their cones alongside a display of a product called, *"Hottest Goat Weed: sex stimulant pills for men and women."* At the assumed-to-be-safe Burger King was a television blaring the images and sounds of a made-for-TV movie scene featuring an unmarried couple in bed together. And then there are the nearly pornographic women's magazines at the grocery store checkout stands or the sexually graphic images gawking back at our children at the video store.[91]

But surely home is a safe haven, right? Not without a heroic *woman-of-dominion* mother *playing her position*, standing her ground, at her post, resolving to fight the good fight for the sake of her children. Remember that strange-looking man wearing the trench coat who lurked in the shadows at the edge of the school playground? Well, he and a whole gang of his friends are now in our homes.

Think of internet filth. Homework isn't the only thing kids are doing online. Solicitations for pornography are legion. Many kids close their bedroom doors and consume hours of sewage. Chat rooms and sites like MySpace.com have become playgrounds for sexual predators.

Think of television trash. "MTV is the number-one viewing choice for teen girls. It's filled with reality-based shows that feature kids dressed in teeny-weeny bikinis licking whipped cream off each other."[92] "Desperate Housewives" is the third most popular show among teens.

Think of video game pollution. "Grand Theft Auto" enables our boys to vicariously become a character who steals cars, rapes women, has sex with a prostitute (to gain more strength), and then clubs her to death. Afterwards, he can decapitate a policeman. "Halo" desensitizes them to the sanctity of life by rewarding them with adrenalin rushes for shooting up an orgy of fantasy foes.

Think of book corruption. Summer reading is a wise idea. A good mom might take her kids to the library so that they a good book to read when they get bored. But the shelves weren't stocked by "your mother's librarian." An American Library Association book title may contain anything from a hyphenated slang term describing incestuous intercourse to descriptions of a sexual encounter between fourth graders.

Think of the music madness. Regardless of race and socioeconomic status, rap and hip-hop, with all their violence and verbal pornography, are the *"genre of choice"* for today's youth. The billions of dollars behind this whole cultural blitzkrieg are teaching our girls that *"sexual power"* strutted with tight and skimpy fashions is where it's at, and our boys that *"crude irresponsibility"* is the ultimate cool. We're witnessing diabolical forces striving toward the systematic moral degradation of humanity (Revelation 18:2-4).

It doesn't "take a village' to protect our children and take back our homes. An act of Congress is not the answer. A mother of *womanly dominion* is. She's better than a mother bear escorting her cubs (Proverbs 17:2). She's a club-swinging woman in shark- infested waters. She realizes that thirteen-year-old boys can't buy video games unless their parents give them the sixty bucks, that eleven-year-old girls can't drive themselves to the mall to buy *"prostitot"* clothes, that internet connections and cable TV contracts are paid and so must be supervised by *"subduing and ruling"* parents. She understands children don't need more trendy friends but godly parents who plant themselves between their precious children and the butchering culture.[93]

Rebecca Hagelin says it well:

> The best tool we can use is our expression of love for them. And sometimes, that commitment is difficult. I know what it's like to have my 13-year-old daughter look at me with tears streaming down her face and say, "But Mom, all my friends are going to that movie." It rips my heart out. But in those moments, I sit Kristin down and say, "You know what, Kristin? God made me your mom, and I love you more than anybody else in the world could possibly love you. I have to do what I think is best for you. Please allow me to be your Mom, allow me to love you, allow me to protect you the best way I know how. I might make mistakes, but *as long as there is breath in me*, I will be here for you." And then, we always find something else to do that's fun for her.
>
> Those situations could easily turn into ugly scenes where I scream, "No you're not going to that movie and I don't care what you say! Go to your room!" Or they can turn into moments where I give in, *too tired to fight another battle*, sending my daughter off with the message that standards only apply when I'm not worn out. [94]

Mom, your little ones are a culturally-threatened brood! They desperately need your conviction, your resolve, your fearlessness, and your strength. They need a *mother of dominion* who's willing to stand firm, to fight on, to shed blood, sweat, and tears in this good fight. They need you to be *"more than a gentle and quiet spirit"*!

4. Running a Dynamic Household

Jean Fleming describes a common experience of a dedicated mother of many who is finally able to crawl into bed after an exhausting day:

> On a winter night the air in our bedroom is frigid.
>
> I slid under the blankets, even covering my head, hoping my warm breath will thaw my nose. At last a toasty warmth envelopes me I drift toward sleep.
>
> Then a hacking cough disturbs the silence. I wait. Maybe it will go away in a minute or so. I struggle with ambivalent feelings: *Poor Beth, I guess I should fetch her some cough medicine. But I dread that shivering walk to the kitchen, now that I'm finally warm.*

If she coughs three more times I'll get up. Oh Lord, please help her stop coughing. One more cough. "Please, Beth, stop coughing," I whisper. Two more coughs. That makes three. I can delay no longer. Reluctantly I pull on socks and a robe and drag myself to her aid.[95]

Upon arriving at such bedsides after a late-night awakening, mothers have found anything from coughing mouths, to runny or bloody noses, to dirty diapers, to wet beds, to vomit-soaked sheets, to tear-filled faces. This motherhood thing can be a very messy business.

Well, to such child-preoccupied servants of God, Proverbs 14:4 provides volumes of encouragement:

Where no oxen are, the manger is clean,
but much increase comes by the strength of the ox.

A. Its Agricultural Picture
This proverb contrasts two barns.

1. The Immaculate but Unproductive Barn
Ancient barns or stables were often dug into the sides of hills. It is possible Jesus was born in such a cave-like barn and laid there in a manger (Luke 2:7). Sometimes barns were attached to a farmer's dwelling like a garage. They could also be free standing (Luke 12:18). In such places, livestock would be housed and fed.

Step into an "oxless" barn. Look, there are no muscular beasts which do the great work of plowing up a field for planting. But it's immaculate here. The manger (feeding trough) is perfectly clean—no feed slop, corn dust, or beastly saliva. In fact, everything is spic and span. You could eat off the floor—no hay or mud. There are no unsightly hoof prints, manure piles, urine puddles, or buzzing flies. The smell is antiseptic and fresh. Everything is in perfect order.

But there is a downside to this tidiness. Outside the barn, the acreage is overrun with weeds. The fields are untilled and uncultivated. The grain cribs are empty. You see, there's no ox to cut open the soil with the plow blade. And so, no seed was hidden, and no harvest was reaped. There's no *"increase"* here. Poverty reigns and the cupboards are bare.

2. The Soiled but Profitable Barn
Step into the "ox-inhabited" barn. Whew! The manure, urine, hay,

mud, and flies make it anything but fresh and sweet in here. Here comes Farmer Elimelech with a shovel over his shoulder to clean up the mess. He's late this morning. He was up at two a.m. to help deliver an ox calf. It's a huge task to feed, house, and look after these enormous beasts. Why does he put up with all the grief, messiness, and aggravation? It's as the Proverb says, because *"Much increase comes by the strength of the ox."* *"Increase"* is revenue, yield, income, harvest, or gain. These mighty plodders knife open the soil, enabling the nestling of the seed in rows, resulting in the eventual swaying of wheat and barley, the overflowing of barns, the rolling of full wagons to the marketplace, the piling of the kitchen table high with bounty, and the providing of riches for one's family and heritage.

Sure, the barn is not very tidy, immaculate, or fresh smelling, but the yield, *the increase* makes it a far better barn than the first.

B. Its Profound Principle
In a nutshell, Proverbs 14:4 teaches that enduring and worthwhile gain comes only at the cost of draining upheaval. The modernized version is: *"No pain, no gain."*

Derek Kidner entitles this proverb, *"Neat but Negative."* Think of the dear woman who dreams of an immaculate house, uncluttered by the tramplings and inconveniences of a small herd of messy offspring. Kidner comments: "Orderliness can reach the point of sterility (uselessness). This proverb is not a plea for slovenliness, physical or moral, but for the readiness to accept upheaval, and a mess to clear up, as the price of growth." Kidner concludes by encouraging us "to foster a farmer's outlook, rather than the curator's."[96]

A curator is the manager of an art gallery. Stereotypically, he's so obsessed with the tidiness, neatness, and quietness of his realm that he's actually irritated by the trampling of little visitors, to whom he compulsively snaps, "Do not touch!" He's more committed to cosmetic compliments than educational benefits.

C. Its Maternal Implications
Instead of contrasting barns, let's contrast two homes.

1. The Immaculate but Unproductive Home
The mistress of this home has the curator's mindset. Approaching her house, we stroll by her perfectly manicured lawn; step inside her vanilla candle-scented living room onto her spotless and perfectly

combed carpet. It's immaculate and gorgeous like an art gallery. How does she do it? Well, Tiffany and Randy absolutely love style, neatness, and order. Such things are a high priority with them. So frankly, they don't want their lives, careers, and home, cluttered with the messiness of kids. They think that maybe someday they'll have a child, but honestly, such thoughts make Tiff break out in a rash.

They enjoy cutting-edge curtains, a fashionable wardrobe, and sharp, late-model cars. They're able to channel their dual incomes to the acquiring of their wants. The coffee table was imported from South America. The blown up black and white framed photograph on the wall is from last winter's Hawaii vacation. The kitchen calendar is quite clean and unsullied, with the exception of Randy's scheduled softball games on Monday, Wednesday, and Friday, during which Tiffany does her workouts with her personal trainer at the fitness club. On Saturday, Tiff shops while Randy golfs. The rest of the time they have for just being alone together and falling more in love with each other!

2. The Soiled but Profitable Home

The mistress of this home has the farmer's mindset. Approaching her house, we stroll by her lawn which is blemished by four unsightly bare spots which suspiciously give her front yard the look of a baseball diamond. We step inside onto her carpet marred by some pretty heavily worn traffic areas. That scratch in the wall over there came from her son Tom's banging his science project when he tripped on his little brother Joe's baseball glove. You see, Rick and Joan have five children. Joan's wardrobe is very pleasant, but not cutting edge. In the garage, their not-so-late-model cars reflect the high cost of kids. In the laundry room are three baskets-full of clothes waiting to be folded. On the kitchen table is a pile of books, as Rick and Joan spend much time helping the children with studies and homework. The calendar is cluttered with child-enriching events, such as music and swim lessons, baseball and soccer practices, caddying and paper route duties, and next Saturday's 5K run, for which the whole family is signed up.

D. Its Lifestyle Applications

1. Resign yourself to a degree of upheaval.

With the oxen of children in our domestic barns, the immaculate lifestyle of Tiffany will surely prove illusive.

Now, remember Kidner's important qualification: "This proverb is not a plea for slovenliness."[97] A *woman of dominion* will strive to maintain an orderly household. An overgrown yard, ransacked rooms, and a sink stacked high with dirty dishes do not glorify the God who loves things being *"done properly and in an orderly manner"* (1 Corinthians 14:40; also numerous Proverbs). The immaculate tranquility of Tiffany's house will be an impossible achievement for a woman committed to the rearing of mighty creatures who will *plow hard* for the kingdom.

Oh, I suppose a mother could keep things *"neat as a pin"* if her goal was to have just one or two "low maintenance" children of the "sheltered" variety to whom she selfishly communicated, "Just go to your room and don't bother us." But if a mother is bent on raising up mighty children, capable children, bold, brave, daring, adventuresome, God-fearing, *dominion-minded* children, then she needs to "kiss good-bye" any aspirations of immaculate tranquility. Oxen who go out and turn the soil over, and children who go out and turn the world upside down, make messes. But the *woman of dominion* is willing to pay the price of domestic upheaval for the prospects of kingdom profit.

There will be more corner cobwebs than you'd like, because instead of obsessively cleaning, you'll be nursing, teaching to read and ride bikes, and telling bedtime stories. Your front lawn may be blemished with dandelions because your husband assigned your thirteen-year-old son (who needs to learn responsibility) to spray weed killer on the grass instead of Dad's doing it perfectly himself. Because you let the children finger paint and do Play-Doh today, your kitchen won't pass a white glove inspection tonight. Your Lord's Day mornings aren't as tranquil as you'd like, because it takes time before Sunday School to find a matching sock, help polish the memory verses, and get the munchkins all into the car on time. And now that we've mentioned the car, it's not as new as you'd like, due to the dollars and time poured into feeding, educating, nurturing, and rounding out the kids.

Yes, you do want well-rounded kids. You're not content to have them just aimlessly kicking up dust in the backyard, sitting around playing computer games, or sequestered away in their sheltered bedrooms. That's why your calendar may be cluttered with soccer, basketball, or baseball games. It's much easier to just relax at home. You may be convinced that athletics can be greatly used to cultivate important character traits, like submission to authority, self discipline and control, a hard-working spirit, courage, teamwork, endurance, focus, and poise. Convinced that pressure brings character issues to the surface, you may use music lessons, boy scouts, or 4H projects to accomplish the same character-molding results.

You may spend much time driving your teenage son way across town for his job, rather than to the nearby MacDonald's, because you want him to be mentored by a godly boss in a work environment with wholesome peers.

Your evening schedules are clogged by a commitment after dinner to spend time reading and discussing the Bible, then praying for the needs of family, friends, and church.

Your vacations are spent in tents and on campgrounds rather than in five-star hotels.

Your sleep schedule is often *messed up* by a coughing child, a crying infant, a fearful daughter, or a late-night talk. Their hiding *owl-like* personalities often come out at night. Their teen problems often heat up later in the evenings, and you've got to strike while the iron is hot, though your body is really weary. Then you don't sleep so well, because concerns for their young souls haunt you in the dark. Morning comes too soon, and you've got to rise up in time to read and pray so you'll have something to give during the dawning new day. Of course, such a commitment takes its toll on your health spiritually, physically, mentally, and emotionally, as you may be plagued by enduring fatigue and a lowered resistance to illness.

None of these things helps your *love life* with your husband. Romantic rendezvouses with your spouse (dates and quiet nights) often must take a back seat to the nurturing of your little herd.

Of these upheavals, the Tiffany's of this world know nothing. But they are also strangers to your greatness.

2. Let go of your right to personal leisure.

This oxen proverb struck me years ago when our children were still quite young. I'd just returned from a marathon weekend of ministry out West. I boarded the plane before dawn on Friday, hit the ground running with draining meetings and counseling sessions, preached three times Sunday, counseled late into the night, awoke at four a.m. to drive hours to catch a plane back home where I arrived around 5:30 p.m. Monday absolutely frazzled, fatigued, and exhausted. I craved, body and soul, to crash in relaxation. But then after my dinner, my bride wondered if I'd be interested in taking the boys to the seminary indoor pool to continue the swimming lessons I'd been giving them. This suggestion was like fingernails on the chalkboard. My emotions shrieked in protest. This meant I'd have to pack up the towels and suits, bundle them up, drive through the snow, etc. But there stood the three boys, all staring at me. All were eager to go. One had just started doggy paddling. All needed endurance training. And it hit me. I've not been commissioned at this stage in my life *to enjoy leisure*, but *to be a father*. My goal is not to raise low-maintenance children, but lion-hearted ones. As a friend of mine has said, "I want to train up thoroughbreds to the glory of God."

We went to the pool. It was a defining moment for me as a parent. One of my sons actually soiled his suit due to after-dinner swimming, and I found myself cleaning his loose stool droppings off the shower, locker-room, and bathroom floors.

> *Where no oxen are, the manger is clean,*
> *but much increase comes by the strength of the ox*
> *(Proverbs 14:4).*

My defining moment is a mother's continuous experience. Nancy Wilson writes about motherhood:

> It can mean little time for novel-reading, not too many long phone calls, and not much socializing. The home and the children are the first priority. Bathing the children, keeping their clothes clean, feeding them, and teaching them are all part of a full-time job that requires planning, stamina, and a heart that is committed to work.[98]

Motherhood is much like Savior-hood. The Lord Jesus needed rest and a vacation but was compelled to do otherwise.

> *And He said to them, "Come away by yourselves to a lonely place and rest a while." (For there were many people coming and going, and they did not even have time to eat.) And they went away in the boat to a lonely place by themselves. And the people saw them going, and many recognized them, and they ran there together on foot from all the cities, and got there ahead of them. And when He went ashore, He saw a great multitude, and He felt compassion for them because <u>they were like sheep without a shepherd</u>; and He began to teach them many things (Mark 6:31-34, emphasis added).*

Keeping livestock, nurturing children, and saving sheep all require the relinquishment of well-deserved leisure.

3. Meditate on your worthwhile harvest.

Tiffany may relish her shallow and temporary self-indulgence. Her *"increase"* and harvest are fleeting and short-lived. Her designer curtains and expensive wardrobes won't rise up and bless her (Proverbs 31:28). When the summer of her jet-set youth dwindles away, and she enters the autumn of middle-age and winter of senior citizenry, her empty soul will gnaw within while gazing over unplowed fields and poverty of heart.

Not so with the selfless mother of dominion who was willing to endure decades of *"upheaval."* God willing, she will be able to watch from the grandstands the *"increase"* of her thoroughbred training. Look how her high-spirited and accomplished horses run the race in such a way as to win the prize! The breathtaking sight brings to her a fullness of soul that causes all the years of *"upheaval"* to evaporate into a fleeting vapor. She is able to feast all winter long on the *"fruit of her hands"* (Proverbs 31:31).

5. Rearing Sons

Christina Hoff Sommers has written a book entitled, *The War Against Boys, How Misguided Feminism is Harming our Young Men.* She delineates the systematic cultural attempts to feminize our sons by seeking to remove from their characters the unsightly blemishes of aggressive manhood. She jousts with Harvard's Carol Gilligan who "calls for a fundamental change in child rearing that would keep boys in a more sensitive relationship with their feminine side." Gilligan claims: "We need to free young men from a destructive culture of manhood." Sommers concludes: "What Gilligan and her followers are proposing is . . civilizing boys by diminishing their masculinity." As Gloria Steinem bluntly advises: "Raise boys like we raise girls."[99]

Such socializing trends are a direct assault against God's created order. "*And God created man in His own image, in the image of God He created him; male and female He created them*" (Genesis 1:27, emphasis added).

A *woman of dominion* resists this philosophy which is promoted in books, magazines, movies, radio shows, public and even Christian schools, and, yes, in some churches, too. Resolve to raise your boys to be men. *"Act like men, be strong"* (1 Corinthians 16:13).

Toughen your sons.

A mother's tenderness and softness are very important in developing the character of her sons, but it is possible to overdo a good thing. *"Have you found honey? Eat only what you need, lest you have it in excess and vomit it"* (Proverbs 25:16).

Years ago, there was a dead skunk in the middle of the road in front of our home. It was stinking to high heaven. It had to be dealt with. Here was an excellent teachable moment for Nathan, our eight-year-old. He was presented with the challenging dilemma and informed that he was *the man for the hour.* He was to dig a suitably deep hole near the ditch, scoop up and drag the foul carcass about 80 feet to the hole, then cover the grave with dirt. He dry heaved a few times during the process, but his mother refused to rescue her *"little boy"* from such a horrible and *"dirty job."* Mothers, don't be guilty of molly-coddling by taking sides with your son against Dad when a peculiarly difficult chore has been assigned.

Train your sons to face tough obstacles head on, work hard through thorns and thistles, and *"find a way"* to get jobs done. They need to become bread-winning providers in a cursed world. Train them to be tough, not fragile.

A three-year-old boy gets bonked in the head by the refrigerator door. He begins to scream bloody murder. The wise mother gives him a brief hug, and then says, "Show me tough!"

The seven-year-old boy gets hit smack in the face with a soccer ball during a Saturday game. Mom doesn't run out to scoop him up in her arms. She's thankful for the principled coach who, from the sidelines, encourages her weeping son to: "Settle down!" and "Stay out there, because we need you on the field!" Nancy Wilson writes in *Praise Her in the Gates*: "Don't tolerate a cry baby. Although it is understandable to see tears in young boys, older boys should not normally cry from pain. This may be an attention-getting device. Don't overdo on the comfort."[100]

When a teen son fails a test or loses a neighborhood lawn-mowing job, it's not Mom's role to go to the teacher or homeowner to plead for mercy or patch things up. Let him endure the pain of reaping what he's sown. *No pain, no gain!*

Dignify your sons.

Men, both young and old, thrive on being recognized as courageous, brave, and valiant. It's emboldening for a son to hear notes and tones from his mother that communicate, "You're my hero!" instead of "You're such a wimp!"

King David made sure to record and publish the names and deeds of his Mighty Men (see 2 Samuel 23), knowing that such recognition would inspire them to even greater feats of valor. He was even careful to *heap commendation* not only on spectacular exploits like *killing a lion in a pit on a snowy day* (2 Samuel 23:20), but also for mundane duties like *guarding the baggage* behind the battle lines (1 Samuel 30:24). In so doing, *he lionized his men.* Mothers must *lionize their sons* by dignifying them with their respect.

Commend your sons for doing noble things like getting the mail in a blizzard, shoveling heavy or deep snow, emptying the mousetrap, walking home into the teeth of a frigid wind, and staining the deck on a sweltering afternoon.

Cloak your son with a big jacket of respect in his childhood, and he'll seek to grow into it in his manhood. Teach him how to deserve, receive, and handle respect. Don't get caught up in the modern self-esteem craze that lavishes praise apart from genuine accomplishment. Don't detach commendation from true achievement. They'll learn to disregard your praising as patronizing—"Oh, that's just Mom!"

A mother's dignifying her sons with admiration must also be flanked by her abstaining from anything that would cause their unnecessary humiliation.

> A mother who makes fun of her son in public or tells others of his weaknesses or failures in casual conversation is showing disregard and disrespect... When a mother shares things about her son, whether he is small or grown, that would embarrass him, she is tearing down her house. Telling people about his interest in a girl before it is public knowledge, laughing about his big ears, sharing about his concern over his acne—these are all examples of discourtesy and disrespect to sons.[101]

Dominionize your sons.

Don't let them grow up to be *Passive-Purple-Four-Balls.* Teach them to subdue and rule in their lives (Genesis 1:28). Men don't hide behind their mother's skirt. They boldly and daringly *"go forth." "Man goes forth to his work and to his labor until evening"* (Psalm 104:23, emphasis added).

Here's the thesis of *Manly Dominion, In a Passive-Purple-Four-Ball-World*:

> I must subdue and rule, and not permit myself to be subdued and ruled. We have been commissioned by God to go out and aggressively assert ourselves as masters over every realm of our lives. I have not been assigned to stare out my bedroom, living room, or office window, passively daydreaming about what I *might* do, *if only* there weren't so many obstacles. Rather I am to get out there, so help me God, and plan it, clear it, and *do it*, with all my might, to the glory of God.[102]

And here's a special emphasis for mothers of *man cubs*:

> Boys should *not* be trained to be home-centered. Even if they are home-schooled, they should be taught that the pattern of the home is not the pattern of their future life. They are to grow up prepared to go out into the world to conquer it. If they are domesticated, they will be unfit to do battle with the world on any level. Boys need the rough and tumble of getting their heads knocked once in a while, and Mom cannot be there to pick up the pieces every time... If they spend all their days in Mom's environment, they will not have a good picture of what it means to be a man. This is a very real threat to the church;...That's why we have terms in our language like *sissy, tied to the apron strings*, etc. Boys like to be coddled and mothers like to coddle, but this has devastating and long-term consequences.[103]

Consider the implications here, especially for teenage boys!

6. Raising Daughters

There's not only a "War Against Boys," there's also a "War Against Girls." Sure, society is trying to *feminize* our boys, but it is also trying to *masculinize* our girls.

Take, for instance, the athletic scene. I think sports can be a wonderful training ground for the development of godly womanliness (See *A Woman Athlete?* in chapter 13). But I am deeply disturbed by the intense pressure placed on some high school girls by their coaches to train for and play their sports like male wannabes. Girls' pumping heavy iron daily in the weight room with the boys has become standard training in some schools. Could it be that such rough unisex whip-cracking is draining from a generation of women the tender *"milk of human kindness"* that ought to characterize the fairer sex?

Somehow, it's now become shameful for a girl to act like a lady and aspire toward biblical womanhood.

> "What do you want to be when you grow up?" asked the lady with the funny glasses.
>
> Bethany smiled and looked affectionately at her mamma. "I want to get married, be a mommy and have babies."
>
> The lady with the funny glasses wrinkled her nose and looked irritated. "Yes, you may choose to marry and have a baby…or so, but what do you want to _be_," glancing at Bethany's mother impatiently, the inquisitor added, "after college?"
>
> Changing her manner to a more persuasive and gentle tone, she went on questioning the little girl, "Don't you know that you can be _anything_ you want—an astronaut, a doctor, a soldier—what do you want to _be_?"[104]

It's very common for parents who are themselves committed in theory to biblical womanhood to unwittingly find themselves wearing the *"funny glasses"* of the feminist.

I admit to occasionally lapsing into a feminist mindset myself. Our daughter is a very competent and gifted young woman. I enjoy seeing her compete and succeed in school-centered endeavors. The question often naturally arises: "So what are Abbie's plans?" It's very easy to get swept up in the modern current and answer: "Well, we're encouraging her to secure an athletic/academic scholarship. With her abilities, she'd make a great attorney or even a politician (See *A Woman President?* in chapter 13)."

Here's where Christian parents need to stop, take a breath, and ask themselves an important question. Are we directing and equipping our daughters to be godly helpmeets and mothers or independent career women who loathe wifehood and motherhood? It's very possible to unwittingly do the latter by haphazardly sending them into the heavy current of today's educational system and youth culture.

Even in Christian high schools and colleges, the feminism suction is strong. I earlier mentioned a professor at a college who held a Bible study for over a dozen undergraduate girls. The gathering began by going around the room with each girl's sharing her goals and aspirations for life. Every one of them spoke of a prestigious career, such as doctor, lawyer, journalist, marketing executive, etc. However, by the end of the session, when the relational defenses had dropped, each young woman admitted that her chief aspiration was to marry a godly man and be a stay-at-home-mom! But they were at first socially ashamed to admit it. This was at a Christian college.

I know. There's no guarantee that any woman will marry. I firmly believe that every young woman should have a career contingency plan (See *A Woman Worker?* in chapter 13). At present, our daughter is interested in nursing. But we need to be careful that our contingency plans don't eclipse the priority plan. A disproportionate emphasis on profession could be mentally confusing and even heart redirecting.

> *Train up a child in the way he should go,*
> *Even when he is old he will not depart from it*
> *(Proverbs 22:6).*

If I believed that my son was called to be a medical doctor, would I be wise to encourage him to spend 95% of his time and energies pursuing NASCAR racing? No, I'd seek to direct his mind and efforts toward the actual goal. Sure, I'd be wise to encourage him to diversify his interests and acquire skills as a mechanic for a contingency plan. But if I continuously put him behind the wheel of a racing car, I shouldn't be surprised if he became bored with medicine!

Likewise, if we totally immerse our daughters in the highly competitive full-time career current, we shouldn't be surprised when they become so totally preoccupied with grooming themselves for marketplace success that they lose any appetite for their priority role as a wife and mother. I've seen many a promising woman's appetite for domestic greatness irreparably spoiled by years of unguarded swimming in the current of feminist-saturated higher education. Furthermore, laboring valiantly as a stay-at-home-mom won't help her husband pay off her $70,000 worth of school loans.

I've also seen well-degreed women who've *"found their way home,"* but due to a neglect of any homemaker training, they are inept in the kitchen and in the nursery. For years they were so obsessed with their GPA, SAT, GRE, and MCAT scores that they never took the time to cultivate skills in meal preparation, nutritional planning, household organization, infant nurture, child discipline, or husband cultivating. They can grow fungus in a test tube or give a slick power-point presentation, but they can't bake bread or burp a baby!

Women of dominion will prudently train their daughters for greatness.

Please understand. I'm not calling for *sofa sitting*—dressing pretty and pink and waiting for Prince Charming to come by to sweep her off Dad's living room couch. I'm strongly encouraging my daughter to get a college education. I believe that higher education is an excellent way to prepare a daughter for excellence in wifehood and motherhood. It's said of the excellent wife of Proverbs 31 that *"her husband is known in the gates, when he sits among the elders of the land"* (31:23).

Her husband is one of the community's noblest, most influential men. As I've written earlier, *"Behind every great man is an even greater woman."* Dianne, my wife, is my best and most influential advisor and counselor. I desperately need a wife who is well-educated, well-read, precise thinking, culturally aware, financially shrewd, and theologically mature. Such a wife is a potent force of inestimable value in the lives of her husband and children.

> *An excellent wife, who can find? For her worth is far above jewels.*
> *The heart of her husband trusts in her, and he will have no lack of gain.*
> *She does him good and not evil all the days of her life (Proverbs 31:10-12).*

A college education can go a long way in training a young woman to be an excellent helpmeet and mother. But she needs her mother continuously at her elbow saying: "Now remember, my dear, that you're not chiefly grooming yourself for a role at Mayo Clinic, on Wall Street, or at the United Nations, but in the home, as a helpmeet, nurturing children. For this great vocation you were chiefly created, as a woman made in the image of God."

Let's go back to the lady with the funny glasses.

> Busily, Bethany tucked her baby doll into her carriage and lovingly patted the handmade doll blanket. She looked puzzled and asked, "Can they teach me how to be a good mommy in college?"

Bethany's mother smiled and took her little girl by the hand, "No," she interjected. "That's my job."[105]

7. Dealing with Offspring Disappointment

I wish I could assure every selfless and dedicated mother that all of her sons and daughters will turn out to be noble-minded and godly Christians. Sadly, there are no such guarantees.

It's true:

Train up a child in the way he should go,
even when he is old he will not depart from it.
(Proverbs 22:6).

But it's also true:

For though the twins were not yet born, and had not done anything good or bad, in order that God's purpose according to His choice might stand, not because of works, but because of Him who calls, it was said to her, "THE OLDER WILL SERVE THE YOUNGER." Just as it is written, "JACOB I LOVED, BUT ESAU I HATED (Romans 9:11-13)."

Ultimately, it's God's sovereign grace, and not a mother's faithful diligence, that saves and sanctifies her children. And the Lord works in mysterious ways to keep us dependent and on our knees rather than proud and on our soap boxes. Sometimes, He does this by crossing His hands (Genesis 48:13-14). God's normal and customary way of working is to bless the nurturing of wise and dedicated mothers with the harvesting of good and godly offspring (Proverbs 22:6). I've seen this general promise fulfilled at a wonderful rate of frequency. But I've also seen the occasional exception strike with painful agony.

I've seen a highly esteemed model of a Christian mother give birth to a son, raise him in the fear and instruction of the Lord, then watch him go off to become a liar, drunkard, and adulterer. I've also seen a godless heathen of a mother give birth to a son, abandon him by her neglect and worldliness, then watch him go off to become the faithful pastor of a God-honoring church. Yes, this is abnormal. But sometimes God, for His own glory, purposefully crosses His hands in these ways.

But oh, how painful it is for the mother of a wayward fool. As William

Shakespeare said in *King Lear: "How sharper than a serpent's tooth it is to have a thankless child"* (Act 1, Scene 4).

Every godly mother who stretches herself out for the prosperity of her children is appallingly vulnerable to horrible piercings of her soul (Luke 2:34-35). Mother takes disappointments harder than Father. Her life is peculiarly bound up with her children. They hold her heart strings. *"A wise son makes a father glad, but a foolish son is <u>a grief to his mother</u>"* (Proverbs 10:1, emphasis added).

John Abbott wrote back in 1833 in his book, *The Mother At Home*:

> This is a dreadful subject; but it is one which the mother must feel and understand. There are facts which might here be introduced, sufficient to make every parent tremble. We might lead you to the dwelling of a clergyman, and tell you that a daughter's sin has murdered the mother, and sent paleness to the cheek, and trembling to the frame, and agony to the heart of the aged father.... .
>
> No matter what your situation in life may be, that little child, not so innocent, whose playful endearments and happy laugh awaken such thrilling emotions in your heart, may cause you years of most unalleviated misery.[106]

Though none of our children has run off to the far country of rebellion, I've watched my bride's heart absorb piercings and achings during times of offspring folly and disappointment. The discovery of a pattern of deceit in one of her young calls from her heroic feats of disciplinary action, but later sends her into our bedroom, where, like a deer shot with an arrow, she goes to bleed alone.

Awhile back one of our older children managed to do something breathtakingly foolish. We confronted him, and the result was a weak repentance. Two days later, I looked over at my wife sitting in the window seat of an airplane. Tears were rolling down her cheeks! Shocked, because I thought we were enjoying a romantic get-a-way of sorts, she explained herself by simply whispering the name of the offending child.

My wife goes out to walk/run nearly every morning. But when her heart is heavy with a sin issue in the life of one of her five, jogging on a flat country road is like climbing Mt Everest. She uses the time to pour out her griefs and concerns to her heavenly Father who alone can lift suffocating burdens from a mother's heart (1 Peter 5:7).

Mothering is not for the faint of heart. It requires courage of steel, relentless stamina, and tenacious faith. It requires a *woman of dominion* who won't throw in the towel or curl up into a ball of depression, but who will resolve to *subdue* and *rule* in the face of soul-withering disappointments, so help her God (See *Facing your Fears* in chapter 11).

Consider these brief words of counsel for times of disappointment:

Reject the lie of fatalism.

In times of disappointment, the enemy will whisper into your pretty ear that your maternal efforts are all in vain. "Look how many good moms have bad kids. Don't waste your life with dedicated mothering. Those kids could tear your heart out regardless of what you do. "

Don't be taken by this scheme (2 Corinthians 2:11). Though God does occasionally cross His hands, the *"train up in the way he should go"* pattern of Proverbs 22:6 is His normal and customary way of working. "Immoral children are *generally* the offspring of parents who have neglected the moral and religious education of their family." [107]

Remove any cause for regret.

John Abbott puts it well:

> A pious and faithful mother may have a wicked child. He may break away from all restraints, and God may leave him to "eat the fruit of his own devices." The parent, thus afflicted and brokenhearted, can only bow before the sovereignty of her Maker, who says, "be still and know that I am God." *The consciousness, however, of having done one's duty, divests this affliction of much of its bitterness.* [108]

Pour out your heart to God.

Hannah's wonderful experience inspires ladies to believe that the Lord peculiarly cups His ear to motherly women who cry out to Him with wet eyes and distressed hearts (1 Samuel 1:9-11, 27). God remarkably responds to such pleading women.

8. Handling Personal Disillusionment

Meet Diana. By age 24, this slender, bright, and beautiful young woman was a newlywed with a BA in Speech Communication and a BS in Education. She loved her husband and the prospects of wifehood and motherhood. At the age of 25, Diana gave birth to a son. About two years later, she birthed a second son. At first the novelties of motherhood and homemaking were quite exhilarating. She felt blessed of the Lord to be living her fondest dreams.

> *He raises the poor from the dust, and lifts the needy from the ash heap, to make them sit with princes, with the princes of His people. He makes the barren woman abide in the house as a joyful mother of children. Praise the* LORD *(Psalm 113:7-9).*

But soon the exhilaration wore off. Every morning, she faced dirty diapers, runny noses, food messes, temper tantrums, discipline problems, clothing piles, and kitchen clutter. Another son was born. Claustrophobic with cabin fever and boredom doldrums, she sighed, "Any twelve-year-old could wash these dishes, wipe these fannies, mop that floor, and pour these Cheerios onto this high chair tray."

Her mind often drifted back to her high school and college years. "Back then, I was the center of *my* world. I decided what I wanted to do for *myself. My* decisions were based on what would please and broaden *me.* People applauded *me* on the stage, commended *me* for my well-delivered speeches, and discussed with *me my* future goals and aspirations in life. I enjoyed expressing *my* creativity in the classroom, discussing profound literary themes with *my* students, and checking off *my* responsibilities on each day's challenging to-do list.

"But it's not about *me* anymore. Now, I watch my husband every morning escape out into the wild blue yonder where *he* meets exciting people, *he* goes out for lunch, and *he* checks off challenging tasks, and he enhances *his* career and *his* potential. Then he returns home to this less-than-immaculate house and is puzzled about what I did all day, why dinner's not ready yet, and why I don't make a fuss about his return.

"Though I've given up everything for my husband and my children, I get no applause or *atta-boys.* I've lost center-stage preeminence and become a back-stage nobody."

Her years in the feminism-infested current had given her glamorous dreams of personal glory. And now those dreams were dashed. Diana was downcast and heavy. She felt trapped. This was her lot for the rest of her life. She was grieving the death of her youthful dreams.

"I basically spiraled down into a depression. I resented my husband's success and my children's thanklessness. I questioned if all of this self-denial was really necessary. It just seemed as if it was asking too much of me.

"Theoretically and theologically, I held to the biblical role of selfless wifehood and motherhood. But internally and emotionally there was deep-seated resistance in my heart. Feminism was like fluoride in the water of my youth, and now I was feeling its poison in my soul. Why must I give up my life to make my husband and his children look good? What about *my* aspirations, *my* abilities, *my* yearnings for influence and significance? What am I, chopped liver? Have I become my husband's medieval slave? *I* want to be somebody. *I* want to be recognized. *I* want to be applauded too."

Years later, Diana, who now has five children, admits, "I was in mild rebellion against God. And I stayed there for a while, until I saw those wants for what they really are—the display of my idolatrous, selfish, sinful pride. It was only when I took those deep personal longings and put them on the altar of consecration to God that I began to make spiritual headway."

Meditations on her Savior burned away her rebellion and brought peace to her soul. In the garden of Gethsemane, the Lord Jesus looked into the appalling cup of self-sacrifice that His Father had poured for Him. He staggered at the thought of drinking it down to its last painful dregs. Instead of resentfully protesting, *"What am I, chopped liver?"* He submitted saying, *"Father, if Thou art willing, remove this cup from Me; yet not My will, but Thine be done"* (Luke 22:42).

It's my understanding that every biblically committed wife and mother must pass through a personal Gethsemane of sorts, needing to come to grips with the cup her Father has poured for her.

Think, dear sister, how the Lord Jesus selflessly served you. *He laid down His life to make you look good. He laid it down on crucifixion day, so that you'd look good on judgment day.* He was spat upon, beaten, scourged, mocked, stripped, spiked, hung, and forsaken. Then He breathed His last so that you wouldn't forever weep, wail, and gnash your teeth in hell. *He was born, lived, and died with the sole object that you would look good forever.* Could it be that this wifehood and motherhood thing is calling you to higher ground, conforming you more to His glorious image?

My bride shared with me an illustration that has helped her. It came from the movie *Chariots of Fire.* The British Olympic sprinter, Eric Liddell, was strolling on the Scottish Highlands, explaining to his sister the reason why he ran: "I believe God made me for a purpose, but He also made me fast. And *when I run I feel his pleasure.*"

The thought of God's face smiling at him drove him down the track.

My bride confided: "*The Lord made me for His purpose, too. He made me a woman, a wife, and a mother. He made me to serve. And when I serve, I feel His pleasure.* And regardless of society's face, my child's face, or even my husband's face, it's my Heavenly Father's face that drives me on. I know that when He sees me serving, He smiles and says, 'This is my beloved daughter in whom I am well pleased.' *When I serve, I feel His pleasure.*"

Sharon, a highly esteemed mother of many in our church, slipped to me a few years ago this anonymously written poem. She finds it useful in her ongoing battle against the accusing ghosts of buried aspirations.

She came tonight as I sat alone, the girl I used to be...
And she gazed at me with her earnest eye and questioned reproachfully;

Have you forgotten the many plans and hopes that I had for you?
The career, the splendid fame, and all the wonderful things to do?
Where is the mansion of stately height with all of its gardens rare?
The silken robes that I dreamed for you and the jewels in your hair?

And as she spoke, I was very sad for I wanted her pleased with me ...
This slender girl from the shadowy past the girl that I used to be
So gently rising, I took her hand, and guided her up the stair
Where peacefully sleeping, my babies lay innocent, sweet, and fair.

And I told her that these are my only gems, and precious they are to me;
That silken robe is my motherhood of costly simplicity.
And my mansion of stately height is love, and the only career I know
Is serving each day in these sheltered walls for the dear ones who come and go.

And as I spoke to my shadowy guest, she smiled through her tears at me.

And I saw that the woman that I am now, pleased the girl I used to be.

Author Unknown

CHAPTER 10:
WOMANLY DOMINION
IN MARITAL LIFE

Consider this account from an unknown eyewitness:

While waiting to pick up a friend at the airport in Portland, Oregon, I had a life-changing experience. This one occurred a mere two feet away from me. Straining to locate my friend among the passengers deplaning through the jet way, I noticed a man coming toward me carrying two light bags. He stopped next to me to greet his family. First, he motioned to his youngest son (maybe six-years-old) as he laid down his bags. They gave each other a long, loving hug. As they separated enough to look in each other's face, I heard the father say, "It's so good to see you, son. I missed you so much!" His son smiled shyly, averted his eyes and replied , "Me, too, Dad!" Then the man stood up, gazed in the eyes of his oldest son (maybe 9 or 10), and while cupping his son's face in his hands said, "You're already quite the young man. I love you very much, Zach!" They, too, hugged a most loving, tender hug. While this was happening, a baby girl (perhaps 1 or 1½) was squirming excitedly in her mother's arms, never once taking her little eyes off the wonderful sight of her returning father. The man said, "Hi, baby girl!" as he gently took the child from her mother. He quickly kissed her face all over and then held her close to his chest while rocking her from side to side. The little girl instantly relaxed and simply laid her head on his shoulder, motionless in pure contentment. After several moments, he handed his daughter to his oldest son and declared, "I've saved the best for last," and proceeded to give his wife the longest, most passionate kiss I ever remember seeing. He gazed into her eyes for several seconds and then silently mouthed, "I love you so much!" They stared at each other's eyes, beaming big smiles at one another, while holding both hands. For an instant they reminded me of newlyweds, but I knew by the age of their kids that they couldn't possibly be. I puzzled about it for a moment then realized how totally engrossed I was in the wonderful display of love not more than an arm's length away from me. I suddenly felt uncomfortable, as if I was invading something sacred, but was amazed to hear my own voice nervously ask, "Wow! How long have you two been married?" "Twelve years," he replied, without breaking his gaze from his lovely wife's face. "Well, then, how long have you been away?" I asked. The man finally turned and looked at me, still beaming his joyous smile. "Two whole days!"

Now that sounds like the kind of a marriage worth pursuing! We'll return to the Portland airport a little later. But until then, let's consider for a while what practical measures a *woman of dominion* will wisely take to *build a marriage* that's both God-glorifying and personally satisfying. *"The wise woman builds her house, but the foolish tears it down with her own hands"* (Proverbs 14:1).

1. Keep Your Vow to Your Husband

One warm mid-August Sunday night, after our evening service, I sat on a park bench overlooking Lake Macatawa, conducting a premarital counseling session with a young, starry-eyed engaged couple. After praying, I opened with this question: "What will be the foundation of your marriage?" Seth and Marie stared at each other. I knew what they were instinctively thinking of—their strong affections, their romantic feelings, and their sweet chemistry together. Surely such things would provide a Rock-of-Gibraltar stability for their relationship.

But that's not so. Romantic feelings, like beach castles, soon crumble with the shifting sands. A couple needs something more solid on which to build a marriage.

The God-ordained foundation for marriage is the *covenantal vow*. When God brought Eve to Adam, the man bound himself to his bride by a verbal commitment: *"This is now bone of my bones, and flesh of my flesh"* (Genesis 2:23a).

Malachi's rebuke to unfaithful grooms hearkens back to this *promised pledge*: *"Because the* LORD *has been a witness between you and the wife of your youth, against whom you have dealt treacherously, though she is your companion and your wife by covenant"* (Malachi 2:14, emphasis added).

> "I take you to be my lawfully wedded husband (or wife),
> to have and to hold,
> from this day forward,
> for better and for worse,
> for richer and for poorer,
> in sickness and in health,
> to love and to cherish,
> till death do us part."

This is a wonderful, yet fearful, *covenantal vow* to make. You make a lifelong commitment, with a ring as a *sign*, with both God and man as your *witnesses*. And though lightweight humans may look the other way should you prove treacherous to your *covenantal vow,* God will *not* overlook it. *"What therefore God has joined together, let no man separate"* (Mark 10:9).

No soul should dare to break a *solemn covenantal vow* sealed by God's presence and Name. *"When you make a vow to God,...pay what you vow!"* (Ecclesiastes 5:4, emphasis added).

> *If a man makes a vow to the* LORD, *or takes an oath to bind himself with a binding obligation, he shall not violate his word; he shall do according to all that proceeds out of his mouth (Numbers 30:2, emphasis added).*

It may be foolish to camp overnight in the cone of an active volcano. It may be foolish to insert your head into the mouth of a hungry lion. It may be foolish to climb to the top of a cellular telephone tower in the middle of a thunderstorm. But none of these things would be nearly as foolish as taking a *sacred vow* in the presence of Almighty God and premeditatedly breaking it. There's a slim chance you may get away with camping, inserting, and climbing, but not with *breaking covenant.*

> *You shall not take the name of the LORD your God in vain, for the LORD will not leave him unpunished who takes His name in vain (Exodus 20:7, emphasis added).*

Either in this life, or in the next, the ax will fall, and you will sorely regret it.

I hope this makes you shudder and tremble. It makes me afraid! And that's a good thing. *"The fear of the LORD is the beginning of knowledge"* (Proverbs 1:7, emphasis added).

Here, we've laid bare the solid and sturdy foundation for a stable and wonderful marriage. It's not strong affections, romantic feelings, or sweet chemistry. It's *"the fear of the Lord."* A man and a woman have made a solemn *covenantal vow* in the presence of God, and both so fear God that they dare not break this *solemn covenant.* My wife and I so revere the Lord's eyes and delight in His smile that *breaking-up* is not an option. *"For better or for worse,"* we'll work it out, so help us God.

A couple of months after we were married in the summer of 1982, my bride and I had a late-night pillow-talk argument. The silent treatment set in. She fell asleep, but I was wide awake, staring in the dark at the digital clock which announced some time after 1:00 AM. I wasn't happy. She was more difficult than I'd expected. This kind of conflict was not what I'd bargained for. I felt trapped and wanted out. What should I do?

I'd once had a job that became a nightmare, and I had quit. I'd once gone out for a team that didn't work out, and I'd quit that, too. But this was different. Quitting wasn't an option. I was stuck in this marriage. I felt claustrophobic. There was no way out. I had made a lifelong vow to her before God. That was it. There was no way out! God's will, *"till death do us part,"* was perfectly clear: *"Love her as Christ loved the church"* (Ephesians 5:25). I fell onto my pillow and slept like a baby. *"The peace of God that surpasses all comprehension"* (Philippians 4:7) filled my mind and heart regarding my marriage. Covenantal resolution has never wavered since.

Dianne, my bride, has her version of getting down to the bedrock marital foundation. She said to me: "When disappointment set in, and I realized that you weren't the ideal Prince Charming I thought you were, I wondered if I'd married the wrong person." In seeking God's will, she found it clearly in His word: *"What therefore God has joined together, let not man separate"* (Mark 10:9). It became plain to her. As surely as God had brought Eve to Adam, so surely through providence God had brought Dianne to Mark. There was no guesswork. For certain, Mark was the right person!

The *season of inquiry* is *before* the vow is taken. During this *inquiry* time it's wise to critically evaluate such issues as compatibility, chemistry, personality, spiritual caliber, wisdom, beauty, godliness, diligence, etc., in a potential mate. But after the *vow* has been taken, the season of *inquiry* has ended, and the season of *lifelong commitment* has begun.

A note was sent to Reader's Digest:

> We were visiting friends when they received a telephone call from their recently married daughter. After several tense minutes on the phone, the mother told the father to pick up the extension. The newlyweds had had their first big fight.
> In a few moments, the father rejoined us and tersely explained, "Said she wanted to come home."
> "What did you tell her?" I asked.
> "I told her she <u>was</u> home."[109]

For the last twenty five years, my Dianne has been *"home sweet home"* for me. She tells me that less-than-Prince-Charming Mark has been the same for her.

We must build the home of our marriages and families on the rock of a solemn *covenantal vow* before God, and not on the shifting sands of our unstable feelings, emotions, and circumstances.

A *woman of dominion* will not permit herself to be bullied by her feelings, emotions, and circumstances. Instead, she will rule over them and subdue them under her feet, so help her God.

2. Love Your Husband

Dr. Jay Adams writes in *When Your Marriage Goes Sour*:

> Phil and Emily had not come for help in solving the problems in their marriage although they had called the chaplain to ask for marriage counseling. Actually, their minds already were made up—they had

decided to get a divorce. Yet, they were Christians and they knew that a divorce was wrong since they had no biblical grounds for it. There had been no adultery, desertion; only untold misery. "If we can only get him to agree that going on in this marriage would be an impossibility," they thought, "then perhaps he will be able to show us how *in our case* God will make an exception to His law." That was how they were reasoning inwardly when they first told their stories to Chaplain Cunningham.

"So you see," Emily concluded, "there is simply nothing left to our marriage. I don't *feel* a thing for Phil anymore; there is nothing to build on." Phil ended his remarks in a similar vein: "Well, I suppose that it has been a long time since you've heard a story like that, Chaplain. And, while we don't agree on many things, I must say that Emily is absolutely correct when she claims that there is nothing left to our marriage—every drop of love that I once had for her has drained away."[110]

So that's it! The cultural consensus is that love is a feeling, an emotion that's mysteriously delivered, sometimes *"at first sight,"* and when it's run dry, it's over and time to move on. But biblical love defies cultural consensus.

Chaplain Cunningham responded: "I'm sorry to hear about your difficult times... You say there is no love and no feeling left? That's serious. If you don't love each other, there is only one thing to do. ("Here it comes" they thought: "He will advise a divorce.") You will have to *learn* to love one another."

"*Learn* to love?" They retorted almost simultaneously. "What do you mean learn to love?" asked Phil as soon as he was able to gain some measure of composure. "Yeah," offered Emily, cynically, "How can you learn it? You can't produce feelings out of thin air."

"I was not talking about feelings," said Chaplain Cunningham. "I was talking about love. The two are not identical though Hollywood, the T.V., and Playboy might say otherwise. Love is not feeling first. Before all else, it is the determination to do good for another person because God has told you to do so. Love begins, therefore, with a desire to please God. Love toward another is a willingness to give to him whatever you have that he needs, because you know that God wants you to. Where true love exists, the feeling follows soon enough."[111]

That's right. Biblically, love is not primarily an emotion, but a *resolution*, a *decision*, an *action*. Love is not based on *subjective* sentiment, but on *objective* principle. The world's notion of romantic love ("being in love") has distorted the truth of biblical love. Biblical love isn't primarily a feeling or an emotion. It's fundamentally not a noun, but a verb.

> *Love is patient, love is kind, and is not jealous; love does not brag and is not arrogant, does not act unbecomingly; it does not seek its own, is not provoked, does not take into account a wrong suffered, does not rejoice in unrighteousness, but rejoices with the truth; bears all things, believes all things, hopes all things, endures all things (1 Corinthians 13:4-7).*

Love is not a sentiment, but an action. It's not something you feel, but something you do. *Husbands, love your wives, just as Christ also loved the church and gave Himself up for her* (Ephesians 5:25).

We must love our spouses with Gethsemane love ("Not my will, but Thine be done" Luke 22:42), and with Golgotha love ("He breathed His last" Luke 23:46). Christ loved his bride even when she wasn't lovable.

A wife may encounter her husband at a moment when she has anything but affectionate *feelings* toward him. To the contrary, she may *feel* anger, bitterness, and resentment. She must love him regardless. Biblical love isn't exercised only when he's pleasant, I'm inclined, or she's lovable. No! Biblical love kicks in when it's not pleasant (as when absorbing a pillar-scourging), and when I'm disinclined (as when looking into the agonizing cup of the crucifixion), and when its object is unlovable (as when hanging on a cross and watching sinners wag their heads in derision).

Love is chiefly *a decision*, and not *an emotion*.

"Oh come on!" You may say, "I'm supposed to love my husband when he's acting obnoxiously, and wagging his head at me? At times like that, for me to give him kind words and tender kisses would be hypocritical!"

That's right. According to the world it's hypocritical. The world says that warm emotions must precede loving actions. The Bible doesn't. *"But I say to you who hear, love your enemies, do good to those who hate you"* (Luke 6:27, emphasis added).

If we had to wait until we had warm feelings toward our enemies before we loved them, they'd die of thirst or hunger in the waiting.

We're solemnly obligated to do the right thing *whether we feel like it or not*. We daily decide to obey God and love our spouses.

Let's revisit the joyful and romantic reunion at the Portland airport:

> …Two days? I was stunned. By the intensity of the greeting, I'd assumed he'd been gone for at least several weeks, if not months. I know my expression betrayed me. I said almost offhandedly, hoping to end my intrusion with some semblance of grace (and to get back to searching for my friend), "I hope my marriage is still that passionate after 12 years!" The man suddenly stopped smiling. He looked me straight in the eye, and with forcefulness that burned right into my soul, he told me something that left me a different person. He told me, "Don't hope, friend…DECIDE!" Then he flashed me his wonderful smile again, shook my hand, and said, "God bless!" With that, he and his family turned and strode away together.

I know what you're thinking: "But what about feelings? You make marriage sound so mechanical!" Notice how, for the airport couple, *the decision to love* bore the fruit of *passion in love*. It's important to understand that the sweet feelings of affection are not the *root* of a healthy relationship, but the *fruit* of one. In *Solving Marriage Problems*, Jay Adams writes: "When one gives himself to another, feelings of love follow acts of love. So while feelings of love are not essential for establishing a marriage contract, they are an inevitable result of properly pursuing its terms."[112]

Chaplain Cunningham brought sweetening counsel to the sour marriage of Phil and Emily this way: "If you mean business with God, and do as He says, within six to eight weeks, you can have a marriage that sings."[113]

This fits the biblical formula. How did the Lord Jesus get *his bride* (the church) to gush with *constraining* affection toward Him (2 Corinthians 5:14)? He laid down His life for her. *"We love, because He first loved us"* (1 John 4:19).

I've heard of a counselor who prescribes a simple formula for cultivating the affections and feelings of being *"in love."* "Do ten loving things each day for your spouse." Try it! Feelings of love follow acts of love.

> A woman seeking counsel from Dr. George W. Crane, the psychologist, confided that she hated her husband, and intended

to divorce him. "I want to hurt him all I can," she declared firmly.

"Well, in that case," said Dr. Crane, "I advise you to start showering him with compliments. When you have become indispensable to him, when he thinks you love him devotedly, then start the divorce action. That is the way to hurt him."

Some months later the wife returned to report that all was going well. She had followed the suggested course.

"Good," said Dr. Crane. "Now's the time to file for divorce."

"Divorce!" the woman said indignantly. "Never. I love my husband dearly!"[114]

A *woman of dominion* is not pushed around and bullied by her feelings and emotions. On the basis of her solemn covenantal commitment to her husband, she loves him.

3. Be Grateful for Him

Over the years, I've discovered that my bride has certain days when she wakes up in the morning and is not overwhelmed with a deep sense of gratitude for God's having given me to her! Can you believe this?

Furthermore, I've discovered that this quirk is not unique to my wife, but that other men's wives suffer from this same struggle of being somewhat discontent with their men. Complaints come from all across the board. "He doesn't dress right. He doesn't remember special days. He doesn't take me out enough. He's getting a belly. He doesn't pick up as he should. He doesn't talk to me enough. He's not sensitive to my needs."

If the men were here now, I'd go after them to *"subdue and rule"* in these areas, as I did in *Manly Dominion*. But this is a book on *Womanly Dominion*.

Even when Christian women gather together for Bible study, there can be a strong tendency for the conversation to deteriorate into a mutual grumbling session. One woman who attended a Wednesday-morning "Mom's Group" wrote:

> Instead of finding practical ways to become a better mother, the group was a gripe session for women to vent about their husbands' idiosyncrasies, bad attitudes, and failures in general and in specific. I was becoming trained to complain and whine about real or imagined behavior and look for sympathy from other women.[115]

An Internet anecdote humorously unveils this notorious ingratitude problem that wives have with their husbands.

> A new Perfect Husband Shopping Center opened where a woman could go to choose from among many men to find the perfect husband. It was laid out on five floors, with the men increasing in positive attributes as you ascended the floors. The only rule was that once you open the door to any floor, you must choose a man from that floor, and if you go up a floor, you can't go back down except to leave the store. So, a couple of girlfriends go to the store to find a man to marry.
>
> The first-floor sign reads: "These men have high-paying jobs and love kids." The women read the sign and say, "Well, that's wonderful…but," and wonder what's on the next floor.
>
> The second-floor sign reads: "These men have high-paying jobs, love kids, and are extremely good looking." "Hmmmm," say the girls. "Wonder what's further-up?"
>
> The third-floor sign reads: "These men have high-paying jobs, love kids, are extremely good looking, and will help with the housework." "Wow!" say the women. "Very tempting…but there's more further up!"
>
> The fourth-floor sign reads: "These men have high-paying jobs, love kids, are extremely good looking, will help with the housework, and *are very affectionate*." "Oh, mercy me. But just think! What must be awaiting us further up?!" say the women.
>
> So, up to the fifth floor they go.
>
> The fifth-floor sign reads: "This floor is just to prove that women are impossible to please."[116]

Remember, dear married ladies, the great blessing the Lord has provided in giving to you a man. You don't return every night to a deserted apartment, a lonely dinner table, and an empty bed. God has given to you what countless women can only dream about.

> *He makes the barren woman abide in the house as a joyful mother of children. Praise the* LORD! *(Psalm 113:9).*

> *… being content with what you have; (Hebrews 13:5).*

Sure he's a big sinner. But he's God's gift to you.

Dr. Laura Schlessinger received this note of appreciation from a radio listener:

> "I must say that an important turning point for me came when I was listening to you on the radio, Dr. Laura. You were listening to some woman grouse about picky little things, and you asked her, "Does your husband provide well for your family? Are your kids all healthy? Do you get to stay at home with them?" And so forth. She answered yes to all those questions. Then you said, "So stop whining! You have forgotten to be grateful."
>
> It was as though God took me by the shoulders and said, "Hello! This is you, idiot!" Right at that moment, in the car, I began to thank God for my husband and for every excellent quality he has. Since then, I have made a conscious effort to do the following things:
>
> - Thank God daily for such a terrific guy, mentioning specific qualities for which I'm grateful.
> - Look for daily ways to be a blessing to my husband (trying to understand what pleases him, anticipating his needs, etc.).
> - Chart my menstrual cycle and remind myself on the PMS days that what I'm feeling isn't true and to keep my mouth shut and let it pass.
> - Take responsibility for my own emotional well-being: Stay rested, don't over-commit and then complain, stay in touch with friends with a positive influence.
> - Stay focused on making a home for my family and remember that this is my highest calling and responsibility, and that it has eternal value. The more I do this, the happier and more content I am.[117]

4. Respect Him

As a boy, I used to watch the contemporary sitcom "Leave It to Beaver." June Cleaver greatly admired her husband Ward. My children grew up *not* watching contemporary sitcoms. We didn't permit it. Even the occasional commercials for "Everybody Loves Raymond" are like fingernails on the chalkboard to me. Raymond's wife does not love him, but relentlessly demeans him. June could teach Raymond's Debra a lesson or two.

Nevertheless let each individual among you also love his own wife even as himself; and <u>let the wife see to it that she respect her husband</u> (Ephesians 5:33, emphasis added).

Martha Peace, in confessing her own Debra-like tendencies, hit the mark by saying that "as his helpmeet, he needs my *helpful suggestions* and not my *sarcastic putdowns*." [118]

King David's wife Michal had a respect problem toward her husband. When David publicly worshiped the Lord in the humble attire of a simple linen tunic, Michal's tongue lacerated her man.

But when David returned to bless his household, Michal the daughter of Saul came out to meet David and said, <u>"How the king of Israel distinguished himself today!</u> He uncovered himself today in the eyes of his servants' maids <u>as one of the foolish ones shamelessly uncovers himself!"</u> (2 Samuel 6:20, emphasis added).

A *woman of dominion* will seek to *rule over her spirit*, fighting down the common tongue plague of spewing out biting and disrespectful talk to her husband. The Proverbs make no little thing of this besetting sin of belittling talk.

It is better to live in a corner of a roof,
than in a house shared with a contentious woman.
(Proverbs 21:9)

It is better to live in a desert land,
than with a contentious and vexing woman (Proverbs 21:19).

It is better to live in a corner of the roof
than in a house shared with a contentious woman.
(Proverbs 25:24).

A constant dripping on a day of steady rain
and a contentious woman are alike (Proverbs 27:15).

Dr. Laura Schlessinger's book, *The Proper Care and Feeding of Husbands*, grew out of her receiving and evaluating thousands of comments from men all around the country. In her chapter entitled

"You're a Nag," she wrote, "The universal complaint of men who e-mailed my Web site with their opinions about 'The Proper Care and Feeding of Husbands' was that their wives criticize, complain, nag, rarely compliment or express appreciation, are difficult to satisfy, and basically not as nice to them as they'd be to a stranger ringing their doorbell at three A.M.!"[119]

Many men divulged how they were esteemed outside of the home as competent professionals by their colleagues, but were treated inside the home as bumbling buffoons by their wives. Jim wrote:

> I have always had superlative evaluations on my performance. AT HOME, I CAN'T DO ANYTHING RIGHT! I sometimes spend several minutes in thought on a task at hand, trying to decide exactly what to do. After weighing the pros and cons, I make a decision and act. Almost invariably I get, 'What did you do that for? Now I can't ...,' or I hear, "Who put the ... here?" or sometimes I get a straight-out "That's stupid."...It's something that wears you down like erosion.[120]

Jim painfully understands the "constant dripping" water torture experience of Proverbs 27:15 above. A number of men have said to me, "Pastor, I just don't know why she can't be kind. Her contentiousness poisons our marriage."

Remember, ladies of dominion, there's a great upside to the wise bridling and kind using of your tongues. *A soothing tongue is a tree of life*" (Proverbs 15:4a).

Let's say you want the trash taken out after dinner. You could bark out your will and then nag him every five minutes about it. And then when he finally takes care of it, you might mumble, "It's about time."

Or there's another approach. You could sweetly say, "Honey, I've put the bag by the door for you. When you have time, could you take it out to the garage and throw it into the dumpster?" And then when he does it, catch him on the way back, wrap your arms around him, give him a big kiss, tell him how hard it is for you to lift that dumpster lid with one arm, and then lift that heavy bag with the other. Then say, "You're sweet, Babe." Ladies, you've just made your Clark Kent into a Superman.

Men love to be perceived as heroes and dragon slayers. We love to rescue damsels and be admired for our chivalrous feats. That kind of treatment and talk fills our sails. One woman said that she's adopted ways of making her husband feel like her champion, "Because he is!" When you view us like that, you become lovable darlings in our sight. I know you think we're silly for wanting respect. But we think you're silly for wanting flowers!

Your husband wants to be *your man*, not *your boy*. He wants an adoring bride, not a hen-pecking mother. Respect him. The Lord will smile. So will your man, and so will you!

5. Create an Orderly Home for Him

A *woman of dominion* will *subdue and rule* over her household. Sometimes husbands don't appreciate all that their wives do in the home.

WHAT HAPPENED?

One afternoon a man came home from work to find total mayhem in his house. His three children were outside, still in their pajamas, playing in the mud with empty food boxes and wrappers strewn all around the front yard. The door of his wife's car was open, as was the front door to the house. Proceeding into the entry, he found an even bigger mess. A lamp had been knocked over, and the throw rug was wadded against one wall. In the front room the TV was blaring a cartoon channel, and the family room was strewn with toys and various items of clothing. In the kitchen, dishes filled the sink, breakfast food was spilled on the counter, dog food was spilled on the floor, a broken glass lay under the table, and a small pile of sand was spread by the back door. He quickly headed up the stairs, stepping over toys and more piles of clothes, looking for his wife. He was worried she may be ill, or that something serious had happened. He found her lounging in the bedroom, still curled in the bed in her pajamas, reading a novel. She looked up at him, smiled, and asked how his day went. He looked at her bewildered and asked, "What happened here today?" She again smiled and answered, "You know every day when you come home from work and ask me what in the world I did today? "Yes" was his incredulous reply. She answered, "Well, today I didn't do it."[121]

This is humorous. But it's not funny when a husband habitually comes home to plates and debris piled high on the kitchen counters and sink, to toys cluttering the floors of the living and dining rooms, to laundry piled high near the washer and dryer, and to over-the-budget spending on the credit cards. You will wisely cultivate your marriage by seeking to avoid letting your man come home from work to a shambles in the home.

Strive toward the blessed atmosphere of a disciplined orderliness in the home.

> *She rises also while it is still night, and gives food to her household, and portions to her maidens (Proverbs 31:15, emphasis added).*

> *She looks well to the ways of her household, and does not eat the bread of idleness (Proverbs 31:27, emphasis added).*

> *Therefore, I want younger widows to get married, bear children, keep house, and give the enemy no occasion for reproach (1 Timothy 5:14, emphasis added).*

> *To be sensible, pure, workers at home, kind, being subject to their own husbands, that the word of God may not be dishonored (Titus 2:5, emphasis added).*

An older woman (my mother, Dorothy Chanski, in a personal email) provided me with this counsel to younger women for a sermon I was preparing.

> Be organized with cleaning, grocery shopping, laundry, and cooking. As you fulfill your God-given responsibilities, your husband is free to do his work. A godly wife is organized and works hard to operate her home with the least possible chaos. She also creates an optimistic, joyful atmosphere for her family. Organizing a clean, well-run household is a major biblical emphasis in the God-given ministry of the wife. Think of specific ways you can help him. Examples are getting up early in the morning to help him get off to work with a good breakfast (and lunch), taking care to record phone messages for him, seeking to have his laundry folded and his shirts ironed, and keeping careful records of money spent to keep up with the budget.

Martha Peace adds:

> Often tips like "Don't leave the house in the mornings unless the house is straight, the kitchen clean, and the bathrooms given a good 'once over'" can revolutionize housekeeping. Coming home to a clean kitchen surely makes it easier to begin cooking super! Thinking about supper right after breakfast provides a fighting chance to be organized that night. Perhaps meat may need to come out of the freezer or she may need to be home by a certain time to prepare what she has planned. A little bit of prior planning makes all the difference in the world.
>
> A wife should be good and efficient at what she does, not waste time, and not be lazy. If she is lazy, she must repent. A lazy person may always be doing something, but it is frequently self-indulgent activities such as reading, watching television, lying in bed, etc.[122]

A virtuous woman of dominion, *"playing her position"* in the household with a *"win it"* mindset of *subduing and ruling*, brings a blessed windfall to the chemistry of her marriage. When she makes her nest an orderly oasis instead of a chaotic shambles, her man relishes the thought of coming home to her.

6. Stay Attractive for Him

"After marriage, and definitely after having children, too many wives contract *the Frump syndrome*."[123] This unattractive disorder is marked by such symptoms as failing to shower and make oneself up on a daily basis, wearing baggy, sloppy, unstylish clothing, such as sweatshirts and sweatpants, and gaining too much weight "by eating too much and exercising too little."[124] This *"letting oneself go"* is quite counterproductive in the project of cultivating a healthy marriage.

You may say that in your case your husband doesn't mind. *But I'm telling you that he does mind.* Trust me on this. Maybe he just doesn't dare talk to you about it anymore because of the painful price you've made him pay in the past for bringing up the issue. *But I assure you, it's an important issue for him.*

The Song of Solomon celebrates the wonderful and blessed love shared by a maiden and her man. No small dimension of this fascinating attraction is physical beauty. *"How beautiful you are, my darling, how beautiful you are!...You are altogether beautiful, my darling, and there is no blemish in you...How beautiful is your love, my sister, my bride!"* (Song of Solomon 4:1a, 7, 10a)

The excellent wife of Proverbs 31, though matured by age and the bearing of multiple children, keeps a conscientious eye to her own physical appearance. *"She makes coverings for herself; her clothing is fine linen and purple"* (Proverbs 31:22).

Back in 1846, Charles Bridges commented on Proverbs 31:22 and the importance of a godly woman's maintaining her outward beauty for her husband, both in form and attire.

> It is possible to pay too little, as well as too much, attention to this point; and it is not always that Christian women pay to it the regard precisely due, separate from both extremes.... The primary respect instilled by the inward adorning (2 Peter 3:4; 1 Timothy 2:10), in no way renders the exterior grace a nullity (irrelevant)... As commanding a husband's respect, who justly claims, that his wife's exterior, so far as she is concerned, should continue to be not less pleasing, than when at first his heart was drawn to her.[125]

When I do premarital counseling with a couple, I always warn them both, and especially the bride, of deceptive advertising. "Look at yourself *now*, the way you are so lovely and beautiful *now*. You're quite clearly marketing yourself as a very attractive looking wife. Make sure you deliver on your implied guarantee."

When a woman lets her appearance go, it should be no surprise that her husband finds her to be no longer attractive in his eyes. I'm not talking about the general *wear and tear* of childbearing and aging. There's something very alluring and appealing about a maturing woman (my bride of over 25 years) when she maintains herself through the exercise of prudent self-discipline and stylish discretion.

Dr. Laura's research revealed to her that, "Guys have a natural and deep desire to be with a woman who cares enough about herself to look good for her mate.... In reading all the letters from men, I was struck by their depth of sensitivity about the issue of women's appearance." She concluded that a wife who seeks to keep herself beautiful for her husband "feeds his sense of well-being, his feeling of being loved as a husband and valued as a *man*."[126]

I know that Dr. Laura Schlessinger is not a theologically orthodox Christian. She's a converted Jew. But just as Moses had the good sense to pay attention to the wise counsel that came from Jethro, his *less than theologically orthodox father-in-law* (see Exodus 18:1-27), we would do well to carefully ponder the insightful counsel that comes from Dr. Laura, a *less than theologically orthodox mother-in-law* figure!

> I can bet that the reaction of most women (*and especially Christian women*—my comment) upon reading this is to get their hackles up and proclaim her husband as shallow. Frankly, that hostile reaction itself demonstrates a shallow self-centeredness. The impact on our bodies of natural aging, illness, pregnancies, and so forth is a simple fact of life. The inability to accept these realities betrays immaturity or worse. At the same time, though, the unwillingness to accept responsibility for the upkeep of one's physical or emotional well-being should be met with consternation by a spouse because it is an assault on the marital covenant.
>
> … It's not unusual for me to hear women express hostility that their husbands would like them to clean up, dress up, and tone up. They act like their husbands are selfish, sex-crazed, superficial, insensitive barbarians, which isn't the case. If they loved me, they wouldn't make a fuss about such things" point of view is simply irresponsible and destructive… . A lot is said by one spouse to another by the willingness to fulfill each other's needs. Men have the emotional need to see their wives as desiring them, and the way the wives take care of and present themselves expresses that love.[127]

You realize, of course, that there are wonderful romantic dividends to cultivating and maintaining your beautiful mystique. Sam(antha) wrote to Dr. Laura:

> Women expect to be wooed yet to be allowed to look haggish and frumpy. It's hard to romance a hag and come off as being sincere. I will admit that I have fallen into the trap of letting myself go, but I have been clawing my way out of that hole. I now put the extra effort into showering and doing my hair and makeup before my darling comes home from work, and well, it has certainly paid off."[128]

Yes, we men are easily captivated by our brides' looking beautifully feminine and acting *flirtatiously* sweet. Did I say *flirtatious*? That is an important variable, too.

7. Physically Satisfy Him

I'll only dare touch briefly on this theme from a man's perspective.

I once heard a woman caller complain to a female radio counselor that she just didn't feel like giving herself to her husband physically and sexually. She claimed that it didn't *do much* for her. The counselor asked the caller if she *"felt like"* shopping for groceries. The caller said that she didn't, but that she did it anyway because her family's health depended on it. The counselor informed the woman that her marriage's health depended on her giving of herself physically, sexually, and enthusiastically to her husband.

> *But because of immoralities, let each man have his own wife, and let each woman have her own husband. Let the husband fulfill his duty to his wife, and likewise also the wife to her husband. The wife does not have authority over her own body, but the husband does; and likewise also the husband does not have authority over his own body, but the wife does. Stop depriving one another, except by agreement for a time that you may devote yourselves to prayer, and come together again lest Satan tempt you because of your lack of self-control (1 Corinthians 7:2-5).*

Enthusiasm and responsiveness are important in physically expressing love. A wife's willingness is wonderfully important. But so is her enthusiasm. In Elyse Fitzpatrick's *Helper by Design*, she acknowledges the challenge of hormonal and emotional fluctuations, but emphasizes the importance of sex being "enjoyed" and not merely "endured." This actually helps meet a husband's needs.

Listen to the way that the bride in Solomon's song plans out a romantic interlude with her man:

Come, my beloved, let us go out into the country,
Let us spend the night in the villages.
Let us rise early and go to the vineyards;
Let us see whether the vine has budded
And its blossoms have opened,
And whether the pomegranates have bloomed.
There I will give you my love. (Song of Songs 7:11-12)

What do you suppose she had in mind? An agricultural visit? I doubt it. Godly women may and should take the initiative in sexual relations... . As a wife who's been called to help her husband, this is one of the major ways I can fulfill that calling. If I ignore Phil's needs, then I'm answerable for a whole storm of temptations with which he has to struggle.[129]

A *woman of dominion* will seek to overcome hormonal and emotional obstacles, obey God, and physically satisfy her husband. This is very important to your God and to your man.

Years ago, after my bride birthed our fifth child, she was in a hormonal slump and didn't have much physical interest in her heartthrob man. (Can you believe that?) Nevertheless, she physically loved and gave herself to me, understanding her solemn obligation.

I greatly appreciated her willing efforts. She was so sweet. But one afternoon I said to her, "Honey, I was watching you outside playing on the swing set with the kids yesterday. You were laughing and shouting for joy, as if you were having a blast. And they absolutely loved it, because you were enthusiastically participating with them, though you'd probably rather have been gardening. I don't need any shouting, but if you could enthusiastically participate in the bedroom, like you do on the playground, we'd both have a much better time." And we did—both of us.

That talk show host assured the caller that she wouldn't regret her principled investment into her marriage. Brooke gives her experience:

Driving home on the snowy roads, my heart was singing. Tonight I would be alone. Jake had a basketball game with the church league and the children were each invited to a sleepover. An empty house. What a joy! Visions of slipping into a bubble bath with a good book and a cup of hot chocolate danced in my mind.

When the garage door opened, I saw our blue car. Jake was still home. I was totally unprepared for him and his plan for the evening. With a grin, he informed me that a night of lovemaking awaited me in front of the fire. My heart sunk to my feet. I was anticipating aloneness—not togetherness.

I felt sad that my evening alone had vanished. Sex was the last thing on my mind. Perhaps I could get up for hors d'oeuvre sex, but it was obvious Jake wanted Thanksgiving dinner with all the trimmings! I just wasn't in the mood. What was I to do?

My thoughts went to a conversation I'd had with a friend. She told me her husband never wanted her. I should be grateful that after seventeen years of marriage, Jake still yearned for me, that he preferred a romantic evening with me over a basketball game. But I wasn't. Not tonight. *Help, God,* I prayed. *I love this man. Help me want to love him.* One decision followed another. I prayed that Jake would not see how hard this was for me.

I told Jake how much I loved him, told him how I was going to give him pleasure, but my mind and heart were in the bath with my book. I continued to pray and love my husband. *I choose to love him, Lord. Give me desire for him.*

As I write, it's hours later. My Jake is asleep. I can't sleep because I'm still thinking about what happened tonight. It was a beautiful time of lovemaking—exquisite. Afterward we felt so close and intimate.

What a lesson for me. Yes, my plan was shattered, but how grateful I am that I made a choice and went with the new plan. I made one husband very happy, and I'm at peace that I chose to love. And some day, God will even have an evening alone for me.[130]

Eat, friends; Drink and imbibe deeply, O lovers (Song of Solomon 5:1b).

Eating and drinking deeply of delicious romance requires that you be a chef of *womanly dominion*—one who sacrificially *rules and subdues* her feelings and emotions, according to the principles of the Scriptures, to the glory of God and the health of her marriage. You won't regret it. Such culinary skill, ladies, on *your* part inspires us in *our* cooking responsibilities.

> "As a man, I can tell you our needs are simple. We want to be fed, we want our kids mothered, and we want lovin…This will be repaid by (our) laying the moon and stars at your feet for your pleasure."[131]

CHAPTER 11:
WOMANLY DOMINION
IN FACING YOUR FEARS

About twenty years ago, my pregnant wife returned home from her four-month checkup with her obstetrician. The doctor told her that her blood test indicated an abnormally high level of alpha-pheta-protein in her blood and that this might indicate the presence of a severe spinal defect in the child she was carrying. I greeted her teary-eyed and shaken face at the door. She explained the distressing situation by referring to a colorful pamphlet provided by her physician. "Our baby may be born paralyzed from the chest down and never get out of a wheelchair."

Dianne was afraid. As she spoke, I scanned the literature and snagged the interesting statistic that only 2% of the *"high-protein babies"* were actually born with the feared "spina-bifida" birth defect. I told her that statistically the odds were 98% sure that everything would be okay.

But I would not have been wise to have left her emotionally-distraught soul resting simply on the pillow of the percentages. Two days later, as Dianne sat on an ultrasound table, holding my hand, the radiologist sighed and announced, "There is an abnormality! It appears that there's a pretty severe defect in the spine of this fetus."

For a woman, dealing with paralyzing fears is not a rare and isolated problem. Abraham's Sarah was a model woman whose feminine condition as *"a weaker vessel"* made her peculiarly vulnerable to *"being frightened by fear"* (1 Peter 3:6-7). Most women readily admit that they battle with many *"fears."*

Jill confides that the recent spate of lay-offs at her husband's company makes her fear that *he's* next, and so she hasn't been sleeping well. The mother who's recently heard of a young boy's death obsesses that one of *her* sons may be next. The woman in her mid-twenties is consumed with fears that she'll never marry. The pregnant Sheila, who's miscarried before, so fears the possibility of losing this child that she's practically immobilized.

How does a godly *woman of dominion* deal with her frequent fears? How does she counsel and stabilize herself when assaulted by a crippling dread about what *might* happen in days to come? What tactic should she employ when her spiritual adversary tries to chase her away from *playing her position* and doing her duties with a *win it* mindset in the good fight of faith? What is the suitable tranquilizer for the calming of our worried heads, when faced with the prospects of emotional paralysis?

In our day, many trembling women are turning to their *medicine cabinets* rather than their *open Bibles* and the *Throne of grace.* For an alarming number of professing Christian women, *mind-altering, psychotropic drugs,* are replacing *biblical self-talk.* Some physicians are handing out *anti-anxiety* and *anti-depressant* prescriptions to nearly any woman who complains of seasons of emotional discomfort.

Spiritual warfare according to the Bible is being recast in our day as *chemical imbalance* according to the psychiatrists. Though I'm not convinced that *all* modern resorting to such drugs is inappropriate, I am convinced that *most* of it is. Elyse Fitzpatrick and Laura Hendrickson, M.D. have written a very insightful book: *Will Medicine Stop the Pain? Finding God's healing for depression, anxiety & other troubling emotions.*[132]

Beware, dear ladies. The *law of diminishing returns* typically results in the perilous snowballing of medications. The numbing of our emotions is not the solution to our problems. *Emotional pain is God's calling us to draw near to Him.*

> *From the end of the earth I call to Thee, when my heart is faint;*
> *Lead me to the rock that is higher than I. For Thou hast been*

a refuge for me, A tower of strength against the enemy. Let me dwell in Thy tent forever; Let me take refuge in the shelter of Thy wings (Psalm 61:2-4).

When it comes to emotional instability, an open Bible in general is the great tranquilizer, and the Psalms in particular are an excellent *pharmacy*. Consider the counsel of three Psalms which together press our minds to grasp a fundamental principle for the taming of our fears.

The urged strategy is not *to statistically dispel them*: "Oh, the odds are against that calamity's ever happening." It's not *to sentimentally disqualify them*: "Oh, your heavenly Father would never let such a bad thing happen." And it's not *to forgetfully suppress them*: "Oh, just refuse to think about it." Neither is it to *medically numb them*. Instead, the urged strategy is *to courageously face them*. That's right! Face your fears head on, and *subdue* them under your feet, otherwise they'll trample you under theirs.

1. Psalm 46 and the Fear of Circumstantial Disaster

God is our refuge and strength, a very present help in trouble. Therefore we will not fear, though the earth should change, and though the mountains slip into the heart of the sea; though its waters roar and foam, though the mountains quake at its swelling pride. Selah (Psalm 46:1-3).

Its Dangerous Setting

We don't know what specific crisis triggered the penning of Psalm 46. Was it during the era of David, of Solomon, of Hezekiah? We don't know. But it seems clear that the rumble of hoof-beats and chariot wheels was just over the horizon, as verse 9 revels in the God who *"makes wars to cease... breaks the bow... burns chariots with fire."*

Apparently, Jerusalem was buzzing with concern regarding a fierce enemy who was bearing down on her. Was this the fierce surrounding army of the 185,000 Assyrians, who in Hezekiah's day (2 Kings 18-19) was poised to invade, rape, pillage, plunder, and exile the Holy City and her citizens? I suppose a mother of many, hold up in Jerusalem, with her husband positioned on the wall, might struggle with not being able to sleep deeply.

Its Courageous Realism

The Psalm doesn't counsel Israel with statistical optimism: "We'll probably never even see a single chariot; and besides, no army has ever penetrated Jerusalem's walls." It doesn't encourage suppression or denial techniques: "Just don't even think about war." It doesn't provide rosy assurances: "Jehovah would never let Assyria touch and pain the apple of His eye."

Instead, the Psalm calls for *a courageous facing of our worst fears*. It summons us to *face head on* the possibility of the total destruction of our prosperous way of life, to stare down the worst-case scenario. Verses 2 and 3 boldly explore the potential arrival of the ultimate calamity. They say: *"though the earth should change,"* alluding to the shuddering of an earthquake which could make Jerusalem's walls tumble down. *"Though the mountains slip into the heart of the sea"* refers to a catastrophe of eschatological proportions, the unhinging of the earth and crumbling of its most invincible towers. Finally, they say: *"though the mountains quake at its swelling pride,"* bringing to mind volcanic eruptions of Mt. St. Helens-like magnitude, which can result in a Pompeii-like lava flow bringing death and devastation.

The Psalm calls me to boldly entertain the possible prospects of my home being buried, my business going up in flames, my town being leveled in a quake, my children being swept away in a flood, and my spouse being killed in the wreckage. I may shrink back from this approach to dealing with my fears, claiming it's too negative, or morbid, or pessimistic. But this is not morbid pessimism. It's godly realism. These things may indeed happen! And it's not for us to traffic in *deception*, *evasion*, or *suppression*, but in *reality*, *honesty*, and *integrity*.

Charles Spurgeon, whose sermon on this Psalm is entitled, *"Earthquake but not Heartquake,"*[133] well summarizes its thesis: "This is the doctrine of the Psalm: <u>Happen</u> what <u>may</u>, the Lord's people are happy and secure."[134]

Its Satisfying Comfort

Though our world may collapse all around us, *"God is our refuge and strength, a very present help in trouble"* (Psalm 46:1). He will never leave us or forsake us. He'll be our shelter in the quake, our rock in the flood, our friend in the flames. *"Therefore we will not fear."*

Our calming comfort is found not in *statistical probabilities*: "There's only a miniscule chance that would ever happen to your child." It's not found in *human competence*: "There's no way they'd lay off a man of your husband's skill." It's not found in *stock diversification*: "There's little chance that all of these different industries could crash at the same time."

Our true consolation is found when we *face head on the absolute worst case* of what may indeed happen. Then in the midst, we reckon His promise of His presence as *"our refuge and strength, a very present help in trouble."*

Should I need to endure *my worst nightmare*, He'll be there, to uphold me so I don't collapse or breakdown in despair. As Shadrach, Meshach, and Abednego found a sustaining and supporting Helper in their fiery ordeal (Daniel 3:25), so will I not be left to walk alone either. *"Therefore, we will not fear"*! This enables me to eye yonder furnace with a holy calm, to say as I draw potentially near to it, *"It is well with my soul."*

2. Psalm 27 and the Fear of Relational Abandonment

The LORD is my light and my salvation; whom shall I fear? The LORD is the defense of my life; whom shall I dread? When evildoers came upon me to devour my flesh, my adversaries and my enemies, they stumbled and fell. Though a host encamp against me, my heart will not fear; though war arise against me, in spite of this I shall be confident... . For my father and my mother have forsaken me, but the LORD will take me up (Psalm 27:1-3, 10).

David's Trepidation

Psalm 27 is from the pen of David. Again, we don't know for certain the circumstances that triggered its penning, but it seems to have been a time of military danger (see v. 3: *"host encamp against me...war arise against me"*), that made David reflect on the potential loss of his most intimate relations (see verse 10 *"my father and mother have forsaken me"*).

These clues lead us to think on the days when jealous King Saul was in mad pursuit of the young war hero, David. Upon hearing of Saul's intention to kill him (1 Samuel 20:31), David fled to the town of Nob, where the priests provided food and Goliath's sword (21:6-8), resulting in their being brutally executed for the unjust charge of treason against the king (22:18). David then fled to the high ground fortress of Adullam and surrounded himself with a bodyguard of mighty men

(22:1-2). Perceiving the great danger to anyone suspected of giving him aid, David feared for the safety of his own family—his father and mother in particular.

> *And David went from there to Mizpah of Moab; and he said to the king of Moab, "Please let my father and my mother come and stay with you until I know what God will do for me." Then he left them with the king of Moab; and they stayed with him all the time that David was in the stronghold (1 Samuel 22:3-4, emphasis added).*

In this time of mortal opposition, David was emotionally *"on the ropes"*. He felt nearly alone in a hateful world, and even the citadel of his dearest supporters was vulnerable. *Saul might kidnap and execute Mom and Dad.* Or possibly, the royal propaganda machine might lead his parents to conclude that their fugitive son was a despicable traitor who deserved to be disowned. It may be that these kinds of swirling fears drove David to write verse 10, which many commentators believe should be translated as a hypothetical condition (according to the New American Standard marginal reading)[135]: *"If my mother and father forsake me, then the Lord will take me up"*(emphasis added).

David contemplated the possibility of things getting so bad, that the circle of his supporters would be shrunken down to *no man*. He stared in the face an abandonment of unthinkable proportions—being disowned by *his father*, the supportive man who always stood behind him no matter what, and *his mother*, the tender woman who nursed him and always believed in him.

Events had conspired to *haunt David's emotional life* with knee-knocking fears of death and rejection. But instead of *avoiding* his fears, *he faced them head on* and was consoled by the conviction that even such deeply painful tragedies would be survivable.

David's Consolation

He was emboldened like a lion, *not* by convincing himself that his fears would probably never materialize. They might! Rather he calmed his soul by meditating on the covenant love of His God. Though the supporting *arms* of his earthly father and mother might be cut off, the *everlasting arms* of His Heavenly Father would ever be underneath him. *"The eternal God is a dwelling place, and underneath are the everlasting arms"* (Deuteronomy 33:27).

Yes, the kindest and most tender relations of this sinful world may leave me as a helpless infant weeping in a trash dumpster. It may happen. But <u>come what may</u>, the Lord will take me up. I have entrusted my soul to Him. He's promised: *"I will never desert you, nor will I ever forsake you"* (Hebrews 13:5; Deuteronomy 31:6).

In his darkest and loneliest hour, he saw himself embraced by *arms* infinitely more loving than earth's most passionate father and affectionate mother. And so, he reckoned himself well cared for, with nothing to fear. *He dispelled his fears, by facing his fears.*

3. Psalm 23 and the Fear of Physical Death

> *Even though I walk through the valley of the shadow of death,*
> *I fear no evil;*
> *for Thou art with me; Thy rod and Thy staff, they comfort me*
> *(Psalm 23:4).*

Here, David brings us face to face with the Everest of all human fears—death. John Flavel writes: "Death is the dreadful enemy; it defies all the sons and daughters of Adam."[136]

Who doesn't tremble at the thought of facing this king of terrors? Death is profoundly the dark unknown—the bear's growl from inside the black cave, the lion's roar from the pitch dark night, the wolf's snarl from the dim forest, the dragon's shriek from the shadowy valley. And each of us must enter alone.

David calls it the *"valley,"* or *"ravine,"* of the *"shadow of death."* It is figurative language for the descent into an appalling crisis, ultimately a reference to the grave. When put to shaking by the hobgoblins, dragons, and dreads of the black valley, the Psalmist doesn't flee into the *fantasy of denial,* but boldly ventures down to confront them. *"I fear no evil."*

Years ago, I sat at the hospital bedside of a dear Christian wife and mother named Beth. Hodgkin's lymphoma was strangling the life out of her. We talked about her husband, sons, pastors, and friends who'd supported her through the past few harrowing months. Within 48 hours of that talk, Beth breathed her last. At the rim of the dark valley, all of her guides, companions, and friends were forced to turn back— except one. To the Good Shepherd, the saint's heavenly Friend, David joyfully exclaims, *"Thou art with me."* *"Thy rod,"* a club-like weapon worn at the belt, and *"Thy staff,"* a tool for keeping sheep near—*"they comfort me."*

But what did David know about the Lord being a comforting good shepherd in comparison to what we know? The Redeemer has now come and said, *"I am the good shepherd; the good shepherd lays down His life for the sheep"* (John 10:11). And that's just what He did.

John Flavel wrote: "Christ, by dying, went into the very den of this dragon, fought with it and foiled it in the grave—its own territories and dominions, and came out as the Conqueror."[137]

Our Lord Jesus, all alone, faced head on *mankind's greatest fear*, so that none of His lambs *need ever fear*, for He's now able to carry us on His *shoulders through every fear*. Therefore, in facing even the most unnerving experience devised by this wicked generation—*the killing of the body* (Matthew 10:28), we can sing, *"I will fear no evil, for Thou art with me."*

Now let's summarize the *"facing your fears"* combined counsel of these three Psalms. This is what a *woman of dominion* will do when assaulted by crippling fears about what might happen in days to come:

Do what you are responsibly able to do.

The Psalms' chief counsel directs the soul toward God, but not with an irresponsible presumption. Godly trust does not absolve us of our manly responsibilities. We saw how David, faced with fears due to Saul's murderous jealousy, indeed sought *emotional refuge* in the Lord's sovereign care (Psalm 27:1). But he also provided *military refuge* for his own body in Goliath's sword, the Adullam fortress, and a mighty man bodyguard. Further, he provided *asylum refuge* for his parents in the king of Moab's army.

Likewise, Jill may sweetly encourage her could-be-laid-off, on-the-bubble husband to *arrive at work earlier* and *stay a little later* in order to convince management that he's irreplaceable. She may also tactfully counsel him to begin to send out networking feelers in order to possibly secure a more stable employment situation.

The woman who fears for her teenage son's life may employ a conservative curfew and proactively parent to make sure that he has nothing to do with the drinking crowd at school.

The twenty-something woman who dreads being a spinster at age fifty, spending Christmas Eve alone, might consider taking up running to shed some extra pounds, wearing braces to straighten unsightly teeth, or seeking counsel from godly women on how to cultivate a more winsome personality.

Sheila, who's miscarried before, would do well to become a student of pregnancy wellness, reading much on the subject, seeking specific advice from competent physicians, and diligently maintaining dietary, exercise, and sleep habits that nurture healthy gestation.

Heavenly promises and consolations are *never excuses* for our abdicating our earthly duties and obligations.

> *The horse is prepared for the day of battle,*
> *but victory belongs to the* LORD *(Proverbs 21:31).*

But make sure you prepare your horse.

Stare your worst fears right in the eye.

Fretting and paralyzing fear is no condition for a spiritually healthy, well-adjusted child of God. Psalm 37:1 says, *"Do not fret ..."* Psalm 37:7 says, *"Do not fret ..."* Psalm 37:8 says, *"Do not fret ..."* The wise woman will continually tell herself, *"Do not fret."*

> *The wicked flee when no one is pursuing,*
> *but the righteous are bold as a lion (Proverbs 28:1).*

Lion-like confidence is the fitting face and heart for a woman of God. Retreating and paralyzing fear is the handiwork of the Devil (see Genesis 3:8-10). Our enemy, *"the father of lies"* (John 8:44), traffics in falsehood and deception.

When our firstborn son was about six-years-old, we moved into a new house, and he got a new bedroom. But after a while, this became a big *"fear"* problem, for on the west wall was a miniature door that led into the attic. To Jared, the attic became a dark cave filled with bears, wolves, dragons, and other hobgoblins. At any moment, it could swing open into his room, and he'd never be heard from again!

What's a parent to do? Late one night, when Jared was shuddering, I got an extension cord and attached it to an engine repair light. I swung the door open, and, yes, the two of us climbed into the dreaded attic. Pointing the light toward the roof's northern slope, I whispered, "Look Jared, it's the killer playpen! And over there, it's the abominable box of sweaters. And there, it's the deadly carpet-roll. And there, it's the quicksand insulation." We investigated every corner of the attic and discovered that there was really nothing that could hurt him. And having *stared down his fears*, he exorcised them, enabling him to sleep peacefully. We put a flashlight on his dresser, in case the lies returned, enabling him to reinvestigate and again *tell himself the truth.*

Years ago, a twenty-year-old young lady sat in my office sharing with me her oppression and depression stemming from the fear that she'd never marry. She was terrified at the thought of being forbidden the joys of wifehood and motherhood. The thought of living alone in her older years brought on her great emotional agony. My first impulse was to say, "Nonsense, Esther, you've got a nice personality, an attractive appearance, a tender heart, and surely God will send the right man your way." Then I thought, "How do I know that? Sure, the percentages are heavily in her favor. But the *pillow of percentages* provides no true solace to a worried head. My assurances have no guarantees. I could be telling her a lie."

Instead, I gave her the Psalmist's counsel. "Though you have many attractive traits, there is a real possibility that you may never marry. That prospect is like an ominous attic door to you." Then I told Esther about Jared. "You need to climb into that attic. You need to explore your worst fears. There you are, fifty-years-old, on Christmas Eve, sitting on the sofa alongside the decorated tree, all alone in your apartment, without a husband or children. It seems unbearable. But is it really? Shine the light on it. I know it seems unendurably bleak and dark like *'the valley of the shadow of death.'* But shine the light of God's word on it. Look! You're not alone at all. Your Good Shepherd is with you there in that apartment valley. He's pledged, *'Lo, I am with you always, even to the end of the age'* (Matthew 28:20). Your Father promised to provide all of your needs according to His riches in glory in Christ Jesus (Philippians 4:19). If you spend some time meditatively exploring this attic in light of the Scriptures, you'll sleep much better and glorify God much more."

This biblical prescription is a veritable panacea for treating fear. It sedates the anxious and uptight wife who desperately wants to be a mother, but is worried sick over the prospects of a childless marriage, enabling her to sing from the heart: *"Whate'er my God ordains is right."*[138] It remedies the fear of a romance or engagement break-up, enabling the insecure maiden whose clinginess may drive her beau away, to adopt the personality of a well-adjusted *woman of dominion* and dignity. *"Though my mother or my father or my fiancé forsake me, yet the Lord will take me up."* Here is a woman who, by the grace and Spirit of God, is able to *subdue her fears under her feet.*

I'm not prescribing medicine I don't take myself. A few years ago, a close friend of mine lost his firstborn 18-year-old son to death. The whole ordeal plowed me up emotionally. Weeks later, I was preaching at a weekend conference nearly 2000 miles away from home in Oregon. I had just pillowed my head down to sleep near midnight in the home of my host when the phone rang. I wondered who would call so late unless it was an emergency. A fright response of adrenalin hit my blood, and I was wide awake with worry.

"It may be *my* firstborn son. Maybe he's died in some freak accident!"

"Oh, come on, Mark. Don't be ridiculous. Things like that don't happen. Just roll over and go back to sleep."

"But wait a minute, yes they do. It just happened to my friend's son a few weeks ago."

"Okay, Mark, instead of trusting in a fantasy assurance, that has all the comforting support of a spider's web, stare down the real possibility. In a couple of days, you could be back home choosing a casket with Dianne."

The whole contemplation brought over me a tidal wave of grief, but then in the darkness of that bedroom, flashed a light: *"Even though I walk through the valley of the shadow of death, I fear no evil; for thou art with me, Thy rod and thy staff, they comfort me."* Like my son back home, after his attic exploration, I fell into a deep sleep.

After I preached on this theme, a perceptive mother came to me and said, "I think my greatest fears regarding my children involve the fear that I, their mother, might die while they're still young. I shudder at the thought of my three sons (ages 8, 7, and 5) being left to fend for themselves in this world. Who would ever love and care for them like I do?" Surely, this is a valid and wonderful concern of a deeply loving, committed, and conscientious mommy. But remember. The Lord has promised that *His everlasting arms* are a blessed safety net underneath the *parent-forsaken child.*

Andy is a financially successful, personally vivacious and spiritually-minded 85- year-old in our congregation. He's an eye-brightening encourager to everyone he touches—whether it's refurbishing a used bicycle and giving it to a small girl or following up a sermon with an encouraging word to a weary pastor. Andy adopts everyone as his special friend. When Andy was nine-years-old, both of his parents died. Between then and the time he turned eighteen and went into the military, this orphan boy was passed among fourteen different homes of loving friends and relatives. His all-wise Lord, who is the God of the orphan, in this loneliness valley, molded Andy into an extraordinary gift to His church. Who knows what great work the Lord has in store for our sons and daughters, whom the Lord will surely take up in His sovereign good pleasure, should we prematurely perish?

Now understand, I'm not denying that the children of God ought to have a holy optimism about life. David wrote later in Psalm 27:13, "*I would have despaired unless I had believed that I would see the goodness of the LORD in the land of the living.*"

We are not to habitually dwell on or expect "the worst," but surely we are to be healthily bolstered for it.

Experience liberation from paralyzing fears.

Our Lord Jesus said: "*You shall know the truth, and the truth shall make you free*" (John 8:32). Truth of all kinds has a wonderfully therapeutic effect.

Upon the truthful facing of our fears, the bold exploring of our foreboding attics, and the meditative visiting of our haunted valleys of death, our souls can truly experience spiritual peace. This is not only in the hypothetical, but in the actual.

A little over four months after the radiologist's declaration, "There is an abnormality… a pretty severe defect in the spine of this fetus," Dianne gave birth by C-section to 7-pound, 6-ounce Austin. And though his face was beautiful, his lower back wasn't. The sight of it made Dianne cringe with tears.

Within minutes, Dianne had to bid her needy little man farewell, as he was whisked away across town to the children's hospital to undergo two major surgeries. She was forced by her incision to stay behind a couple days at the birthing hospital, grieving in the passionate fires of her raging maternal instincts. The whole ordeal was a dark valley—the surgeries, the weeks in the neonatal intensive care unit, the early days of wondering if Austin would ever get out of a wheelchair. But do you know what? *God was down in there!* His rod and His staff comforted us. Dianne has said that it was, spiritually speaking, the richest time of her life.

After Austin's birth, a genetic counselor encouraged us to consider having no more children. The statistical odds were greatly increased for another spina-bifida baby. We prayed much. Dianne studied much. She discovered that research revealed that a folic acid deficit in the mother was the main culprit in gestating spina-bifida babies. She bolstered her diet with folic acid, and three years later we were expecting again.

For months she faced the statistically heightened possibility that this child, too, might be born with a deformed spine. But as daunting as was the prospect of passing again through that *dark valley*, she was not paralyzed by fear, because she'd passed through it once before and found that her Good Shepherd was down there. So she thought, "Why should I fear?" The *experience* with her God's comforting rod and staff had given her the unnatural boldness of a lion.

In John Bunyan's *Holy War*, Prince Immanuel appointed *Mr. Experience* as Captain in the City of Mansoul. Embossed on his shield was his *coat of arms*. It was the image of a *dead lion* and a *dead bear*, reminding us of David's claim of fearlessness in the face of the giant Goliath.

> *When the words which David spoke were heard, they told them to Saul, and he sent for him. And David said to Saul, "Let no man's heart fail on account of him; your servant will go and fight with this Philistine." Then Saul said to David, "You are not able to go against this Philistine to fight with him; for you are but a youth while he has been a warrior from his youth." But David said to Saul, "Your servant was tending his father's sheep. When a lion or a bear came and took a lamb from the flock, I went out after him and attacked him, and rescued it from his mouth; and when he rose up against me, I seized him by his beard and struck him and killed him. Your servant has killed both the lion and the bear; and this uncircumcised Philistine will be like one of them, since he has taunted the armies of the living God." And David said, "The LORD who delivered me from the paw of the lion and from the paw of the bear, He will deliver me from the hand of this Philistine" (1 Samuel 17:31-37, emphasis added).*

Experience with God's helping rod and staff, in the past, made the otherwise trembling David into a giant-killer, in the present. W. S. Plumer insightfully wrote: "Experience is a great school for Christians. Without it, they would be babes all their days."[139]

Experience with God's faithful shepherding in dark valleys makes the most delicate of women, as bold as lions. They can act as brave David's when facing circumstantial Goliath's. When everyone else is paralyzed with fear, you can stand alone in the valley if the need be, looking up the nostrils of your opposing giant and *fear no evil*. And though with your own eyes may you see very little help in sight—maybe only a sling in one hand and a few pebbles in another—since your Heavenly Father is with you, you can confidently pursue your appointed business of each day and peacefully lie down and sleep each night.

Shudder at the thought of Christless fears.

If you have not yet repented and believed in the Savior, if you've not yet had heart dealings with God, you need to know that you are a stranger to Christ. The God of heaven is not your gracious Father, but your strict Judge. Your gnawing uneasiness of mind and conscience is legitimate. Your fears about days to come are not unfounded. They are very justifiable and rational.

In fact, if you've not yet gotten right with God by embracing Christ as your Savior and Lord, *it's extremely irrational for you to experience any peace right now.* The day is coming when your mother and father *will* forsake you, and no one will be there to take you up. You'll be forced to descend into the valley of the shadow of *death* alone with no one's rod to protect you, and no one's staff to preserve you. When this world collapses and gives way on the last day, when the mountains come crashing down, and the Son of Man appears in the clouds, it will *not* be well with your soul.

Today, he invites you to stop being a stubborn goat and become one of his humble sheep. Why would you insist His being your Executioner instead of your Shepherd?

I know that the enemy is distracting you now with evasive deceptions. He's whispering that *there's no need to face this fear now.* He's telling you that your day of judgment will never come. It will never happen.

But I'm telling you that you do need everlasting arms beneath you. You do need Christ as your only refuge and strength in that day of trouble. His shepherding arms are stretched out to you right now. Why would you turn and walk away. Put the book down right now. Go to Him. *"Believe on the Lord Jesus, and you will be saved"* (Acts 16:31)

CHAPTER 12:
WOMANLY DOMINION
IN THE CHURCH

My automobile is a finely-tuned machine, engineered to precise specifications according to the wisdom of its designers. I am wise to treat this magnificent machine according to the will of the manufacturer as expressed in its original assembly and owner's manual. Each part was carefully designed to perform its own peculiar and crucial function, enabling the car to run smoothly. I can expect problems if I exchange the fuel pump for the water pump, trade the place of the right front wheel with the steering wheel, or replace the transmission fluid with windshield washer fluid. Such foolish and cavalier actions would bring great damage to the car and also bring a frown from the manufacturer, voiding out any warranty. I must keep things in the right places.

The church, the body of Christ, is also a finely-tuned organism, created according to precise specifications, reflecting the wisdom of its Builder. In the Scriptures, the Lord has provided us with His manufacturer's manual. If we desire the Lord's smile and His body's prosperity, we will conduct the activities of His church according to the clear revelation of His will in the Bible. We must keep people in the right places.

This is a crucial issue for godly *women of dominion*. God has tailor-made women for, and appointed them to, vital roles not only in marriage, in the family, and in the community, but also in the church.

God has strategically positioned you. But the shrill voices of feminism are screaming mutinous instructions, telling you to move up, get the ball, and score for yourself. I'm seeking to reinforce the words of your heavenly Coach by telling you to *"Play your position!"* in the church.

In their excellent book, *Life in the Father's House, A Member's Guide to the Local Church*, Wayne Mack and David Swavely have insightfully presented the highly influential roles of women in the church. They recognize that the Scriptures place some restrictions on the ministries of women in the church, but not because women are *inferior* to men, simply *different* from men. (Who's to say a fuel pump is superior to a water pump, or a pastor to a children's Sunday school teacher?) The following survey of female functions borrows liberally from Mack and Swavely.

1. Women as Submissive Learners

When the church is publicly gathered together into a corporate body, the Bible is clear in describing a woman's role to be that of a *submissive learner*, and not of a *vocal teacher*.

> *Let the women <u>keep silent</u> in the churches; for they are <u>not permitted to speak</u>, but let them <u>subject themselves</u>, just as the Law also says. And if they desire to learn anything, <u>let them ask their own husbands at home</u>; for it is <u>improper for a woman to speak in church</u>. Was it from you that the word of God first went forth? Or has it come to you only? If anyone thinks he is a prophet or spiritual, let him recognize that the things which I write to you are <u>the Lord's commandment</u>. But if anyone does not recognize this, he is not recognized (1 Corinthians 14:34-38, emphasis added).*

> *<u>Let a woman quietly receive instruction with entire submissiveness</u>. But <u>I do not allow a woman to teach or exercise authority over a man, but to remain quiet</u>. For it was Adam who was first created, and then Eve. And it was <u>not Adam who was deceived, but the woman being quite deceived</u>, fell into transgression (1 Timothy 2:11-14, emphasis added).*

Note the context of both passages. They're not talking about family devotions, a neighborhood Bible study, or a Sunday evening group discussion around the dining room table. They're envisioning the assembling of the full local church body for corporate public worship. (1 Corinthians 14:26 *"... When you assemble ..."* 1 Timothy 3:15*"... I write so that you may know how one ought to conduct himself in the household of God, which is the church ..."*). In such a church gathering, women are not to be *vocal teachers*, but *submissive learners*.

Many driven by feminism and political correctness have attempted by creative exegetical gymnastics to undermine the clear meaning of these passages. The arguments are dealt with thoroughly elsewhere.[140] However, the practical implications for church life are quite clear:

1. In the corporate life and government of the church, women are obligated to submit to and learn from the teaching of men, rather than being teachers of men.

2. The authority positions of the church (pastor, elder, overseer) are clearly not open to women. (This is reinforced in 1 Timothy 3:2 and Titus 1:6: *"husband of one wife."* Note the same gender assumption in 1 Timothy 3:12 and also in Acts 6:3 *"select from among you, brethren, seven men* (adult males, Greek *andras*) *of good reputation"*).

But remember. Female submission and complementation does not mean inferiority or devaluation.

William Hendriksen sounds the right note:

> Though these words in 1 Timothy 2:11 and 12 and their parallel in 1 Corinthians 14:33-35 may sound a trifle unfriendly, in reality, they are the very opposite. In fact, they are expressive of the feeling of tender sympathy and basic understanding. They mean: let a woman not enter a sphere of activity for which by dint of her very creation she is not suited. Let not a bird try to dwell under water. Let not a fish try to live on land. Let not a woman try to exercise authority over a man by lecturing him in public worship. For the sake both of herself and the spiritual welfare of the church such unholy tampering with divine authority is forbidden.[141]

R. L. Dabney echoes the same biblical perspective:

> Paul does not say that the woman must not preach in public because he regards her as less pious, less zealous, less eloquent, less learned, less brave or less intellectual than man. In the advocates

of women's right to this function there is a continual tendency to a confusion of thought as though the apostle, when he says that a woman must not do what a man does, meant to disparage her sex. This is a sheer mistake…woman is excluded from this masculine task of public preaching by Paul, not because she is inferior to man, but simply because her Maker has ordained her for another work which is incompatible with this. So he might have pronounced, as nature does, that she shall not sing bass, not because he thought the bass chords more beautiful—perhaps he thought the pure alto of the feminine throat far sweeter—but because her very constitution fits her for the latter part in the concert of human existence, and therefore unfits her for the other, the coarser and less melodious part.[142]

Mack and Swavely thoughtfully tie it all together:

Our sinful society (and perhaps our sinful hearts) has convinced many of us that it is more blessed to lead than it is to follow. That is not necessarily true, for leadership brings problems, difficulties, and heartaches that followers never experience. God made women to be dependent upon men, so that men would protect, provide, and care for women. Any husband who truly loves his wife and desires to be the proper head of the home knows that this is no easy task. Sometimes it would be much more enjoyable to follow than to lead. And any elder/*pastor* who truly loves the Lord and desires to be the proper leader of the church knows that his is no easy task. During many difficult times he might desire strongly to relinquish his role to an eager successor!

The direction and instruction of the church are not a burden that women must bear. They should be grateful to God for that, and joyfully seek to fulfill the many other crucial ministries to which they have been called.[143]

2. Women as Influential Teachers

Women are not called by God to preach to the congregation from a pulpit in public worship or teach men in a Sunday school class. But make no mistake. Women are arguably the most highly influential teachers in the church.

Teaching Your Own Children

R. L. Dabney, writing back in 1891, provides us with a telling account.

> A church was rejoicing with its new pastor in an ingathering of souls, and among the converts was one whose appearance was so surprising that it filled them with wondering gratitude. The subject was a man of the world,...who now suddenly manifested a solemn interest in divine things, was constant in God's house, and was found, before long, sitting like a contrite child at the feet of Jesus... There was naturally in the new pastor's heart a curiosity to know how so surprising and gratifying a conversion occurred, and, perhaps, a trace of pride as he argued with himself that this case must be purely a result of his pulpit labors. So, when the convert came to confer with the church elders, he was asked what sermons had been the special means of his spiritual awakening. It seemed hard for him at first to understand the drift of such a question, but at last he answered very simply that his change was not due to any sermons or recent means, but *to his mother*. To his mother? She had died when he was a boy of six years... He stated that now, if he was Christ's, it was the power of her teachings over his young mind,...which were the true instruments for bringing him back; without which all other instruments would have been futile.[144]

Pastors are overrated in the church.

This entire book has been emphasizing the mighty leverage a woman possesses in *subduing and ruling the earth* from the bottom up rather than from the top down. The hand that rocks the cradle is the hand that rules the world. Women who *"play their positions"* with a *"win it"* mindset turn the world upside down in advancing the kingdom. *Women of dominion* wield impressive teaching clout in the church.

In his book, *Female Piety*, John Angell James writes about the mighty drawing power of a woman's teaching, coupled with her feminine love:

> Human nature is made to be moved and governed by love: to be drawn with the cords of affection, rather than dragged with the chains of severity. And woman's heart is made to love; and love is exerted more gently, sweetly, and constrainedly upon her child, by her than by the other sex. It makes her more patient, and more

ingenious, and therefore, more influential. Her words are soft, and her smile more winning, her frown more commanding, because less terrific and repulsive. The little flowerlet she has to nurture opens its petals more readily to the mild beams of her face. Hence, to repeat an expression of Monod, "The greatest moral power in the world is that which a mother exercises over her young child." Nor is there much exaggeration in that other expression, "She who rocks the cradle rules the world."[145]

Teaching the Children of Others

I know that not all women have their own children. But in the church, even for childless women, the teaching fields are white unto harvest. Women who have *"eyes to see"* and *"hands to work"* can mightily influence the souls of countless young ones.

Last night, I noticed that someone had removed from our basement storage closet a colorful selection of toys which hadn't seen action for quite a while. There was a Playschool barn full of livestock, a medieval castle with knights, and trucks, planes, and Hot Wheels cars, etc. I teased our third-born, 19-year-old Austin, who was working on his college marketing class, and asked if he'd been taking a study break. It wasn't until early this morning when my bride brought three little children from our church into the house that I made the connection. Dianne is helping a nearly nine-month pregnant mommy by taking her kids for the day. Those kids will be treated today to stories from the greatest book reader of all times!

Barbara Hughes reminisces:

> Mrs. Coleman, my fourth grade Sunday school teacher, was the "mother" who coached me in Bible memory work. She saw to it that I memorized several Psalms (the 23rd, 100th, and 121st), the Lord's Prayer, and the Beatitudes. She rewarded me then, but many years later I am still reaping the benefit of God's word logged into my memory bank. I thank God for her nurturing of my young soul.[146]

Dedicated, competent, and reliable women Sunday school teachers are a windfall to the church's upcoming generation. Their kingdom contribution is incalculable. In our church, girls clubs and book studies for young ladies sprout up spontaneously on the calendar. Children scarred by broken families and divorce can be spiritually nursed by an adopting older friend. Advice given by a fresh voice like Mrs. Johnston's can sometimes have more of an impact than the overly familiar counsel of parents. After the service, instead of gathering to chat with your cluster of close lady friends, try approaching a teenage girl who could benefit from the friendship of a godly big sister.

Realize that such edifying and evangelizing work can be done not only within the walls of the church, but also far beyond into our lost communities and world. Only the last day will unveil the wonderful teaching influence of such loving and assertive *womanly dominion*.

Teaching Younger Women

John Wooden coached UCLA basketball for twelve years and won ten national championships. He became a coaching legend. He retired in 1980, but he never stopped working. He has spent his latter years teaching his golden nuggets of wisdom to younger coaches through speeches, clinics, and books. *They hang on his every word.*

What a shame it is to see experienced wives and mothers wave farewell to their youngest child, then return to their empty nests and basically say: "Whew, it's great to be retired from the bother of kids. I'm done! I'm on vacation now." A *woman of dominion* won't do that. She'll realize that her experience makes her a repository of valuable golden nuggets of wisdom that she must not *bury in a hole* of self-indulgence (Matthew 25:25). Instead, she'll discerningly think, "My ministry is just beginning!"

> *Older women likewise are to be reverent in their behavior, not malicious gossips, nor enslaved to much wine, teaching what is good, that they may encourage the young women to love their husbands, to love their children, to be sensible, pure, workers at home, kind, being subject to their own husbands, that the word of God may not be dishonored (Titus 2:3-5, emphasis added).*

Avenues of such ministry in the church are uncountable. Mrs. Schmidt may occasionally open up her home for book studies that last for six weeks in a row. Emma may invite a group of young women to her home once a month for a gourmet lunch during which she instructively prepares the meal before their eyes, then at the table discusses a relevant angle on husband loving. Julie may volunteer to come over and help clean the home of an overwhelmed mother of many, creating a day full of teachable moments and insights. After the services, Mrs. Stewart may roam about the sanctuary, discreetly holding informal "counseling sessions" with her grateful yet unofficial flock of younger "clients."

And a mature *woman of dominion* will not merely keep things shallow and "surfacey." Sure, she'll be winsome and sweet. But she'll also be edifying and helpful. Martha Peace writes in *Becoming a Titus 2 Woman*:

> Often I will ask a younger woman, "What sins or what character weaknesses do you think God wants you to work on?" They might reply something like, "pride, anger, fear, gossip, or selfishness." Once I asked a woman what she thought *her* sins were. She could not think of any, so I asked her this, "If I could ask your husband what he would like for you to change, what would he say?" Quickly, she gave me a list.[147]

Younger women, there's an important message for you here, too. If you are a godly woman, wise older women should not need to exert great efforts to *hunt you down*. You should be hungrily and eagerly *seeking them out* for their wisdom. It is a sad evidence of worldly-minded hearts, when younger women disinterestedly rebuff the overtures of older women by detouring opportunities for mentoring relationships, in favor of easygoing shallow chats with the girls.

Imagine the local basketball coaches disregarding a John Wooden clinic at a nearby gymnasium. Unthinkable! *Women of dominion* hunger and thirst after righteousness and will seek out the experienced *legends* who can make them better. What about you? Find at least one and *hang on her words*.

Mack and Swavely nicely conclude our section on the crucial ministry role of *Women as Influential Teachers* in the church. Their words are especially relevant for contemporary Christendom where feminists are chafing against the clear Scriptural regulations regarding gender roles.

> Since there are *more women and children in the world than men*, what a mission field women have! Some women complain, "I don't have anything to do for Christ." But the women who say that usually are looking for an excuse because they do not really want to serve Christ sacrificially. Women can never legitimately say that they have nothing to do for Christ until they have taught every

needy child and every needy woman in the church and in their community everything they know about the Word of God. In fact, these are ministries that women can perform better than men, because there are problems among children and other women that women can deal with better than men. Women may disclose personal problems to women that they would not discuss with men, and women often can understand the emotional makeup and disposition of other women better than men.[148]

3. Women as Hospitality Extenders

Dr. Francis and Edith Schaeffer founded L'Abri in the mountains of Switzerland in 1955. They decided to make their home a place where confused people might find biblical answers to life's gnawing questions. It was called L'Abri, French for "shelter." They wanted their home to be a safe place for people to ask intellectual questions and explore the solid answers provided by biblical Christianity.

Francis was a brilliant philosopher, but much of L'Abri's genius was found in Edith's hospitality and servant's spirit. Betsy Childs writes:

In the early stages of L'Abri, she did all of the cooking and cleaning to make the backpackers, hippies, and university students feel like welcome houseguests. The answers Francis Schaeffer gave to their questions as well as the peacefulness of the Swiss mountain chalet drew visitors in greater and greater numbers. The growing number of guests made a lot of work for Edith Schaeffer who also had to care for four children, two of whom had major health problems. She writes, "Sometimes when difficult times are being lived through it seems as though the difficulties are simply too mundane to be the least bit worthwhile. Martyrs being tortured or persecuted for their faith at least sounds dramatic. Having to cook, serve meals to two sittings at times without ever sitting down to eat in between yourself, having constantly to clean up spilled and broken things, to empty mounds of garbage, and to scrub a stove that things have boiled over on, or an oven in which things have spilled over and baked to a black crust is neither dramatic nor glamorous!" But Edith's mind was not idle as she scrubbed the stove and made the beds. She too engaged in conversation with the guests, helping them probe their existential questions and come to know the one the Schaeffers called "the God who is there." She did not see the material realm as unrelated to the spiritual realm, and she did not describe housework as drudgery. No one can tell how many lives have been changed or how many sons and daughters of God have been born at her table.[149]

Paul writes to Timothy about aged widows who have over the years forged an outstanding name in the church by heroic service, and thus deserve honored treatment in their latter years.

> _Let a widow be put on the list_ only if she is not less than sixty years old, having been the wife of one man, _having a reputation for good works_; and if she has brought up children, if she has_ _shown hospitality to strangers_, if she has washed the saints' feet, if she has assisted those in distress, and if she has _devoted herself to every good work_ (1 Timothy 5:9-10, emphasis added).

The selfless work of domestic hospitality (befriending of strangers) is a vital dimension of an effective church ministry.

Alexander Strauch summarizes in his fine book, _Using Your Home for Christ_:

- Hospitality is a crucial element in building Christian community. Hospitality may well be the best means we have to promote close, brotherly love. It is especially important in churches where people don't know each other or where relationships are superficial, Sunday-morning-only relationships.
- Hospitality is an effective tool for evangelism. Showing Christ's love to others in a home environment may be the only means Christians have to reach their neighbors for Christ. A Christian home can be a lighthouse for God in a spiritually dark neighborhood ...
- Hospitality is a biblical command. Many Christians do not realize what the New Testament teaches about hospitality and what it can do for the local church.150

Though men need to be hospitable as well, the weight of this particular errand chiefly falls into the laps of women. I know that my bride has more practical heart dealings with the passage, _"Be hospitable to one another without complaint"_ (1 Peter 4:9), than I do. In fact, the selfless service of hospitality is presented biblically as the outflow of a heart full of thanksgiving to the Lord Jesus.

> *Now Simon's mother-in-law was lying sick with a fever; and immediately they spoke to Him (Jesus) about her. And He came to her and raised her up, taking her by the hand, and the fever left her, and she waited on them* (Mark 1:30-31, emphasis added).

> *Jesus, therefore, six days before the Passover, came to Bethany where Lazarus was, whom Jesus had raised from the dead. So they made Him a supper there, and Martha was serving; but Lazarus was one of those reclining at the table with Him. Mary therefore took a pound of very costly perfume of pure nard, and anointed the feet of Jesus, and wiped His feet with her hair; and the house was filled with the fragrance of the perfume* (John 12:1-3, emphasis added).

> *And a certain woman named Lydia, from the city of Thyatira, a seller of purple fabrics, a worshiper of God, was listening; and the Lord opened her heart to respond to the things spoken by Paul. And when she and her household had been baptized, she urged us, saying, "If you have judged me to be faithful to the Lord, come into my house and stay." And she prevailed upon us* (Acts 16:14-15, emphasis added).

A godly *woman of dominion* will labor to use her opened-up home as a ministry tool for serving the body of Christ and His kingdom. I understand that this is a Herculean task, requiring great energy output, self-denial, and organizational skills.

Invite church families over to your house on Friday nights. On Sundays, prepare a little extra in the oven so you can freely ask a first-time visitor over for dinner. People who have eventually become members of our church have told me that a lasting impression was made on them the first time they were a guest among us, by their leaving our building with multiple invitations to lunch. I know that such spontaneity requires a disciplined domestic engineer who's able to consistently keep her house in order. It also requires a homemaker of confident realism who's not paralyzed by the pride of perfectionism. A few hot dogs may have to be put on and served alongside a roast and mashed potatoes to feed unanticipated mouths. Such a mature perspective and performance requires a confident and realistic *woman of dominion.*

In our church, certain families have mightily ministered to our youth simply by making their homes available as sites for wholesome social events. The Jones family invites everyone over for volleyball and a campfire. The Smiths purposefully outfitted their basement with a pool table and game room in order to provide a popular venue for teens. The Carpenters just create a relaxed atmosphere that's conducive for good conversation. Mrs. C's snacks contribute to the right climate. The Jacksons open up their pool every Tuesday during the summers as "open swim" for mothers and their young children. When you think of the relationships and friendships that grow out of such experiences, you realize the staggering kingdom profit of the ministry of hospitality.

It's chiefly the *woman* of the house, and not the man, who creates these sweet and hospitable environments. Years ago, one woman came to me spiritually wrestling with the prospects of her husband's purchase of a large, expensive house and surrounding property. She confided that they could only justify this purchase with the intentions of using the estate for kingdom ministry. For many years now, I've watched. She's delivered above and beyond what I ever imagined. But it has required great self-denial and hard work.

Remember the example of Edith Schaeffer?

Only a *subduing and ruling woman of dominion* can make hospitality happen.

4. Women as Foot Washers

Returning to Paul's "honor list" for the church's older women, we discover that another admirable attribute beyond *"hospitality extender"* is *"foot washer."*

> <u>Having a reputation for good works</u>; and if she has brought up children, if she has shown hospitality to strangers, <u>if she has washed the saints' feet</u>, if she has assisted those in distress, and if she has <u>devoted herself to every good work</u> (1 Timothy 5:10, emphasis added).

Foot washing is not a center-stage, limelight position. It's behind the scenes, often in the shadows of anonymity, but very Christ-like (John 13:3f). Women *foot washers* are indispensable to the mission of the church. What the infantry foot soldiers were to the D-Day mission to take Normandy and gain a foothold in France, so the women *foot washers* are to the church's mission to teach sinners and *"make disciples of all nations"* (Matthew 28:19-20).

Sure, big names like Eisenhower, Bradley, Montgomery, and Churchill may have grabbed the D-Day headlines. But it was the heroic feats of anonymous soldiers who waded through the waters, crawled onto the beaches, climbed up the cliffs, and won the landscape acre by acre that ultimately defeated the forces of evil. Such a battle drama has unfolded in church after church over the centuries and across the globe, and it's profoundly the heroism of anonymous *foot-washing* women that has wonderfully pushed down the gates of Hell.

At the last-day victory banquet, when saints come from east and west, north and south to recline at the table (Luke 13:29), King Jesus will hand out the medals of honor according to a far different criterion of heroism than we might expect.

> *And they came to Capernaum; and when He was in the house, He began to question them, "What were you discussing on the way?" But they kept silent, for <u>on the way they had discussed with one another which of them was the greatest</u>. And sitting down, He called the twelve and said to them, <u>"If anyone wants to be first, he shall be last of all, and servant of all"</u> (Mark 9:33-35, emphasis added).*

I frankly don't expect that many pastors or elders will occupy the most privileged seats on that day.

Our churches are teeming with spiritual heroines. Beyond their great works of helpmeeting, mothering, and teaching, I've watched mighty women of dominion

- rise before dawn to prepare mouthwatering Men's Breakfasts.
- spend themselves as tireless church secretaries and pastoral assistants.
- pour themselves out to make sure the building appears spic and span.
- organize and maintain a benevolent meal delivery system.
- form a team that supervises and maintains a children's Sunday school system.
- administer church music ministries.
- give their all as pianists to bring joyful and skillful praise to the Lord.

- wrestle spiritually with sisters given to anorexia and bulimia.
- comprise a gifted team of multitasking wonders who make sure policy decisions made by elders and deacons actually get implemented into the practical life of the church.
- maintain the swarming duties of the church nursery.
- carry the heavy service burden of youth days and retreats.
- whip up massive and lovely impromptu meals for funerals.
- create brilliant flower arrangements and bulletin board designs.
- landscape the church grounds.
- select and systematize books as the church librarian or bookshop consultant.
- write timely letters of encouragement to pastors and fellow members.
- act as peacemakers between Euodia's and Syntyche's and Paul's and Barnabas's.
- function as Priscilla-like, eye-opening counselors to temporarily blinded pastors.

The list goes on and on without limit.

May the Lord enable you, dear ladies, to tune out the sour notes and shrill shouts of God-defying feminists who groan and complain about what God has *not* directed or designed them to do in the church. Don't be a water pump insisting you do the work of a fuel pump. Instead, may you *"play your position,"* with a *"win it"* mindset as you gratefully and enthusiastically perform your God-given ministries. Be a Christlike *woman of dominion* in the church.

CHAPTER 13:
WOMANLY DOMINION
IN THE PUBLIC SQUARE

If one day you saw a woman riding a motorcycle from Lincoln, Nebraska, to Des Moines, Iowa, on Interstate 80, you might notice a bit of curious behavior as she crosses the Missouri River, the border between the states. You might well observe her removing her helmet and releasing her long locks to flutter freely in the wind! You see, in our country, different states have different laws regarding helmet requirements. Nebraska is a *Mandatory Helmet Law State*. Every rider, regardless of age, must wear a helmet. But Iowa boasts itself as a *No Helmet Law State*. No rider is required to wear a helmet. Each state has its own laws. In this case, Iowa allows more liberty than Nebraska.

Life is much like this according to the Bible. Each sphere of life has its own set of restrictions regarding gender roles. In the previous chapter, we saw that the Bible provides certain restrictions for female saints in the sphere of the church. Earlier we saw that the Bible gives principles for women in the sphere of the family as wives and mothers. But as we move into the sphere of the public square, we notice that the Bible is much less precise in regulating the roles and activities of women.

As we cross the river into this final chapter, I believe the Scriptures speak less dogmatically and provide more liberty to women in their decisions about their roles in the *public square* (politics, military service, recreation, employment, etc.). Therefore, I will write this chapter in a more flexible tone. Instead of saying, *"Thus saith the Lord,"* I'll be saying, *"Come, let us reason together."* Notice how each category comes in the form of a question instead of a declaration. You may enjoy the feel of your hair *fluttering freely* in the wind.

But remember, just because a cyclist has the liberty to ride without a helmet, doesn't necessarily mean it's wise to do so. The same is true regarding Christian liberties for women in the *public square*. Liberty doesn't necessarily mean advisability. Simply because *I may*, doesn't mean *I should*.

> *All things are lawful for me, but not all things are profitable (1 Corinthians 6:12).*

1. A Woman President?

Right now, it's January, 2008. The polls indicate that Hillary Clinton is the frontrunner for the Democratic Party's presidential nomination. Past polls have shown that in a general election, pitted against any Republican candidate, Hillary would win. There's also been talk on the Republican side of the nominee possibly choosing the present Secretary of State, Condoleezza Rice, as his running mate, placing a woman a *"heartbeat away"* from the oval office. Setting aside for the moment specific personalities and liberal vs. conservative ideology, would this be a good thing in general, for a woman to become our President?

Important Considerations
1. The Bible views it as a judgment and calamity upon a nation for it to be ruled by women. Isaiah 3:12 reads: *"O My people! Their oppressors are children, and women rule over them. O My people! Those who guide you lead you astray, and confuse the direction of your paths."* Surely here, God views women and children as less than ideal rulers. This probably refers to an inherent constitutional *weakness* in womanhood (1 Peter 3:7, 1 Timothy 2:14), which generally hinders them in high-pressured leadership challenges.

2. Esther was a wise queen, but she did not rule as a monarch. Persian

authority rested with her husband, King Ahasuerus. Her influence on national policy was profound, but as a bold and advising *helpmeet* behind the scenes (Esther 5:1-4; 7:2-6), not as a political ruler. In her we find a noble pattern for our daughters. If George W. Bush is the most powerful man in the world, his wife Laura may arguably be the second most powerful *man* in the world (Esther 4:14).

3. Deborah was indeed God's appointed leader for Israel during the period of the Judges (Judges 4:1-5:31). But this was a morally dark and bleak era for Israel, and Deborah's rise to power was actually an indictment against shameful male dereliction. (See chapter 4 of this book in explaining Deborah.) The accomplished Puritan Poet, Anne Bradstreet, (whose husband Simon Bradstreet and father Thomas Dudley served as governors of the Massachusetts Bay Colony in the 1600's) understood that in trying times God could use a Deborah. In a poem commending the reign of Queen Elizabeth I, Anne Bradstreet penned:

> She hath wiped off th' aspersion of her sex,
> That Women wisdom lack to play the rex…
> Was ever people better ruled than hers?"[151]

4. The Bible looks favorably on the competence of the Queen of Sheba and the legitimacy of her secular rule over her gentile nation (1 Kings 10:1-10). Such national leaders as Elizabeth I in England, Margaret Thatcher in the United Kingdom, and Golda Meir in Israel are examples of competent women who have admirably led their respective nations. It's interesting how the latter two were both given the nickname "Iron Lady," indicating that their mettle was uncharacteristically strong for their gender. Steely firm toughness, an essential trait for effective ruling, is typically more pronounced in men (1 Corinthians 16:13). It's interesting how David Ben Gurion, Israel's first prime minister, called Mrs. Meir "the only *man* in his cabinet." [152]

5. It is difficult to imagine a high-ranking female politician's being able to conscientiously fulfill her priority obligations as a helpmeet to her husband and a mother to her children. Golda Meir broke off her political responsibilities for four years to stay at home and raise her two children. However, upon returning to public life, her enormous workload contributed to the collapse of her marriage in 1945.[153] It is

interesting to note that Condoleezza Rice is presently single.

Summary Opinion

Though I would never vote for a woman as my pastor, I could, under the right circumstances, be persuaded to vote for a woman as my president.

Upon my giving this conclusion in a Sunday school class, a wise and insightful 50ish-year-old grandmother in our church took me aside and said with sparkling and humorous eyes: "I could never vote for a woman for President unless I was assured that she'd already passed completely through menopause." This prudent Priscilla raises an interesting dimension worthy of consideration!

2. A Woman Warrior?

Most countries recruit women to serve in the military, chiefly in support roles. Only a few nations, including Canada, Denmark, Finland, France, Germany, Norway, and Switzerland, permit women to fill active combat roles. Today, the United States allows women into most flying positions, even as combat pilots, but not into combat infantry roles. The wars in Afghanistan and Iraq, however, have pushed the envelope of danger for women. Some governmental officials claim, "They're out there, doing it like never before!" Many are calling for an ending to what are called *"discriminatory policies"* and for the granting of full combat *"rights"* to women on the battlefield.

Would it be wise to promote women into the role of warrior?

Important Considerations

1. *There are biblical concerns.* The Bible presents a comprehensive picture of differentiation between men and women that certainly extends to the battlefield. Men are to protect women and children who are, generally speaking, not as physically strong and militarily brave.

> *"Your wives, your little ones, and your cattle shall remain in the land which Moses gave you beyond the Jordan, but you shall cross before your brothers in battle array, all your valiant warriors, and shall help them, until the LORD gives your brothers rest" (Joshua 1:14-15a, emphasis added).*

> *"Take a census of all the congregation of the sons of Israel, by*

*their families, by their fathers' households, according to the
number of names, <u>every male</u>, head by head from twenty years
old and upward, whoever is able to go out to war in Israel, you
and Aaron shall number them by their armies" (Numbers 1:2-
3, emphasis added).*

*Thus Sarah obeyed Abraham,...and you have become her
children if you do what is right <u>without being frightened by
any fear</u>. You husbands likewise, live with your wives in an
understanding way, <u>as with a weaker vessel, since she is a
woman</u> (1 Peter 3:6-7a, emphasis added).*

*"<u>When you go out to battle</u> against your enemies and see
horses and chariots...Then the officers shall speak further to
the people, and they shall say, '<u>Who is the man that is afraid
and fainthearted</u>? Let him depart and return to his house, so
that he might not make his <u>brothers'</u> hearts melt like his heart'"
(Deuteronomy 20:1a, 8, emphasis added).*

*In that day <u>the Egyptians</u> will become <u>like women</u>, and they
will <u>tremble and be in dread</u> because of the waving of the hand
of the LORD of hosts, which He is going to wave over them
(Isaiah 19:16, emphasis added).*

*The mighty men of Babylon <u>have ceased fighting</u>, they stay in
the strongholds; <u>Their strength is exhausted</u>. They are <u>becoming
like women</u> (Jeremiah 51:30a, emphasis added).*

2. *There are physical concerns.* The Center for Military Readiness
states: "Female soldiers are, on average, shorter and smaller than men,
with 45-50% less upper body strength and 25-30% less aerobic capacity,
which is essential for endurance. Even in current non-combat training,
women suffer debilitating bone stress fractures and other injuries at
rates double those of men."[154]

This is relevant considering that the equipment a soldier carries
into combat can easily approach 100 pounds (flak jacket, rucksack,
weaponry, etc.), and that every soldier should have the capacity to carry
his comrade (of 200 lbs.?) out of harm's way. Private Jessica Lynch, the
soldier who was injured and captured in Iraq during 2003, was "five
foot three and a wispy 100 pounds."[155] Furthermore, menstruation

cycles and pregnancy are also delicate facts of life.

3. *There are psychological concerns.* Do women have an adequate *killer instinct*? Does the presence of women with men damage a combat unit's *esprit de corps*? Do budding romantic relationships between men and women disrupt a unit's fighting capability? Does a man's natural protective instinct toward women suspend a soldier's ability to make wise battlefield decisions? After 1948 Israel Defense Forces policy for many years withdrew women from combat after observing a male infantryman's rage when he witnessed a wounded woman. His uncontrollable, protective, instinctual aggression could have caused a massacre.[156] Real men instinctively run to a woman's rescue, potentially endangering the larger military unit.

4. *There are POW concerns.* Combat assignments place women at high risk of being captured, tortured, and sexually assaulted. Unlike their male counterparts, women are almost always subjected to sexual abuse of varying degrees upon capture. According to the American doctors who examined Pfc. Jessica Lynch after her 2003 rescue by Special Operations forces, she was brutally raped by Iraqi thugs during the three to four hours following her ambush and capture.[157]

5. *There are moral concerns.* It is not prudent to order married men and women to live in close quarters where they are tempted to adultery. The same can be said about singles and fornication.

Summary Opinion
I believe that women should be removed from all combat situations and employed militarily only in non-threatening support roles. This is not sexual discrimination. It is privileged exemption. Our nation should honorably dignify and exalt women by protecting them from cruelty and carnage. Women should fight only as a last resort, when survival demands it, i.e., "when the Indians are circling the ranch and the men are dead and wounded."[158]

My hearts beats with John Piper's on this theme:

> If I were the last man on the planet to think so, I would want the honor of saying that no woman should go before me into combat to defend my country. A man who endorses women in combat is not pro-woman; he's a wimp. He should be ashamed. For most of

history, in most cultures, he would have been utterly scorned as a coward to promote such an idea. Part of the meaning of manhood as God created us is the sense of responsibility for the safety and welfare of our women.[159]

I believe that these basic principles apply as well to women as policemen and firemen.

3. A Woman Athlete?

This book began with the account of my coaching our daughter Abigail's recreational girls' soccer team, and my urging them to *"Play your position!"* and *"Win it!"* Abbie is now sixteen-years-old, a sophomore at a Christian high school, and a member of the girls' varsity soccer team. She also runs like a gazelle on the cross country team.

But is it wise for girls and women to participate in athletics?

Earlier in the book, I wrote that there's not only a "War Against Boys," there's also a "War Against Girls." Sure, society is trying to *feminize* our boys, but it is also trying to *masculinize* our girls.

The athletic scene is an example of this. I think sports can be a wonderful training ground for the development of godly womanliness. But I am deeply disturbed by the intense pressure being placed on some high school girls by their coaches and parents to train for and play their sports like *male wannabe's*. Girls' pumping heavy iron daily in the weight room with the boys has become standard training in some schools. Could it be that such rough unisex whip-cracking is draining from a generation of women the tender *"milk of human kindness"* that ought to characterize the fairer sex?

Does a woman's participation in athletics undermine her God-given femininity?

Important Considerations

1. *The inroads of feminism.* God-defying feminism has forced its way into the athletic sphere of our culture. Feminism-backed Title IX rulings have fundamentally affected the gender chemistry of the public schools, and, yes, the Christian schools, too.

We need to be very discerning here.

Dr. Leon Podles writes about the way historically sports have been utilized to build manhood into boys.

Agonistic masculine play was the origin of civilization. In the modern world, sports are the emotional center of countless men. Sports are a traditional means to attain masculinity... Because sports provide an initiation into masculinity, they can easily become a religion. Sports are often the way the boy puts away the soft, sheltering world of the mother and her femininity and enters the world of challenge and danger that makes him a man... Team sports develop masculinity; they are "the civilized substitute for war" and sublimate male aggression into channels less harmful than crime... Sport forms character, manly straightforward character, a scorn of lying and meanness, habits of obedience and command, and fearless courage.[160]

What are we doing to our girls and women? The past decade has seen the encouraging of high school girls to compete *"right in there"* with the boys in varsity football, hockey, and wrestling. I've read of principled boys forfeiting their high school wrestling matches scheduled against girls on convictions rooted in masculine chivalry and modest purity. Women's hockey and wrestling are now Olympic sports. Action photographs of grimacing muscle-bound women wrestlers twisting each other's bodies into painful contortions are instinctively repulsive. Women's rugby, football, weightlifting, and boxing have now become public spectacles.

Will we ever forget the 1999 FIFA Women's World Cup championship game? After scoring the winning penalty kick, Brandi Chastain, imitating the men, whipped off her uniform shirt, exposing her sports bra-attired torso to a gawking world?

Women's professional sport is disproportionately honeycombed with the plague of lesbianism. The WNBA, for example, is notoriously so.

Surely it is arguable that athletics, as promoted by feminism, has assaulted God's created order of *"in the image of God He created him; male and female He created them"* (Genesis 1:27). Women are to display *"a gentle and quiet spirit"* (1 Peter 3:4) and conceivably highly competitive sports could foster the very opposite—*a brash and contentious spirit.*

2. *The importance of physical fitness.* A Christian's body is a temple of the Holy Spirit (1 Corinthians 6:19). Though they are not the chief priorities in life, physical exercise and bodily discipline are indeed profitable (1 Timothy 4:8). The *"excellent wife"* of Proverbs 31 daily ran a marathon of a domestic race, and needed adequate physical strength and stamina to handle it.

> *She girds herself with strength, And makes her arms strong (Proverbs 31:17).*

> *Let our sons in their youth be as grown-up plants, and our daughters as corner pillars fashioned as for a palace (Psalm 144:12, emphasis added).*

Sadly in our day, physical strength and sturdiness have been replaced by bodily frailty and flabbiness. Obesity has become a national epidemic. *Junk food* consumption and *couch potato* lifestyles have become the norm. This is dishonoring to God.

A dear woman in our church has conducted seminars with our teen "Girls' Club" and with our "Ladies Fellowship" on the theme of physical fitness. She stresses the importance of women keeping their bodies in tiptop shape. She teaches the importance of diet, jogging or running, and stressful exercising. She may ask aloud important questions like: "Do you want to have the energy to be productive in your labors? Do you want to be able to carry your babies full-term? Do you want to be able to finish all of your daily chores? Do you want to avoid being weak and sickly? Do you want to be able to play outdoors with your children? Do you want to maintain a high degree of emotional resilience? Do you want to avoid flabbiness and keep your body tone? Do you want to grow old enough to see your grandchildren? Do you want to fend off osteoporosis? Do you want to stay attractive for your man? Do you want to attract a man?"

She firmly believes that a sober-minded participation in athletic recreation can be a great help to a woman's achieving the goal of God-honoring physical fitness. A team or individual sport can create an enjoyable atmosphere for the development of physical fitness. Our daughter Abigail's cross country experience has been wonderful in spurring her on to superior eating habits and a year-round running regimen that promotes healthful conditioning. The fitness benefits of this athletic experience will probably be life-long. My almost fifty-year-old wife runs-walks-jogs nearly every morning and supplements this with various specially tailored fitness exercises.

You say that you have small children and *just can't* find time to exercise? I've seen a mother of three little ones running briskly down on our street. She was pushing two in a large-wheeled stroller while the third rode along on a bike. A *woman of dominion* finds a way!

3. *The building of character.* Speaking about the Christian life, the Apostle Paul writes:

> Do you not know that those who run in a race all run, but only one receives the prize? Run in such a way that you may win. And everyone who competes in the games exercises self-control in all things. They then do it to receive a perishable wreath, but we an imperishable (1 Corinthians 9:24-25).

Notice how he uses the athletic imagery of a *marathon runner*. Paul appeals to our instinctive awareness that athletic endeavors train and challenge people to achieve a level of excellence that positions them to achieve high and lofty goals.

Athletics promotes the development of such character virtues as discipline, self- denial, stamina, confidence, selflessness, initiative, assertiveness, boldness, submission to authority, endurance of pain, the will to fight against great odds, the resolve to finish an endeavor, and the determination to do what you don't feel like doing.

Women, as much as men, need to develop these godly character traits. Athletics, properly directed, can become an important piece in the great project of training up, and maintaining *women of dominion.*

4. *The exercise of caution.* Though I believe a godly woman may indeed avail herself of the enjoyments and benefits of athletics, I recommend she do so only with careful discretion. She must not conform to the pattern of the world as saturated by radical feminism. She should participate in athletics *in a distinctly feminine manner.*

There's a third slogan that I've taught Abigail beyond *"Play your position"* and *"Win it."* That slogan is: *"Play like a lady!"* On the soccer field, we have noticed those girls who seem resolved to *"play like bruisers"* and *"shove like bulls."* We've mutually concluded that such a style of play for a lady *"is disgusting"* and not in keeping with *"a gentle and quiet spirit, which is precious in the sight of God"* (1Peter 3:4).

On occasions I've said to her, "Abbie, I'd much rather see you lose the game than watch you play like a man." She knows exactly what I mean. Women's soccer, properly played, looks more like ballet than football. Women need to be convinced that maintaining their God-given femininity is more important than gaining the scoreboard victory. Christian parents and coaches as well are obligated to communicate the same. Victory, or even a scholarship, at a *defeminizing* cost, isn't worth it.

Summary Opinion

I believe that a female athlete can indeed be a godly *woman of dominion*. But she should be very conscientious about avoiding *sports idolatry* and maintaining her distinct femininity. I seriously wonder if this can be accomplished while playing at a highly competitive college or professional level.

What sports would harmonize quite well with femininity and womanhood? How about sports like cross country, track, tennis (minus the groaning—though Abbie argues women groan in childbirth!), swimming (minus the muscle bulking up), golf, volleyball, and horseback riding.

Other sports, like soccer, basketball, and softball, may require additional effort on the part of the female participant to spurn the tendency toward masculine behaviors and mindsets.

Martial arts may be an excellent discipline for a woman to stay in shape and learn to defend herself in a dangerous and threatening world. But I would encourage the avoidance of striking and absorbing blows in competitive competitions and gender intermingling in training.

I have a very difficult time encouraging women to participate in wrestling, rugby, hockey, or heavy weightlifting.

Modesty in attire must be a non-negotiable. Don't conform to the world.

4. A Woman Worker?

My bride is a wife and mother of five, placing her on a demanding and exhausting 24/7 vocational schedule. Over the years, she has filled out various insurance forms. Inevitably, they'll ask her, "Do you work?" She shows the form to me, and then frowns. They really want to know if she's employed in the marketplace outside the home. That's my meaning here—*working women*.

Is it appropriate for a woman to be gainfully employed outside of the home in the pursuit of financial income? Earlier, we established that *man* was assigned by God to the role of *"breadwinner"* and *woman* to the role of *"child nurturer."* But does this prohibit women from laboring in the field of the marketplace for monetary profit?

Important Considerations
1. *Consider a single woman.* Both men and women are created in God's image (Gen1:27) and are solemnly obligated to imitate their glorious Maker who labored for six days and rested on the seventh (Genesis 1:31-2:3; Exodus 20:8-11). Both males and females must be *"workers."* For such a reason, Paul wrote:

> For even when we were with you, we used to give you this order: *if anyone will not work, neither let him eat.* For we hear that some among you are leading an undisciplined life, *doing no work at all,* but acting like busybodies (2 Thessalonians 3:10-11, emphasis added).

Rebekah, as a virgin, was employed in drawing water at the community well, not only for her father, but also for the camel-riding stranger. It was her *womanly dominion* work ethic that attracted the eyes of Abraham's matchmaking servant (Genesis 24:13-20).

Rachel was a "shepherdess" (Genesis 29:9). Diligent and loyal *"maidservants"* were of noble stature in Israel (Deuteronomy 15:17; Ruth 2:8).

Ruth was highly esteemed by Boaz for her conscientious gleaning in the fields (Ruth 2:7-8).

Lydia was a successful and commended *"seller of purple fabrics,"* an entrepreneur whose financial profit enabled her to extend extraordinary hospitality to Paul and his entourage (Acts 16:14-15).

A *woman of dominion* will be a *hard worker.* A godly single woman is not to sit on a porch swing, looking pretty, holding a parasol, waiting for a suitor to sweep her off of her feet into marriage and motherhood. No woman is guaranteed a husband. Her *plan A* may be a wedding, but she needs a *plan B.* She needs to train herself to become a productive, self-supporting member of society. Furthermore, great men like Boaz aren't attracted to parasol holders, but to focused laborers. God calls *workers* like Rebekah, and not *sitters,* to accomplish great things (Moses in Exodus 3:1-2; Elisha in 1 Kings 19:19; etc.).

A single woman should train herself for gainful employment in the marketplace. I believe that *nurturing* vocations like teaching and nursing are wonderful options. Certifying college degrees can be acquired in four years qualifying her for fulfilling work at a handsome wage. But surely other fields are wide open. I know of very competent women interested in medicine and law opting for the less consuming (educationally, chronologically, and financially) positions of "physician's assistant" and "paralegal," rather than "doctor" and "lawyer." Excellent "executive assistants" and "secretaries" are always in demand. Such positions allow much flexibility for the *plan A* hope of eventual courtship and marriage.

The kingdom mission field is wide open and white unto harvest.

For some, the position of "nanny" constitutes a satisfying vocation.

A woman may eventually come to believe that God has called her to extended or lifelong singleness. Then, she could choose to immerse herself educationally and vocationally and become an attorney like Harriet Miers (George W. Bush's Supreme Court nominee) or a statesman like Condoleezza Rice.

In summary, a *"woman of dominion"* will find something to do, and then *do it with all her might* (Ecclesiastes 9:10).

But remember. We live in an *"evil and adulterous generation"* (Matthew 12:39; 16:4; Ruth 2:15) where impurity abounds in the business world through the indiscreet mingling of men and women in injudicious situations. A *"subduing and ruling"* woman must be selective and discriminating in her career decisions. Sexual purity is a crucial variable.

2. *Consider a married woman.* Upon our marriage at age 23, our plan was that my certified teacher bride would teach full time for a couple of years before we had children. In retrospect, I believe that this was a reasonable plan. But the Lord had different plans (Proverbs 16:9). Dianne was soon diagnosed with *endometriosis*, and her gynecologist recommended the immediate pursuit of pregnancy as the best therapy for long-term health and fertility. Eighteen months after our wedding day, Jared, our firstborn, was in her arms.

I believe it is typically wise and prudent for a married woman who is yet without children to "work" in the marketplace. The Titus 2:5 encouragement for women to be *"workers at home"* assumes the presence of *"children"* who need to be *"loved."* Without the workload crush of motherhood, I do not believe that *homemaking* necessarily requires full-time, undistracted attention. You can only paper the cupboards, dust the furniture, and fluff the pillows so many times, right?

But I caution young, dual-income couples. Beware of the worldly tendency to become *self-indulgent*. Remember, God hasn't given you to each other to seek out and hoard mutual pleasures for yourselves—constant dining out, luxury vacations, late-model cars, a fashionable home, etc. Such partaking can be addictive. Your adopting and maintaining an unrealistic standard of living may push back indefinitely your solemn obligation to selflessly serve through *procreating* and *childrearing*.

It's sad to listen to a childless, young married couple sharing their family philosophy while mutually petting their purebred dog in the front yard of their stylish suburban home: "You know, we really feel good about our lifestyle right now. Our careers are going well. We've achieved a reasonable comfort level financially, recreationally, and relationally. We're just not ready to disturb everything with the hassle of kids." Avoid this unbiblical mindset like the plague!

Nevertheless, a childless couple may, for God-glorifying reasons (like paying off college debts, building a down payment for a home, etc.), choose to have the wife work even full time in the marketplace. I recommend she take on employment roles which avoid such high stress and pressure that would cause the helpmeet to "bring home" heavy anxieties from the workplace.

The husband's vocation must be established as *primary* and *supporting*, while the wife's as merely *secondary* and *supplemental*. She needs to be available to *"help"* him handle his great breadwinning project rather than being consumed and thoroughly preoccupied in handling her own. Your man is running a grueling vocational marathon. He needs you, his helpmeet, riding your bicycle alongside him, offering him water, oranges, and encouragement. He doesn't need you off somewhere running your own separate, grueling marathon.

Furthermore, University of California, Davis, conducted a study on "Female Lawyers and Stress." Consider its findings:

> Women lawyers working more than 45 hours a week are five times as likely to feel high stress at work and three times more likely to experience a miscarriage in the first trimester than women who work less than 35 hours a week, say occupational health epidemiologists at UC Davis School of Medicine and Medical Center. The findings are reported in the June issue of the Journal of Occupational and Environmental Medicine.[161]

For many reasons, titles like Doctor, Lawyer, CEO, and Sales or

Project Manager, may be far less suitable than roles like Physician's Assistant, Nurse, Dental Assistant, Paralegal, Secretary, Teacher, and Hair Stylist.

3. *Consider a mother of children.* The economic pressures of American culture have begun to strangle the very heart and soul of the Christian family. A global marketplace and industrial outsourcing have forced us to wave farewell to an abundance of high-paying jobs with hefty benefit packages, including fully-funded health insurance coverage. Corporations have been forced to become more competitive and thus *"lean and mean,"* resulting in increased employee demand and reduced remuneration, lagging way behind the rate of inflation. Gas prices at the pump are sky-rocketing. Many families are feeling it—in the pocketbook and in the throat.

In some circles, the surrender flag has gone up the pole. They've concluded: "We need dual incomes. Our men can't carry the breadwinner ball all alone. Our mothers must work! Yes, even full time. We don't want to do it. But we must. If we're going to make ends meet, provide an acceptable standard of living, give our kids reasonable opportunities in life, and provide them with tuition for a Christian education, we've got to both go off to work."

I'm very uneasy with this surrender of the precious ground of *stay-at-home motherhood.* I fear we're welcoming in a Trojan horse. The earlier chapters of this book have thoroughly treated this theme. As previously stated, *I do not believe that the Bible absolutely prohibits a mother from ever working outside of the home.* See Proverbs 31:14, 16, 24. But also remember that a married mother's focus and headquarters is her home and not her office or work station. See Proverbs 31:15, 21, 27-28. Modest amounts of part-time work (ideally) from the home are far different from consuming amounts of full-time work totally away from the home.

Let me here bring to bear some important considerations:

A. *You need to understand men.*
We're supposed to be the heroic providers, caring for you, as *our wives.* But if you create the right dynamics, we become the passive victim, letting you care for us as if you were *our mothers.*

I once heard two women talking. The younger woman said that she had to take a full-time job because her husband just didn't make enough money to make ends meet. The older woman responded: "Maybe if you didn't jump in and come to his rescue, he'd *find a way* to make more money to adequately provide for his family by himself."

Nancy Leigh DeMoss wrote: "In some situations, I think women have not discovered what God might do in motivating their husbands to provide if the wife wasn't stepping in to fill the vacuum."[162]

You see, ladies, some men don't exercise *manly dominion* in their vocational life. They're content with mediocrity rather than excellence. Promotions and pay increases aren't a priority for them. Intensely hard work is irksome. Overtime isn't pleasant. They like hunting, sports, video games, and relaxation. There's no urgency. They know that their wives will bail them out by taking care of the financial shortfall. It's not necessary for them to really push themselves very hard. "Mom will take care of us," they think.

Shame on such pathetic Passive-Purple-Four-Ball wimpiness!

Now, I realize that not every man whose wife works falls into that pathetic category. I know that times are tough. But when it comes to deciding to separate our children from their mother, we men need to rise up with a sense of heroic and holy urgency. We need to go to the mirror, look at ourselves straight in the eye, and say, "What can I possibly do to keep my children's mother at home? I need to *find a way!*" My own dad sometimes worked up to three jobs back in the 1960's to make it happen!

Don't be guilty, ladies, of cultivating unmanly passivity in your husband by prematurely volunteering to come to his rescue and going off to work.

B. You need to count the cost.

Scott W. Danger, a certified public accountant, has illustrated the surprisingly low net financial gain of many mothers who work full time.

> Let's use an example. Joe and Julie are married and expecting their first child in three months. They live in a modest house in the suburbs. Joe is an electrician with good benefits, including family health insurance. Julie is an office manager downtown. Joe and Julie would like her to be able to stay home with the new baby, but they don't see how they can make it work. How could they ever get by without her $25,000 salary? Let's look at how much of that $25,000 salary they would actually see:

Gross Salary $25,000

⊖ Taxes ($7,500)
15% Federal, 7% State, and 8% FICA and Medicare

⊖ Daycare ($6,250)
$2.50 per hour x 10 hours per day x 5 days x 50 weeks

⊖ Commuting ($2,500)
$.25/mile x 40-mile round trip x 5 days x 50 weeks

⊖ Work Clothes ($1,200)
$100 per month

⊖ Meals out ($1,000)
Twice a week at $10 each time x 50 weeks

⊖ Other ($500)
Office gifts, professional fees, convenience items

_____

⊜ **Net Income $6,050**

Of Julie's $25,000 salary, they would only see $6,050. Based on a 40-hour work week, this is only $2.91 per hour. The difference of $18,950 is Julie's cost of work. Julie may be able to find work at home to make up the $6,050 gap in their earnings. [163]

But there's an even heavier cost factor. Here's an abbreviated list from Nancy Leigh DeMoss' catalogue of the *"unintended consequences"* of mothers going off to work full time:

- millions of infants and toddlers being dropped off at day care centers before daylight and being picked up after dark;
- millions of children coming home from school to empty houses or being relegated to after-school child care programs;
- mothers giving their best energy and time to persons other than

their husbands and children, leaving those women perpetually exhausted and edgy;

- families that seldom sit down and have a meal together;
- children subsisting on frozen dinners and fast food eaten on the run;
- emotional and physical affairs being fanned by married women spending more quality time with men at work than they do with their own husbands;
- women who don't have enough time or energy to cultivate a close relationship with their children and who end up permanently estranged from their grown children;
- children spending countless hours being entertained by videos, TV, electronic games, and computers;
- inadequately supervised children becoming exposed to and lured into pornography, alcohol, drugs, sex, and violence.[164]

Mary Beeke provides timely straight talk:

> There is a price. It is inherent in parenting to make sacrifices. If you aren't willing to give up many of your own desires for the welfare of your child, then please don't bring a child into this world. Don't burden yourself, your child, or others by having a baby just "because that's what every other couple does." [165]

C. You need to consider economizing.

A reliable older vehicle is much more cost effective than an impressive newer one. A used sofa from an estate sale costs only a fraction of a new one from a furniture store. Designer clothing labels are really overrated and overpriced.

Home schooling two children, instead of paying their Christian school tuition, can save you anywhere from $10,000 to $20,000 per year.

Are some of our necessities really luxuries? Was I deprived of the essentials back in the 1960's living a simpler lifestyle? Do our houses really need to be so large? Does every family member really need a cell phone? Is cable TV indispensable? Do we need to go on costly vacations? Are expensive birthday and Christmas gifts all that important?

Books and articles abound in providing wise counsel for homemakers seeking to make ends meet. Remember what the old Dutch woman said about life among the early Midwest settlers: "*A woman in an apron was more valuable than three men in boots.*" She went on to explain that a skilled household mistress was capable of stretching a pound of butter, a sack of flour, and a portion of meat into an unthinkable number of meals. It's still true today!

4. *Consider an empty nester.* When the children are grown and married, certainly a mother enjoys the experience of facing the unfamiliar sight of vast and wide open spaces of free time. But a *woman of dominion* will be very conscientious with the use of these precious hours. She surely has the liberty to labor for financial profit and personal fulfillment in the marketplace. But she remains a mother to her grown children who are slugging-it-out in the trenches of young family life and a grandmother to a newly hatching generation. An *available* and servant-hearted mom and grandma is an incalculable windfall. Furthermore, the church of Christ can be mightily empowered by older women who pour their time, energies, and wisdom into the ministries of their local congregations.

Planted in the house of the LORD, *they will flourish in the courts of our God.* They will still yield fruit in old age; *they shall be* full of sap *and very green (Psalm 92:13-14, emphasis added).*

Let a widow be put on the list only if she is not less than sixty years *old, having been the wife of one man, having* a reputation for good works; *and if she has brought up children, if she has shown hospitality to strangers, if she has* washed the saints' feet, *if she has* assisted those in distress, *and if she has* devoted herself to every good work *(1 Timothy 5:9-10, emphasis added).*

For I am mindful of the sincere faith within you, which first dwelt in your grandmother *Lois, and your mother Eunice, and I am sure that it is in you as well (2 Timothy 1:5, emphasis added).*

Older women *likewise are to be reverent in their behavior, not malicious gossips, nor enslaved to much wine, teaching what is good, that they may* encourage the young women *to love their husbands, to love their children (Titus 2:3-4, emphasis added).*

Summary Opinion
Should a woman work outside the home?

I believe that a godly *woman of dominion*, who is a mother, will fight with all her might to avoid working outside of her home. However, in some circumstances, part-time work may become a budgetary necessity.

In this cyberspace computer age, much gainful employment can be accomplished in the home. Creative and entrepreneurial *women of dominion* have devised wonderful and profitable businesses that can be run from the home. A mother may secure a cleaning job in the evenings and even take a rotating schedule of the older children with her. A nurse may work an occasional or part-time schedule to supplement the family income. A mom of dominion may negotiate an employment niche where she can wave goodbye to her school-bound children in the mornings and be waiting for them with welcoming arms at home in the afternoons. Any job ought to be scheduled in such a way as to produce minimal disruption in the God-ordained mother-child relationship priorities.

I understand that some women have been placed in emergency situations, requiring extraordinary *womanly dominion*. They've been widowed, sometimes by divorce, and have been dealt a bitter hand by providence. There is no man in the house to be *the breadwinner*. Like Ruth, such heroines are forced into the field of labor to provide for their dependents. But, dear ladies, remember, the Lord is the God of the orphan and the widow (Deuteronomy 10:18). He is *Jehovah-Jireh* (Genesis 22:14). He will provide (2 Kings 4:1-7). May the Lord bless you, dear husbandless mothers, in your valiant daily battles.

I am very uneasy, however, with ever recommending that any mother with a husband, abandon her homemaking mission and calling (Titus 2:5), to seek full-time employment outside of her home. In my mind, the greatness of her motherly mission makes her indispensable in her home.

In a wonderful chapter entitled, "Mommy, please don't go!" Mary Beeke compellingly urges women to stay home from work and *"play their positions."*

> My career begins at the top of the corporate ladder, and it stays there until the end of my life. The name of my corporation is *My Family*. I am a mother.[166]

May the Lord make you a God-honoring *woman of dominion.*
Play your position!
Win it!
So help you God, *subdue* and *rule* your life to His glory.

ENDNOTES

INTRODUCTION

1 Robert L. Dabney, *The Life and Campaigns of Lieutenant General Thomas J. Stonewall Jackson* (Harrisonburg, VA: Sprinkle Publications, 1866 reprint), p. 222.

2 Ibid., pp. 222-223.

3 Ibid., p. 2.

4 Ibid., pp. 2-3, 5.

5 Charles Bridges, *A Commentary on Proverbs* (Carlisle, PA: Banner of Truth Trust, 1846, reprinted 1979), p. 626.

6 George Lawson, *Commentary on Proverbs* (Grand Rapids, MI: Kregel Publications, 1829, republished 1980), pp. 564, 568.

7 Mark J. Chanski, *Manly Dominion* (NY: Calvary Press, 2004), p. 12.

CHAPTER 1

8 Ibid., p. 18.

CHAPTER 2

9 Louise Story, "Many Women at Elite Colleges Set Career Path to Motherhood," New York Times 20 Sept. 2005.

10 Jessica L. Allen, "Mother Knows Best," Wheaton Winter 2007, p. 27.

11 Anthony Hoekema, *Created in God's Image* (Grand Rapids, MI: Eerdmans Publishing Co., 1988), p. 14.

12 Matthew Henry, *Commentary on the Whole Bible* (New York: Fleming H. Revell, 1935), p. 11.

13 Michael Meyers, "Birth Dearth: Remember the Population Bomb?" Newsweek International 27 Sept. 2004.

14 Sarah Womack, "Mohammed Overtakes George in List of Most Popular Names," The Daily Telegraph (London) 21 Dec. 2006.

15 Joel Belz, "The New Baby Boom: Remember all the Jokes about Big Families?" World Magazine 6 May 2006, p. 6.

16 Ibid., p. 6.

17 Hoekema, p. 77.

18 John S. C. Abbott, *The Mother at Home* (Sterling, VA: Grace Abounding Ministries,1833, reprinted 1984), p. 7.

19 Abbott, p. 7.

20 Ilion Jones, Morning Glory, January 8, 1994.

CHAPTER 3

21 Edward J. Young, Genesis 3, *A Devotional and Expository Study* (Carlisle, PA: Banner of Truth Trust, 1966), p. 19.

22 Ibid., p. 19.

23 Nancy Leigh DeMoss, *Lies Women Believe* (Chicago: Moody Press, 2001), p. 20.

24 Ibid., p. 71.

25 Ibid., p. 72.

26 Ibid., p. 72.

27 Ibid., p. 71.

28 Ibid., p. 72.

Endnotes

29   Chanski, pp. 21-22.

30   DeMoss, p. 219.

31   Chanski, pp. 174-75.

32   DeMoss, p. 145.

33   Ibid., pp. 137, 138, 140.

34   Media Matters for America, 3 Apr. 2006, 27 Feb. 2008, http://mediamatters.org/items/200604030002.

35   Allen, p. 27.

36   Jeanne Sahadi, "Being a Mom Could be a 6-Figure Job," CNNMoney.com, 3 May 2006, 29 Feb. 2008, http://money.cnn.com/2006/05/03/pf/mothers_work/index.htm.

CHAPTER 4

37   John Bunyan, *Grace Abounding to the Chief of Sinners* (Grand Rapids, MI: Baker Books, 1978), p. 123.

38   John Piper, "To Live Upon God that is Invisible, Suffering and Service in the Life of John Bunyan," 1999 Bethlehem Conference for Pastors, 2 Feb. 1999.

39

   Wayne Grudem, 1 Peter (Grand Rapids, MI: IVP-Eerdmans Publishing Co., 1989,), p. 141.

40   Courtney Anderson, To the Golden Shore (Valley Forge, PA: Judson Press, 1987), p. 83.

41   Ibid., p. 83.

42   Ibid., p. 86.

43   Grudem, p. 141.

44 Anderson, p. 328.

45 Walt Kaiser, *The Expositors' Bible Commentary, Exodus, Vol. 2* (Grand Rapids, MI: Zondervan, 1990), p. 333.

46 Thomas Scott, *Scott's Bible, Vol. 1* (New York: Collins and Hannay, 1832), p. 432.

47 George Grant, *Carry a Big Stick*, (Nashville, TN: Cumberland House Publishing, Inc., 1996), p. 145.

48 Ibid., p. 145.

49 W. G. Blaikie, *The First Book of Samuel* (Minneapolis, MN: Klock & Klock Christian Publishers, 1887, reprinted 1983), pp. 384-85.

50 *Henry Commentary, Volume 2*, Fleming H. Revell Company, New York, original 1708, 1 Samuel, chapter 25.

51 Derek Kidner, *Proverbs, An Introduction and Commentary* (Downers Grove, IL: Inter-Varsity Press, 1964), p. 184.

CHAPTER 5

52 William Hendriksen, *The Gospel of Luke* (Grand Rapids, MI: Baker Books, 1978), p. 90.

    DeMoss, p. 13.

53 J. C. Ryle, *Expository Thoughts on the Gospel of Luke* (Hertfordshire, England: Evangelical Press, 1879, reprinted 1985), p. 21.

54 Ibid., pp. 183-184.

55 John Angell James, *Female Piety* (Pittsburgh, PA: Soli Deo Gloria Publications, 1860, reprinted 1994), p. 304.

56 DeMoss, pp. 121-122.
    Ibid., pp. 123-124.

59   Chanski, p. 135.

60   Geoffrey Wilson, *Romans* (Carlisle, PA: Banner of Truth Trust, 1977), p. 242.

61   The Savannah News-Press, June 1975.

62   Wayne Mack and David Swavely, *Life in the Father's House* (Phillipsburg, NJ: Presbyterian & Reformed Publishing, 1996), p. 85.

63   Jacob W. Kapp, *The International Bible Encyclopedia, Vol. 1* (Grand Rapids, MI: Eerdmans Publishing Co., 1939), p. 211.

64   Alexander Maclaren, *Expositions of the Holy Scripture, Vol. 12* (Grand Rapids, MI: Baker Books), p. 359.

65   Charles Spurgeon, *Metropolitan Tabernacle Pulpit, Sermon on Romans 16:1-16*, Ages Software, Sermon #1113, p 357.

CHAPTER 6

66   Nightline, ABC, Making Hillary Clinton an Issue, 26 March 1992.

67   James B. Hurley, *Man and Woman in Biblical Perspective* (Grand Rapids, MI: Zondervan, 1981), p. 222.

68   William Hendricksen, *Thessalonians, Timothy, and Titus* (Grand Rapids, MI: Baker Books, 1979), p. 111.

69   A. T. Robertson, *Word Pictures in the New Testament* (Grand Rapids, MI; Kregel Publications, 2003) on 2 Timothy 2:15, Vol 4.

70   Hurley, p. 223.

CHAPTER 7

71   Dr. Laura Schlessinger, *Proper Care and Feeding of Husbands* (New York: HarperCollins Publishing, Inc., 2004), pp. 168-169.

72   John Newton, *Out of the Depths* (Chicago: Moody Press), pp. 15-17.

73   Martin V. Melosi, *Thomas A. Edison and the Modernization of America* (Glenview, IL: Scott, Foresman/Little, Brown Higher Education, 1990), p. 8.

74   Arnold Dallimore, *Susanna Wesley, The Mother of John & Charles Wesley* (Grand Rapids, MI: Baker Books, 1993), pp. 57-61.

75   Edna Gerstner, *Jonathan and Sarah: An Uncommon Union* (Morgan, PA: Soli Deo Gloria Publications, 1996), p. v.

76   John Flavel, *The Works of John Flavel, Vol 1* (Edinburgh: Banner of Truth Trust, 1968), p. 270.

77   Walter Chantry, *The High Calling of Motherhood* (Carlisle, PA: Banner of Truth Trust, 2000), p. 8.

78   J. C. Ryle, *The Duties of Parents* (Choteau, MT: Christian Heritage Publisher, 1888, reprinted 1983), p. 8.

CHAPTER 8

79   Victor Hugo, Ninety Three.

80   Elizabeth Harvey, New Study Finds No Harm to Children of Working Moms (CNN.com, February 28, 1999)

81   Dr. Laura Schlessinger (Daily Radio Talk Show Broadcast).

82   Ann Crittenden, *The Price of Motherhood* (New York: Henry Holt and Company, LLC, 2001), p. 1.

83   Patricia Holland.

84 Bruce Hafen, *The Importance of Motherhood* (North Melbourne, Victoria: The Australian Family Association, April, 2000), p. 11.

85 Ibid., p. 11.

86 John MacArthur, "How to be a Godly Mother," 1 Sam. 1-2, Tape GC 1279.

87 Anonymous Mother, *Letters on Christian Education* (Avinger, TX: Simpson Publishing Company, 1993), pp. 13-14.

88 T. W. Talmage, *Sermons Delivered in the Brooklyn Tabernacle* (London, R. D. Dickinson, 1872), p. 228.

89 Albert N. Martin, "Dealing with Your Spiritually Awakened Children #1," Trinity Pulpit, Montville, NJ.

90 Fox News, Fox News Network, Liza Kappelle, May 18, 2007.

91 Rebecca Hagelin, "Taking Back Our Homes," Imprimis, April 2006, pp. 1-2.

92 Ibid., p. 2.

93 Ibid., p. 7.

94 Ibid., p. 8.

95 Jean Fleming, *A Mother's Heart* (Colorado Springs, CO: Navpress, 1996), p. 121.

96 Kidner, p. 106.

97 Ibid., p. 106.

98 Nancy Wilson, *The Fruit of Her Hands* (Moscow, ID: Canon Press, 1997), p. 76.

CHAPTER 9

99   Christina Hoff Sommers, "The War Against Boys," The Atlantic Monthly, May 2000, pp. 73-74.

100   Nancy Wilson, *Praise Her in the Gates* (Moscow, ID: Canon Press, 2000), p. 62.

101   Ibid., p. 59.

102   Chanski, p. 18.

103   Wilson, Praise Her, pp. 62-63.

104   Stacy MacDonald, "What Do You Want to Be When You Grow Up?" Homeschooling Today, Jan/Feb 2004, p. 1.

105   Ibid., p. 14.

106   Abbott, pp. 12-13.

107   Ibid., pp. 9.

108   Ibid., pp. 8-9.

CHAPTER 10

109   Larry Cunningham (Billings, Montana), Reader's Digest

110   Jay E. Adams, *When Your Marriage Goes Sour* (Phillipsburg, NJ: Presbyterian & Reformed Publishing Co., 1972), p. 1.

111   Ibid., pp. 1-2.

112   Jay E. Adams, *Solving Marriage Problems* (Grand Rapids, MI: Baker Books, 1983), p. 28.

113   Adams, When Your Marriage Goes Sour, p. 4.

Endnotes

114 Jack L. Canfield, *Chicken Soup for the Romantic Soul: Inspirational Stories about Love and Romance* (Deerfield Beach, FL: Health Communications, Inc., 2003), p. 259.

115 Schlessinger, p. 51.

116 Ibid., pp. 7-8.

117 Ibid., p. 13.

118 Martha Peace, *The Excellent Wife* (Bemidji, MN: Focus Publishing, 1999), p. 107.

119 Schlessinger, pp. 37-38.

120 Ibid., p. 40.

121 Anonymous.

122 Peace, p. 74.

123 Schlessinger, p. 120.

124 Ibid., p. 125.

125 Bridges, p. 624.

126 Schlessinger, p. 125.

127 Ibid., pp. 125-126.

128 Ibid., p. 120. .

129 Elyse Fitzpatrick, *Helper by Design* (Chicago: Moody Press, 2003), pp. 104-105

130 Linda Dillow and Lorraine Pintus, *Intimate Issues, Conversations Woman to Woman* (Colorado Springs, CO: Water Brook Press, 1999), pp. 49-50.

131 Schlessinger, p. xiii.

CHAPTER 11

132 Elyse Fitzpatrick and Laura Hendrickson, MD, *Will Medicine Stop the Pain?* (Chicago: Moody Publishers, 2006).

133 Charles Spurgeon, *Metropolitan Tabernacle, Sermon #1950 on Psalm 46:1-3*, p. 158.

134 Charles Spurgeon, *Treasury of David, Vol. 1* (McLean, VA: MacDonald Publishing Co.), p. 339.

135 Derek Kidner, *Tyndale Old Testament Commentaries, Psalms 1-72* (Downers Grove, IL: InterVarsity Press 1981), p. 121.

136 John Flavel, *The Works of John Flavel, vol 1* (Carlisle, PA: Banner of Truth, 1820, reprinted 1982), p. 496.

137 Ibid., p. 496.

138 Samuel Rodigast, "Whate'er My God Ordains is Right," Trinity Hymnal (Suwanee, GA: Great Commission Publications, Inc., 1995), p. 94.

139 David Dickson, *Psalms* (Carlisle, PA: Banner of Truth Trust, 1867), p. 525.

CHAPTER 12

140 George W. Knight, *The Role Relationship of Men and Women* (Phillipsburg, NJ: Presbyterian & Reformed Publishing, 1989) and Wayne Grudem, *Evangelical Feminism & Biblical Truth* (Sisters, OR: Multnomah Books, 2004).

141 William Hendriksen, *The Exposition of the Pastoral Epistles* (Grand Rapids, MI: Baker Books, 1964), pp. 108-109.

142 Robert L. Dabney, *Discussions: Evangelical and Theological, Vol.2* (London: Banner of Truth Trust, 1967), p.96.

Endnotes

143 Mack and Swavely, p. 85.

144 Dabney, Discussions, Vol. 1, p. 600.

145 James, p. 317.

146 Barbara Hughes, *Disciplines of a Godly Woman* (Wheaton, IL: Crossway Books, 2001), p. 124.

147 Martha Peace, *Becoming a Titus 2 Woman* (Bemidji, MN: Focus Publishing, 1997), p. 19.

148 Mack and Swavely, p. 88.

149 Betsy Childs, "Edith Schaeffer: The Hospitable Soul," 27 Feb. 2008, http://www.rzim.org/slice/slicetran.php?slideid=903.

150 Alexander Strauch, *Using Your Home for Christ* (Littleton, CO: Lewis and Roth, 1967), p. 96.

CHAPTER 13

151 Anne Bradstreet, *The Works of Anne Bradstreet*, Jeannine Hensley, ed. (Cambridge, Mass.: Harvard University Press, 1967), p. 196.

152 BBC News Profile, BBC, Golda Meir, 21 April 1998.

153 Ibid.

154 "Women in Combat," Center for Military Readiness, 22 Nov. 2004, 27 Feb. 2008, http://www.cmrlink.org/WomenInCombat.asp?DocID=237.

155 David Lipsey, NY Times.

156 Lt. Col. Dave Grossman, *On Killing: The Psychological Cost of Learning to Kill in War and Society* (Bel Air, CA: Back Bay Press, 1996), p. 43ff.

157 "Women in Combat," R. Cort Kirkwood, "What Kind of Nation Sends Women into Combat?" 11 Apr. 2003, 27 Feb. 2008, http://www.lewrockwell.com/orig3/kirkwood.html.

158 John Piper, World Magazine, "Combat and Cowardice," 10 November 2007, p. 43.

159 Leon Podles, *The Church Impotent: The Feminization of Christianity,* (Dallas, TX: Spence Publishing Company, 1999).

160 Carole F. Gan, News from UC Davis Health System, Davis, CA, 1 June 1997, 27 Feb. 2008, http://www.ucdmc.ucdavis.edu/news/medicalnews/womenlawyers.html.

161 Nancy Leigh DeMoss, "Taking Inventory," "First Things First" series (Revive Our Hearts).

162 Scott W. Danger, CPA, "The Cost of Work: How Much Do You Really Earn?" 27 Feb. 2008, http://www.mommysavers.com/family-finances/cost-of-work.shtml.

163 DeMoss, Lies, pp. 125-126.

164 Mary Beeke, *The Law of Kindness, Serving with Heart and Hand* (Grand Rapids, MI: Reformed Heritage Books, 2007), pp. 221-222.

165 Ibid., pp. 215-216.